WORKING PAPERS, CHAPTERS 15-26
to accompany

FINANCIAL and MANAGERIAL ACCOUNTING

JERRY J. WEYGANDT Ph.D., C.P.A.
Arthur Andersen Alumni Professor of Accounting
University of Wisconsin—Madison
Madison, Wisconsin

PAUL D. KIMMEL Ph.D., C.P.A.
Associate Professor of Accounting
University of Wisconsin—Milwaukee
Milwaukee, Wisconsin

DONALD E. KIESO Ph.D., C.P.A.
KPMG Peat Marwick Emeritus Professor of Accountancy
Northern Illinois University
DeKalb, Illinois

Prepared by
Dick D. Wasson, M.B.A., C.P.A.
Southwestern College
San Diego State University
University of Phoenix

John Wiley & Sons, Inc.

COVER PHOTO: © Bill Stevenson/Aurora Photos

ISBN-13   978-1-118-23345-0

Printed in the United States of America

10 9 8 7 6 5 4 3 2 1

Printed and bound by EPAC Technologies, Inc.

CONTENTS

Working Paper templates are provided for end-of-chapter brief exercises, Do it! exercises, exercises, problems, and broadening your perspective problems. Working Paper templates are not provided for solutions that are textual in nature.

BE15-7

		Product Costs		
		Direct Materials	Direct Labor	Factory Overhead
1	(a)			
2	(b)			
3	(c)			
4	(d)			
5				
6				

BE15-8

				Factory Overhead
7				
8	(a)			
9				
10				
11				
12				
13	(b)			
14				
15				

BE15-9

Ruizz Company
Balance Sheet
December 31, 2014

1 Current assets		
2		
3		
4		
5		
6		
7		
8		
9		
10		
11		
12		
13		
14		
15		

BE15-10

	Direct Materials Used	Direct Labor Used	Factory Overhead	Total Manufacturing Costs
(1)	$ 40 0 0 0	$ 61 0 0 0	$ 50 0 0 0	
(2)		$ 75 0 0 0	$ 140 0 0 0	$ 296 0 0 0
(3)	$ 55 0 0 0		$ 111 0 0 0	$ 310 0 0 0

BE15-11

	Total Manufacturing Costs	Work in Process (January 1)	Work in Process (December 31)	Cost of Goods Manufactured
(1)		$ 120 0 0 0	$ 82 0 0 0	
(2)	$ 296 0 0 0		$ 98 0 0 0	$ 321 0 0 0
(3)	$ 310 0 0 0	$ 463 0 0 0		$ 715 0 0 0

Fishel Company
Cost of Goods Manufactured Schedule
For the Month Ended April 30

1				
2				
3				
4				
5				
6				
7				
8				
9				
10				
11				
12				
13				
14				
15				
16				
17				
18				
19				
20				
21				
22				
23				
24				
25				
26				
27				
28				
29				
30				
31				
32				
33				
34				
35				
36				
37				
38				
39				
40				

1	(a)		1
2			2
3			3
4			4
5			5
6			6
7			7
8			8
9			9
10	(b)		10
11			11
12			12
13			13
14			14
15	(c)		15
16			16
17			17
18			18
19			19
20			20
21			21
22			22
23			23
24			24
25			25
26			26
27			27
28			28
29			29
30			30
31			31
32			32
33			33
34			34
35			35
36			36
37			37
38			38
39			39
40			40

E15-7

1	(a) Delivery service (product) costs:
2	
3	
4	
5	
6	
7	
8	
9	
10	(b) Period costs:
11	
12	
13	
14	
15	
16	
17	
18	

E15-8

20	(a) Cost of goods manufactured:
21	
22	
23	
24	
25	
26	
27	
28	
29	
30	
31	
32	
33	
34	(b) Cost of goods sold:
35	
36	
37	
38	
39	
40	

E15-9

Molina Company
Cost of Goods Manufactured Schedule
For the Year Ended December 31, 2014

1	Work in process (1/1)		$21 0 0 0 0
2	Direct materials:		
3	Raw materials inventory (1/1)		
4	Add: Raw materials purchases	1 5 8 0 0 0	
5	Total raw materials available for use		
6	Less: Raw materials inventory (12/31)	2 2 5 0 0	
7	Direct materials used	$1 9 0 0 0 0	
8	Direct labor		
9	Manufacturing overhead:		
10	Indirect labor	1 8 0 0 0	
11	Factory depreciation	3 6 0 0 0	
12	Factory utilities	6 8 0 0 0	
13	Total overhead	1 2 2 0 0 0	
14	Total manufacturing costs		
15	Total cost of work in process		
16	Less: Work in process (12/31)		8 1 0 0 0
17	Cost of goods manufactured		$5 3 0 0 0 0

E15-10

		Case A	Case B	Case C
21	Direct materials used		$6 8 4 0 0	$1 3 0 0 0 0
22	Direct labor	5 7 0 0 0	8 6 0 0 0	
23	Manufacturing overhead	4 6 5 0 0	8 1 6 0 0	1 0 2 0 0 0
24	Total manufacturing costs	1 9 5 6 5 0		2 5 3 7 0 0
25	Work in process 1/1/12		1 6 5 0 0	
26	Total cost of work in process	2 2 1 5 0 0		3 3 7 0 0 0
27	Work in process 12/31/12		1 1 0 0 0	7 0 0 0 0
28	Cost of goods manufactured	1 8 5 2 7 5		

	Alternative Approach to Solving for Missing Data	
1	CASE A:	1
2	(a)	2
3		3
4		4
5		5
6		6
7	(b)	7
8		8
9		9
10		10
11	(c)	11
12		12
13		13
14	CASE B:	14
15	(d)	15
16		16
17		17
18		18
19		19
20	(e)	20
21		21
22		22
23		23
24	(f)	24
25		25
26		26
27	CASE C:	27
28	(g)	28
29		29
30		30
31		31
32		32
33	(h)	33
34		34
35		35
36		36
37	(i)	37
38		38
39		39
40		40

Name

Section

Date

Exercise 15-11

Colaw Company

(a)

	Direct Materials Used	Direct Labor Used	Manufacturing Overhead	Total Manufacturing Costs	Work in Process 1/1	Work in Process 12/31	Cost of Goods Manufactured
(1)	$ 127000	$ 140000	$ 87000		$ 33000		$ 360000
(2)		200000	132000	450000		40000	470000
(3)	80000	100000		255000	60000	80000	
(4)	70000		75000	288000	45000		270000

(b)

Colaw Company

Cost of Goods Manufactured Schedule

For the Year Ended December 31, 2014

(a)

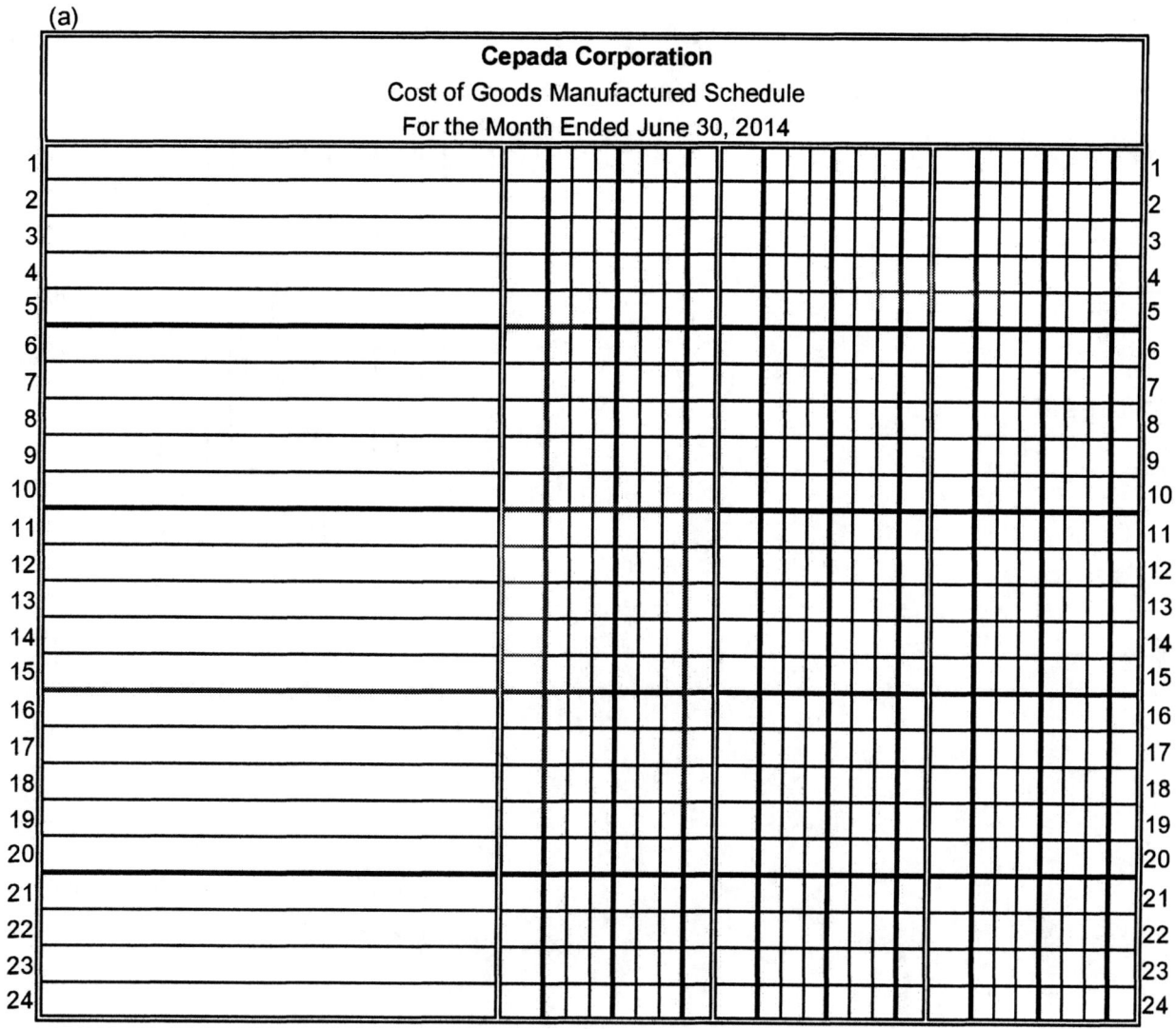

Cepada Corporation
Cost of Goods Manufactured Schedule
For the Month Ended June 30, 2014

(b)

Vargas Corporation
Income Statement (Partial)
For the Month Ended June 30, 2011

Net sales	$	8 7 1 0 0

Name _____

Section _____

Date _____

(a)

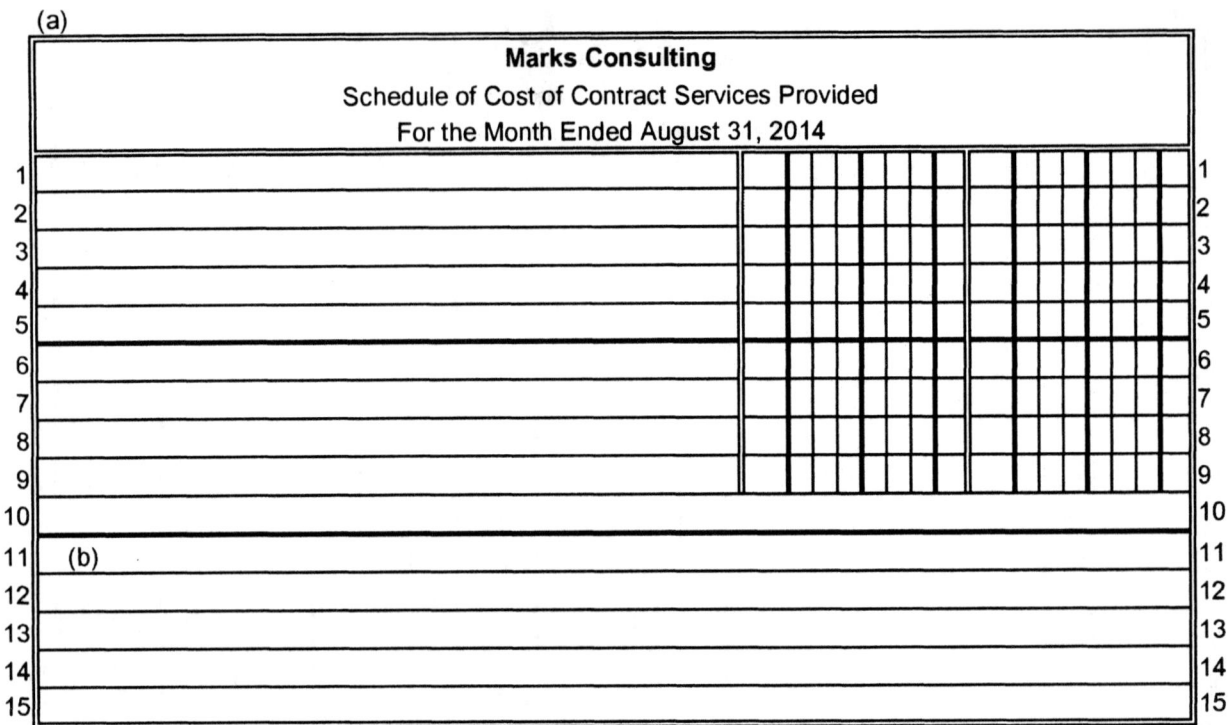

	Marks Consulting	
	Schedule of Cost of Contract Services Provided	
	For the Month Ended August 31, 2014	
1		
2		
3		
4		
5		
6		
7		
8		
9		
10		
11	(b)	
12		
13		
14		
15		

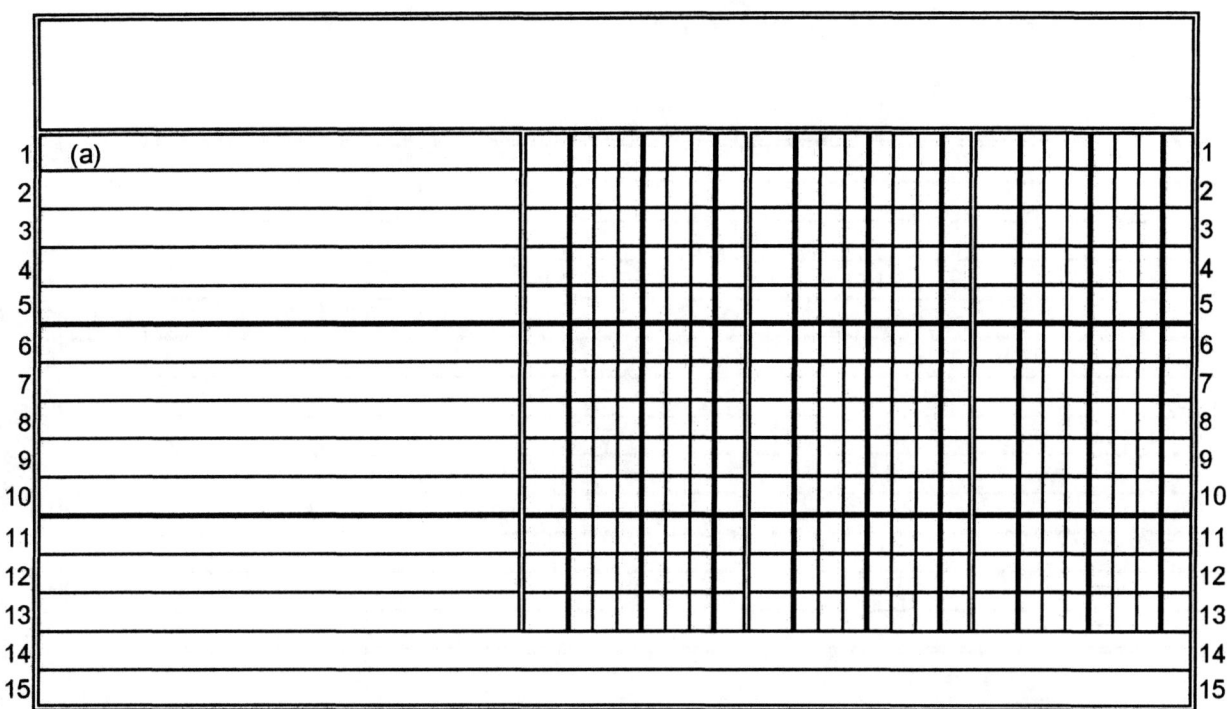

(a)

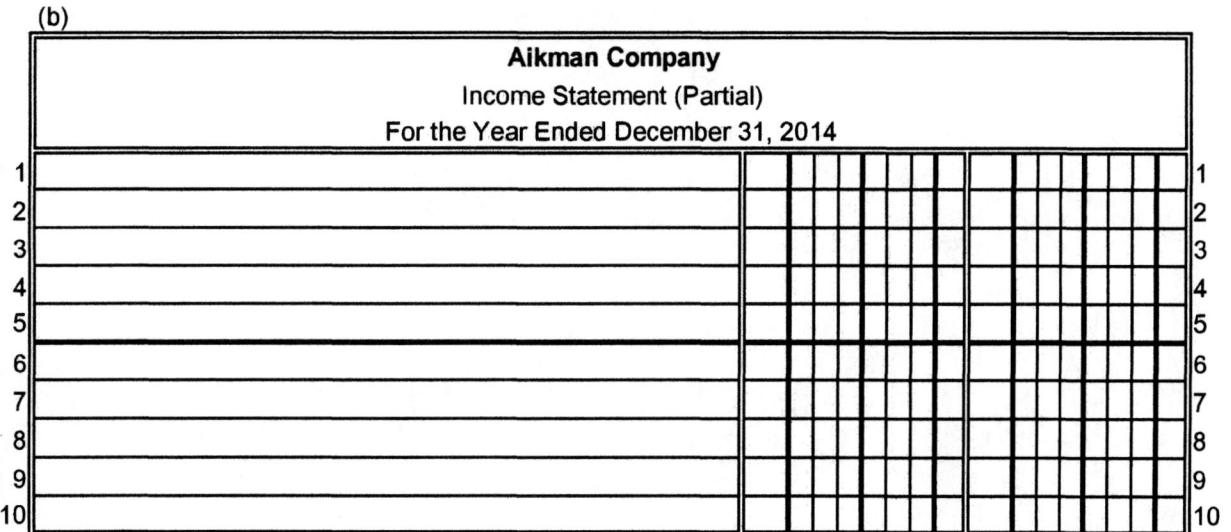

(b)

Aikman Company

Income Statement (Partial)

For the Year Ended December 31, 2014

(c)

	Current assets:		
1			1
2			2
3			3
4			4
5			5
6			6
7	(d)		7
8			8
9			9
10			10
11			11
12			12
13			13

(a)

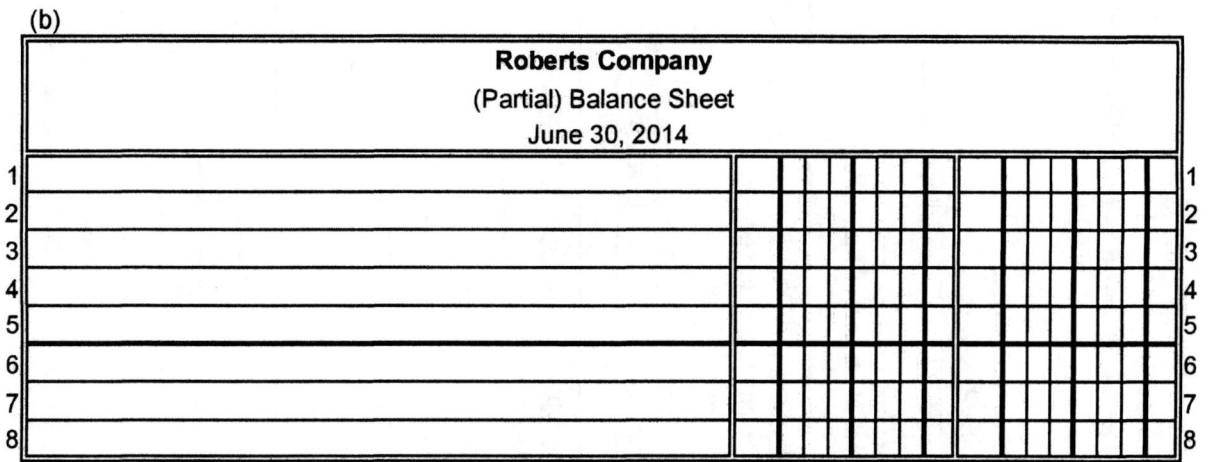

Roberts Company				
Cost of Goods Manufactured Schedule				
For the Month Ended June 30, 2014				

(b)

Roberts Company			
(Partial) Balance Sheet			
June 30, 2014			

(a)

Cost Item	Product Costs			Period Costs
	Direct Materials	Direct Labor	Manufacturing Overhead	
1 Rent on factory equipment				
2 Insurance on factory building				
3 Raw materials				
4 Utility costs for factory				
5 Supplies for general office				
6 Wages for assembly line workers				
7 Depreciation on office equipment				
8 Miscellaneous materials				
9 Factory manager's salary				
10 Property taxes on factory building				
11 Advertising for helmets				
12 Sales commissions				
13 Depreciation on factory building				
14 Totals				
15				
16				
17				
18 (b)				
19 Total production costs:				
20				
21				
22				
23				
24				
25 Production cost per helmet:				

(a)

Cost Item	Product Costs			Period Costs
	Direct Materials	Direct Labor	Manufacturing Overhead	
1 Raw materials				
2 Wages for workers				
3 Rent on equipment				
4 Indirect materials				
5 Factory supervisor's salary				
6 Janitorial costs				
7 Advertising				
8 Depreciation on factory building				
9 Property taxes on factory building				
10 Totals				
11				
12				
13				
14				
15				
16				
17 (b)				
18 Total production costs:				
19				
20				
21				
22				
23				
24 Production cost per system:				
25				

(a)

	CASE 1	
1		1
2		2
3		3
4		4
5		5
6		6
7		7
8		8
9		9
10		10
11		11
12		12
13		13
14		14
15		15
16		16
17		17
18		18
19		19
20		20
21	CASE 2	21
22		22
23		23
24		24
25		25
26		26
27		27
28		28
29		29
30		30
31		31
32		32
33		33
34		34
35		35
36		36
37		37
38		38
39		39
40		40

(b)

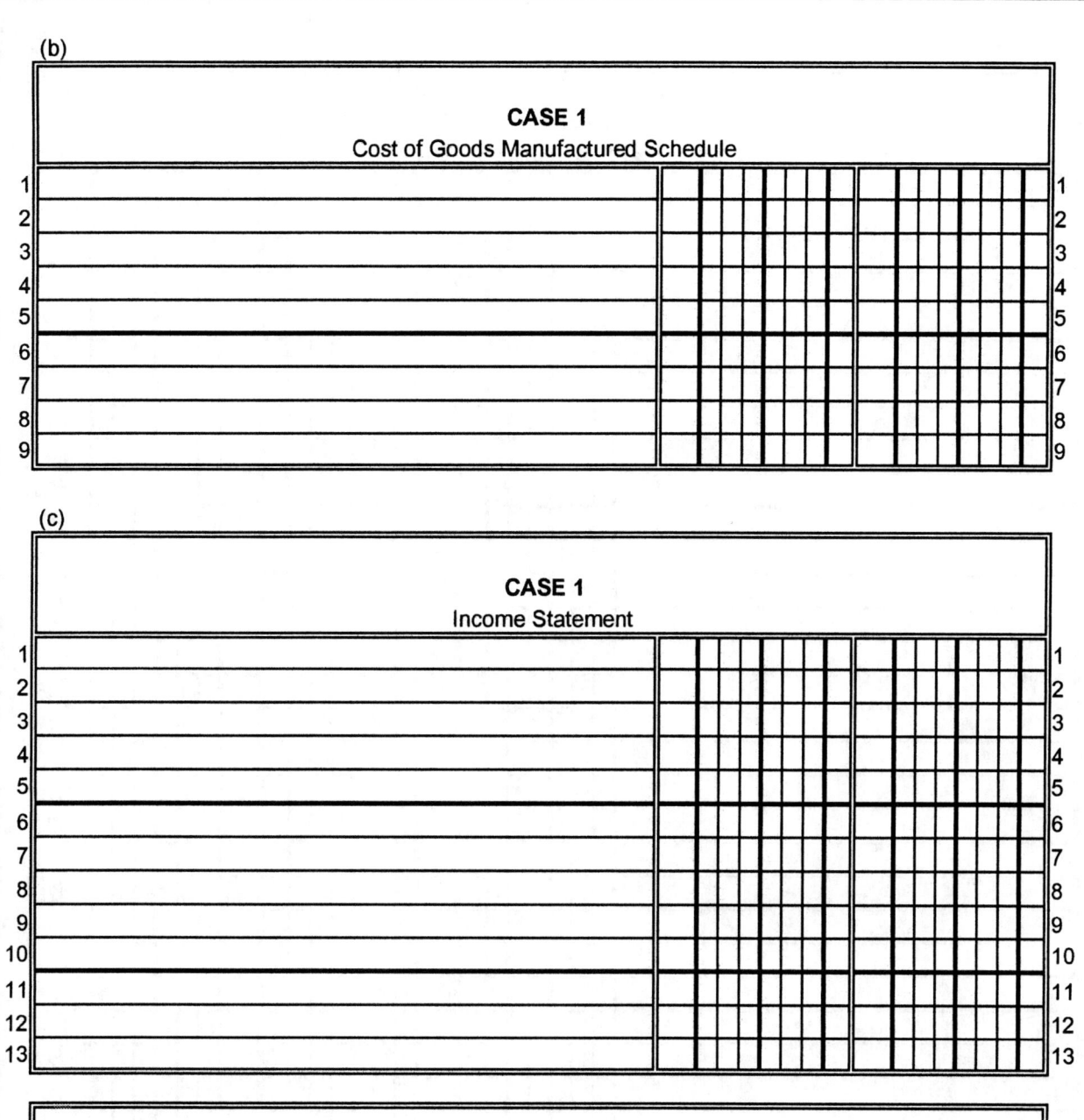

CASE 1

Cost of Goods Manufactured Schedule

(c)

CASE 1

Income Statement

CASE 1

(Partial) Balance Sheet

Current assets:

(a)

Clarkson Company
Cost of Goods Manufactured Schedule
For the Year Ended June 30, 2014

(b)

Clarkson Company
(Partial) Income Statement
For the Year Ended June 30, 2014

1		
2		
3		
4		
5		
6		
7		
8		
9		
10		
11		
12		
13		
14		
15		
16		
17		
18		

(c)

Clarkson Company
(Partial) Balance Sheet
June 30, 2014

Current assets:		

(a)

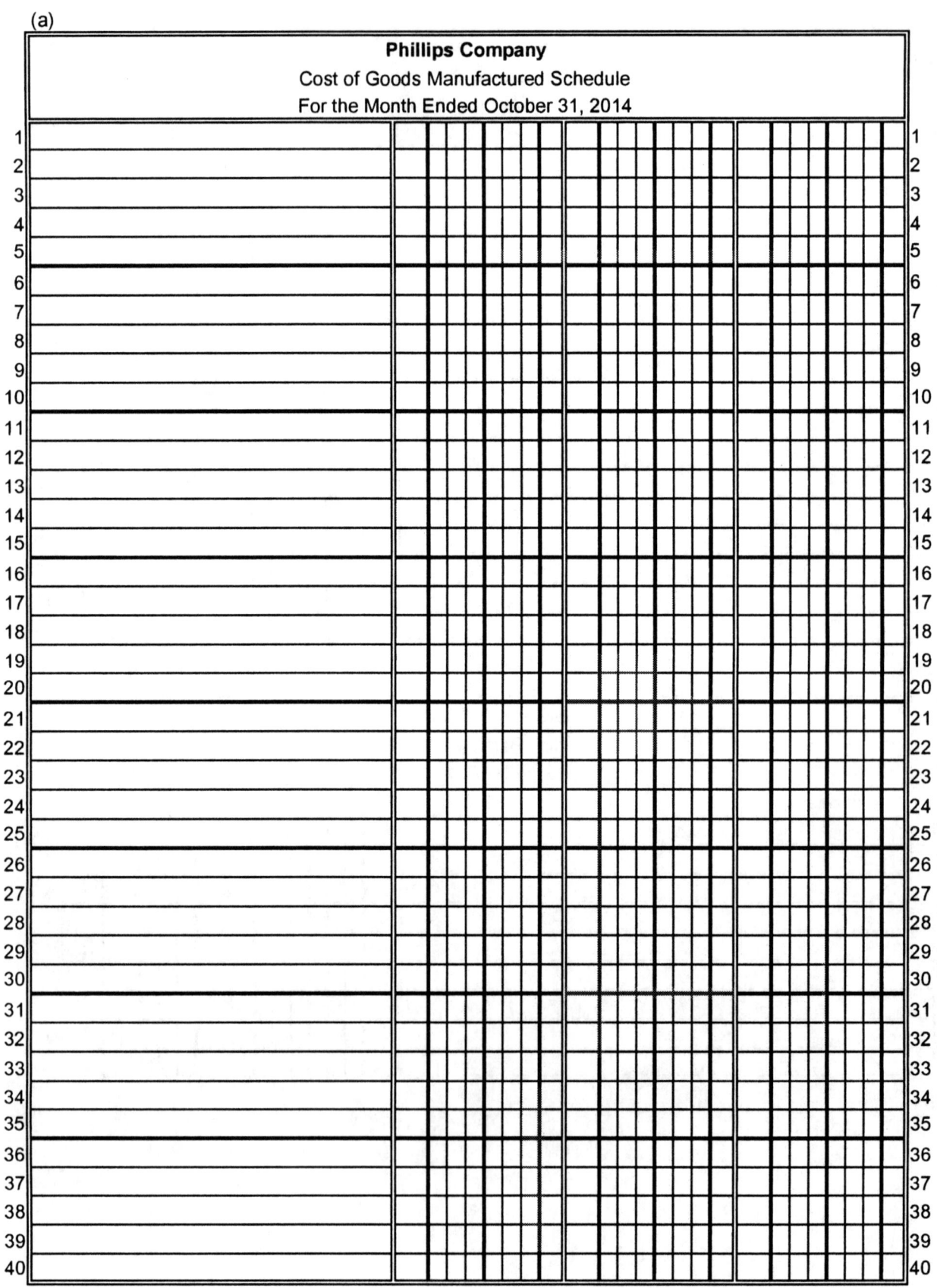

Phillips Company				
Cost of Goods Manufactured Schedule				
For the Month Ended October 31, 2014				

(b)

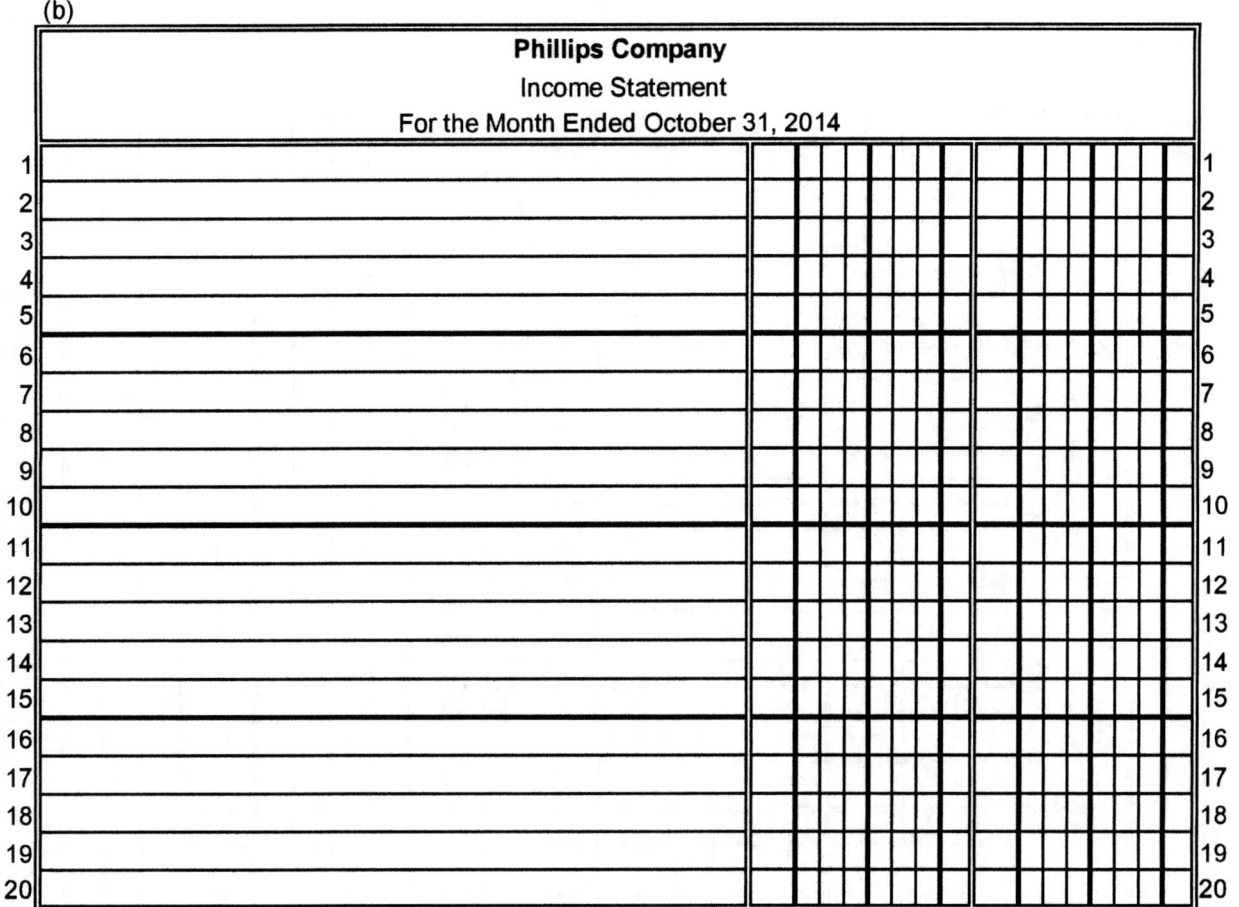

	Phillips Company				
	Income Statement				
	For the Month Ended October 31, 2014				
1					1
2					2
3					3
4					4
5					5
6					6
7					7
8					8
9					9
10					10
11					11
12					12
13					13
14					14
15					15
16					16
17					17
18					18
19					19
20					20

(a)

Cost Item	Product Costs			Period Costs
	Direct Materials	Direct Labor	Manufacturing Overhead	
1 Maintenance costs on factory building					1
2 Factory manager's salary					2
3 Advertising for helmets					3
4 Sales commissions					4
5 Depreciation on factory building					5
6 Rent on factory equipment					6
7 Insurance on factory building					7
8 Raw materials					8
9 Utility costs for factory					9
10 Supplies for general office					10
11 Wages for assembly-workers					11
12 Depreciation on office equipment					12
13 Miscellaneous materials					13
14 Totals					14
15					15
16					16
17 (b)					17
18 Total production costs:					18
19					19
20					20
21					21
22					22
23					23
24 Production cost per motorcycle helmet:					24
25					25

(a)	Product Costs			Period Costs
Cost Item	Direct Materials	Direct Labor	Manufacturing Overhead	
1 Raw materials				
2 Wages for workers				
3 Rent on equipment				
4 Indirect materials				
5 Factory supervisor's salary				
6 Janitorial costs				
7 Advertising				
8 Depreciation on factory building				
9 Property taxes on factory building				
10 Totals				
11				
12				
13				
14				
15				
16				
17 (b)				
18 Total production costs:				
19				
20				
21				
22				
23				
24 Production cost per racket:				
25				

(a)

CASE 1

1	1
2	2
3	3
4	4
5	5
6	6
7	7
8	8
9	9
10	10
11	11
12	12
13	13
14	14
15	15
16	16
17	17
18	18
19	19
20	20

CASE 2

21	21
22	22
23	23
24	24
25	25
26	26
27	27
28	28
29	29
30	30
31	31
32	32
33	33
34	34
35	35
36	36
37	37
38	38
39	39
40	40

(b)

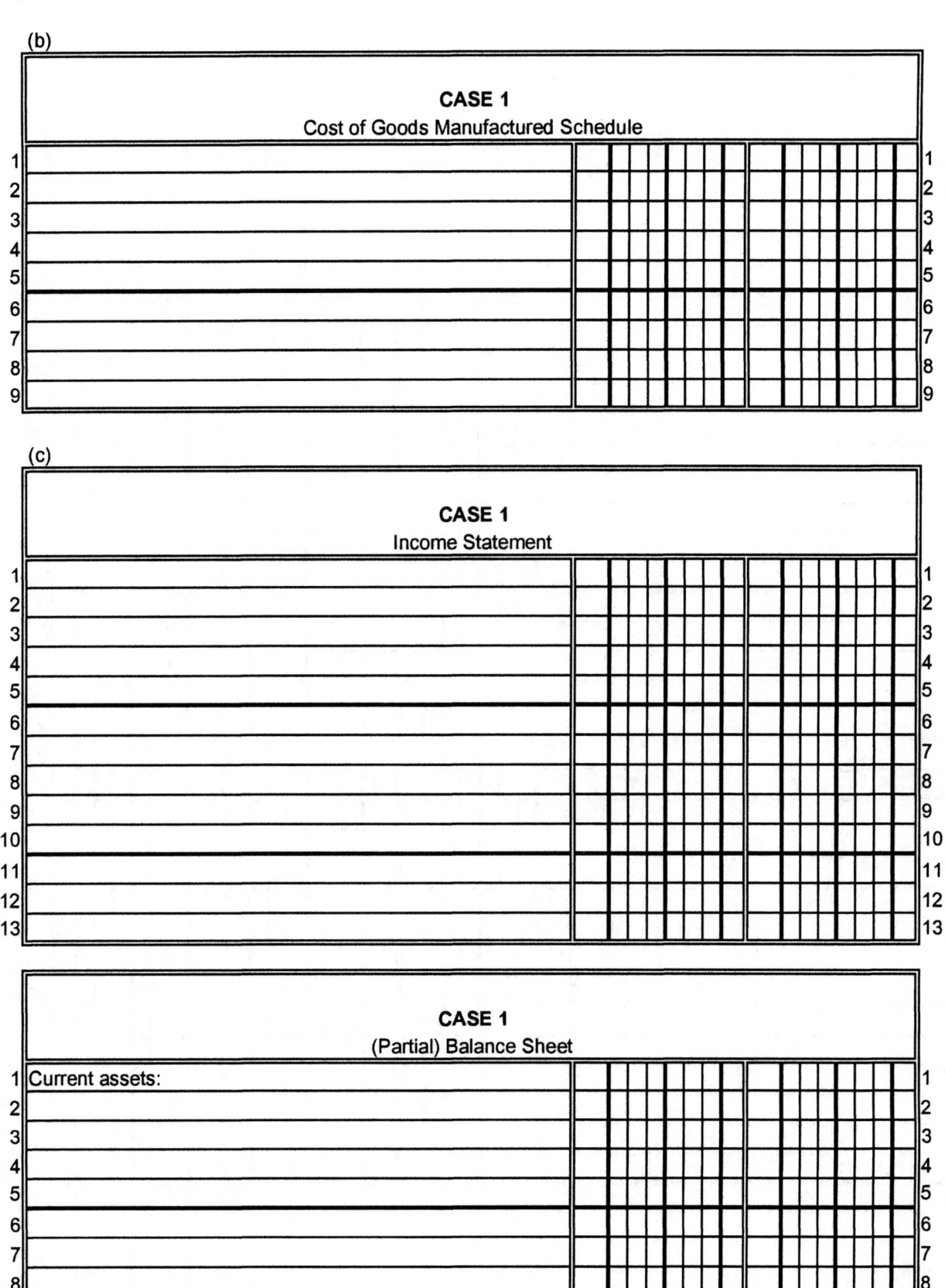

CASE 1
Cost of Goods Manufactured Schedule

(c)

CASE 1
Income Statement

CASE 1
(Partial) Balance Sheet

Current assets:

(a)

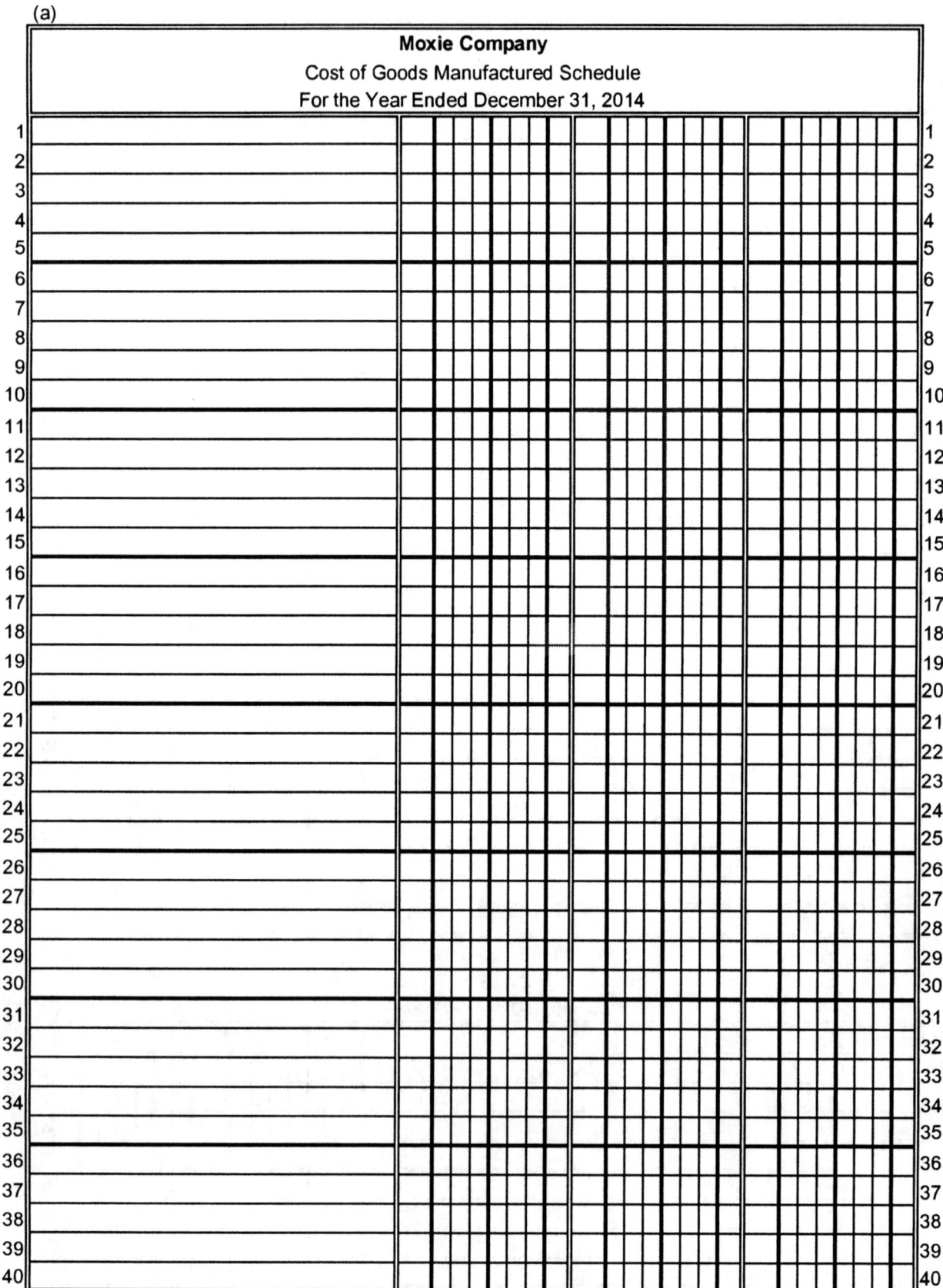

Moxie Company
Cost of Goods Manufactured Schedule
For the Year Ended December 31, 2014

(b)

Moxie Company (Partial) Income Statement For the Year Ended December 31, 2014					
1					1
2					2
3					3
4					4
5					5
6					6
7					7
8					8
9					9
10					10
11					11
12					12
13					13
14					14
15					15
16					16
17					17
18					18

(c)

Moxie Company (Partial) Balance Sheet December 31, 2014					
1	Current assets:				1
2					2
3					3
4					4
5					5
6					6
7					7
8					8
9					9
10					10

(a)

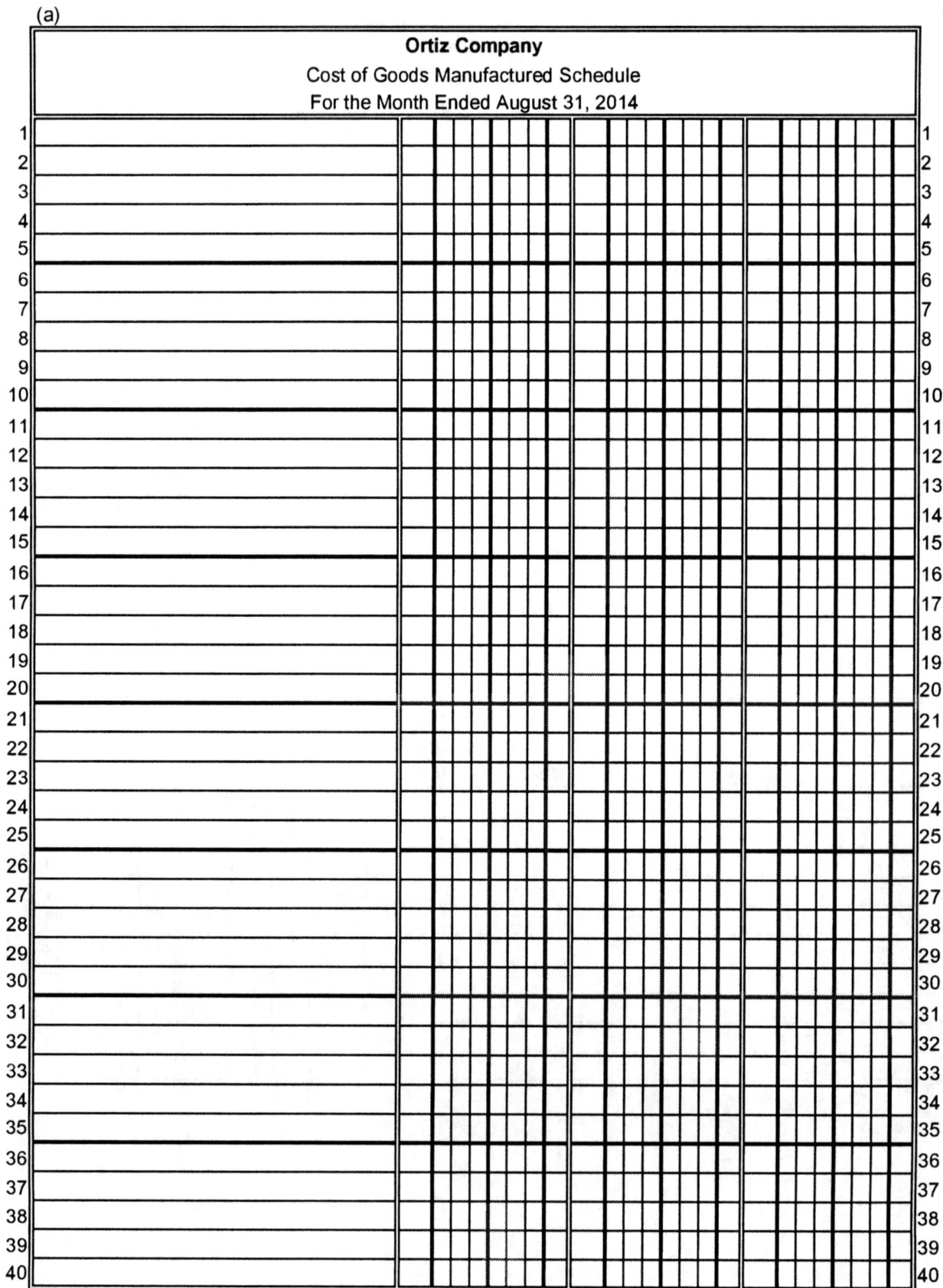

Ortiz Company

Cost of Goods Manufactured Schedule

For the Month Ended August 31, 2014

(b)

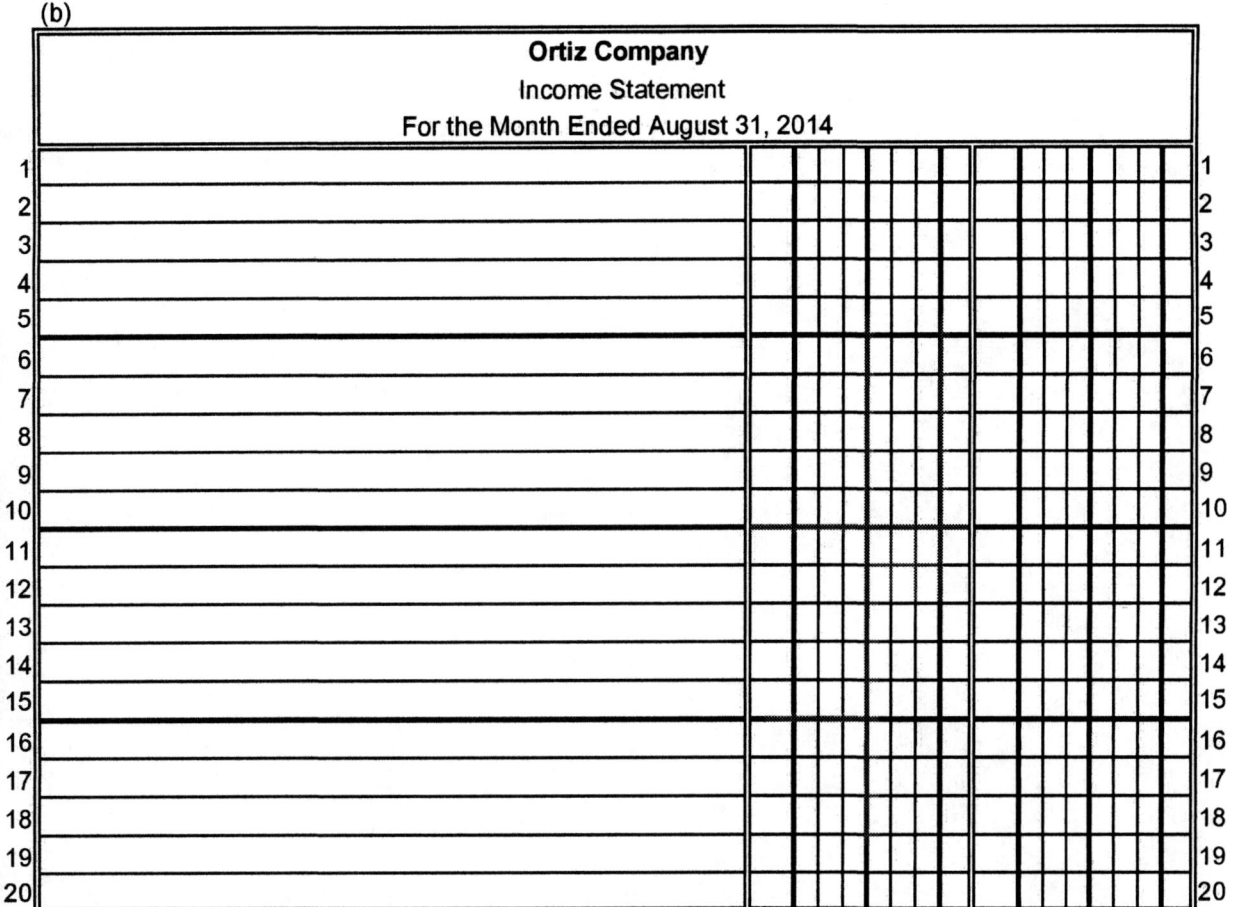

Ortiz Company
Income Statement
For the Month Ended August 31, 2014

BE16-2

	Date	Account Titles	Debit	Credit	
1	Jan 31				1
2					2
3					3
4	31				4
5					5
6					6
7					7
8	31				8
9					9
10					10

BE16-3

	Date	Account Titles	Debit	Credit	
11					11
12	Jan 31				12
13					13
14					14
15					15
16					16

BE16-4

	Date	Account Titles	Debit	Credit	
17					17
18	Jan 31				18
19					19
20					20
21					21
22					22
23					23
24					24
25					25

BE16-5

	Job 1			Job 2		
	Date	Direct Materials	Direct Labor	Date	Direct Materials	Direct Labor

Job 3		
Date	Direct Materials	Direct Labor

31

BE16-7

	Date	Account Titles	Debit	Credit	
1	Jan 31				1
2					2
3					3
4					4
5	Feb 28				5
6					6
7					7
8					8
9					9
10	Mar 31				10
11					11
12					12
13					13
14					14
15	**BE16-8**				15
16	Mar 31				16
17					17
18					18
19					19
20	31				20
21					21
22					22
23					23
24					24
25	31				25
26					26
27					27
28					28
29					29
30					30
31					31
32					32
33					33
34					34
35					35
36					36
37					37
38					38
39					39
40					40

BE16-9

	Date	Account Titles	Debit	Credit	
1					1
2					2
3					3
4					4
5					5
6					6
7					7
8					8
9					9
10	**BE16-10**				10
11		Shimeca Company			11
12	Dec 31				12
13					13
14					14
15		Garcia Company			15
16	Dec 31				16
17					17
18					18
19					19
20					20
21					21
22					22
23					23
24					24
25					25
26					26
27					27
28					28
29					29
30					30

DO IT! 16-1

		Account Titles	Debit	Credit	
1	(a)				1
2					2
3					3
4					4
5	(b)				5
6					6
7					7
8					8
9					9
10	(c)				10
11					11
12					12
13					13
14					14
15					15
16	**DO IT! 16-2**				16
17	The three summary entries are:				17
18					18
19					19
20					20
21					21
22					22
23					23
24					24
25					25
26					26
27					27
28					28
29					29
30					30
31					31
32					32
33					33
34					34
35					35
36					36
37					37
38					38
39					39
40					40

Name

Section

Date   Reyes Corporation

		Account Titles	Debit	Credit	
1					1
2					2
3					3
4					4
5					5
6					6
7					7
8					8
9					9
10					10
11					11
12					12
13					13
14					14
15					15
16					16
17					17
18					18
19					19
20					20
21					21
22					22
23					23
24					24
25					25
26					26
27					27
28					28
29					29
30					30

E16-1

	Date	Account Titles	Debit	Credit	
1	(a)				1
2					2
3					3
4					4
5					5
6					6
7					7
8	(b)				8
9					9
10					10
11					11
12					12
13					13
14					14
15					15

16	**E16-3**				16
17	(a) 1.				17
18					18
19					19
20					20
21	2.				21
22					22
23					23
24					24
25	(b)				25

	Date	Account Titles	Debit	Credit	
26	Date	Account Titles	Debit	Credit	26
27	Jan 31				27
28					28
29					29
30	31				30
31					31
32					32
33	31				33
34					34
35					35
36	31				36
37					37
38					38
39					39
40					40

(a)

	Date		Debit	Credit	
1	May 31				1
2					2
3					3
4					4
5					5
6	31				6
7					7
8					8
9					9
10					10
11	31				11
12					12
13					13
14					14
15					15
16	31				16
17					17
18					18
19					19
20					20

(b)

WORK IN PROCESS INVENTORY

Cost Sheets

	Job No.	Beginning WIP	Direct Materials	Direct Labor	Manufacturing Overhead	Total	
34							34
35							35
36							36
37							37
38							38
39							39
40							40

E16-5

1	(a)				1
2					2
3	(b)				3
4					4
5					5
6					6
7	(c)				7
8	Date	Account Titles	Debit	Credit	8
9					9
10					10
11					11
12					12
13					13
14					14
15					15
16	**E16-6**				16
17	(a) (1) The source documents are:				17
18					18
19					19
20					20
21					21
22	(2)				22
23					23
24					24
25					25
26	(3) The total cost is:				26
27					27
28					28
29					29
30					30
31					31
32					32
33	(b)				33
34	Date	Account Titles	Debit	Credit	34
35	July 31				35
36					36
37					37
38					38
39					39
40					40

	Trans-action	Account Titles	Debit	Credit	
1	1.				1
2					2
3					3
4	2.				4
5					5
6					6
7					7
8	3.				8
9					9
10					10
11					11
12	4.				12
13					13
14					14
15					15
16	5.				16
17					17
18					18
19					19
20					20
21	6.				21
22					22
23					23
24					24
25					25
26	7.				26
27					27
28					28
29					29
30					30
31	8.				31
32					32
33					33
34					34
35					35
36					36
37					37
38					38
39					39
40					40

Section

Date   Enos Printing Corp.

	Trans-action	Account Titles	Debit	Credit	
1	1.				1
2					2
3					3
4					4
5					5
6					6
7	2.				7
8					8
9					9
10					10
11					11
12					12
13					13
14					14
15	3.				15
16					16
17					17
18	4.				18
19					19
20					20
21					21
22	5.				22
23					23
24					24
25	6.				25
26					26
27					27
28					28
29					29
30					30
31					31
32					32
33	Computation of cost of jobs finished:				33

	Job Number	Direct Materials	Direct Labor	Manufacturing Overhead	Total	
34						34
35						35
36						36
37						37
38						38
39						39
40						40

(a)

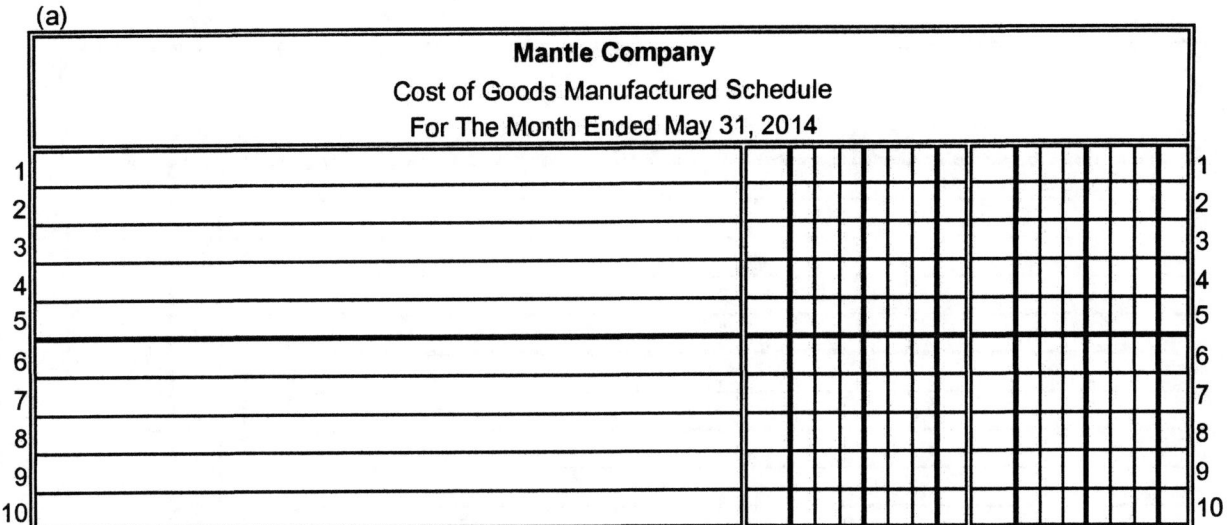

Mantle Company
Cost of Goods Manufactured Schedule
For The Month Ended May 31, 2014

(b)

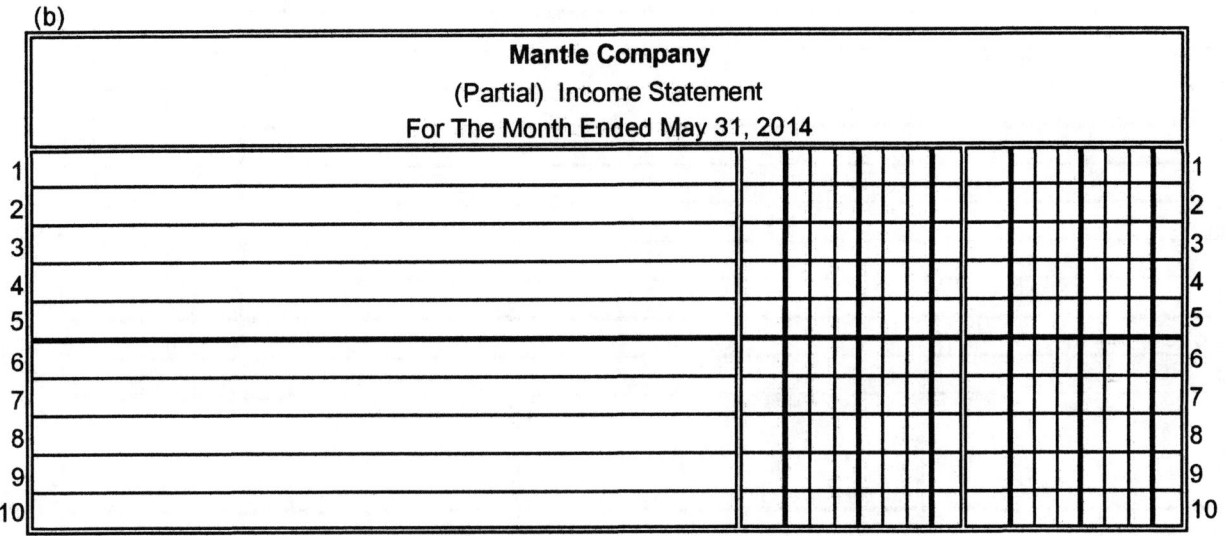

Mantle Company
(Partial) Income Statement
For The Month Ended May 31, 2014

(c)

(a)			
1	Work in Process Inventory:		1
2			2
3			3
4			4
5			5
6			6
7			7
8			8
9			9
10			10
11	(b) Finished Goods Inventory:		11
12			12
13			13
14			14
15			15
16			16
17			17
18			18
19			19
20			20
21	(c) Gross Profit:		21
22			22

	Month	Job Number	Sales	Cost of Goods Sold	Gross Profit	
23						23
24						24
25						25
26						26
27						27
28						28
29						29
30						30
31						31
32						32
33						33
34						34
35						35

(a)

	Trans-action Number	Account Titles	Debit	Credit	
1	1				1
2					2
3					3
4	2				4
5					5
6					6
7					7
8	3				8
9					9
10					10
11					11
12	4				12
13					13
14					14
15	5				15
16					16
17					17
18	6				18
19					19
20					20

(b)

WORK IN PROCESS INVENTORY

21	21
22	22
23	23
24	24
25	25
26	26
27	27
28	28
29	29
30	30
31	31
32	32
33	33
34	34
35	35
36	36
37	37
38	38
39	39
40	40

E16-12

(a)	Lynn	Brian	Mike
1			
2			
3			
4			
5			

(b)

(c)

E16-13

(a)   Predetermined overhead rate =

(b)   Applied overhead:

Account Titles	Debit	Credit

(c)   Under-or-overapplied overhead:

(a)

(b) and (e)

Job Cost Sheets

JOB NO. 50

Date	Direct Materials	Direct Labor	Manu-facturing Overhead

Cost of completed job

JOB NO. 51

Date	Direct Materials	Direct Labor	Manu-facturing Overhead

Cost of completed job

JOB NO. 52

Date	Direct Materials	Direct Labor	Manu-facturing Overhead

Account Titles	Debit	Credit
1 (c)		
2		
3		
4		
5		
6		
7		
8		
9		
10		
11		
12		
13		
14 (d)		
15		
16		
17		
18		
19		
20		
21		
22		
23 (e)		
24		
25		
26		
27 (f)		
28		
29		
30		
31		
32		
33		
34		
35		
36		
37		
38		
39		
40		

(g)

	FINISHED GOODS INVENTORY		
1			1
2			2
3			3
4			4
5			5
6			6
7			7
8			8
9			9
10			10
11	Components of account balance:		11
12			12
13			13
14			14
15			15
16			16
17			17
18			18

(h)

	MANUFACTURING OVERHEAD		
1			1
2			2
3			3
4			4
5			5
6			6
7			7
8			8
9			9
10			10
11			11
12			12
13			13
14			14
15			15
16			16

(a)

	WORK IN PROCESS INVENTORY	
1		1
2		2
3		3
4		4
5		5
6		6
7		7
8		8
9		9

	Supporting calculations for five postings to Work In Process Inventory:				
10					10
11	(1)		(3)		11
12					12
13					13
14					14
15					15
16	(2)		(4)		16
17					17
18					18
19					19
20					20
21	(5) (a) Job 7640				21
22					22
23					23
24					24
25					25
26					26
27					27
28	(b) Job 7641				28
29					29
30					30
31					31
32					32
33					33
34	(c) Total cost of completed work				34
35					35
36					36
37					37
38					38
39					39
40					40

(a) (Continued)

	Proof of ending Work In Process Inventory balance:		
1			1
2			2
3			3
4			4
5			5
6			6
7			7
8			8
9			9
10			10
11	(b) Actual overhead costs		11
12			12
13			13
14			14
15			15
16			16
17			17
18	Applied overhead costs		18
19			19
20			20
21			21
22			22
23			23
24			24
25			25
26			26
27			27
28			28

	Date	Account Titles	Debit	Credit	
29					29
30					30
31					31
32					32
33	(c)				33
34					34
35					35
36					36
37					37
38					38
39					39
40					40

Stellar Inc.

Account Titles	Debit	Credit
			1
			2
			3
			4
			5
			6
			7
			8
			9
			10
			11
			12
			13
			14
			15
			16
			17
			18
			19
			20
			21
			22
			23
			24
			25
			26
			27
			28
			29
			30

Job	Direct Materials	Direct Labor	Manufacturing Overhead	Total Cost
					1
					2
					3
					4
					5

(b)

1	1
2	WORK IN PROCESS INVENTORY	2
3	3
4	4
5	5
6	6
7	7
8	8
9	9
10	10

(c) Components of account balance:

11	11
12	12
13	13
14	14
15	15
16	16
17	17
18	18

(d)

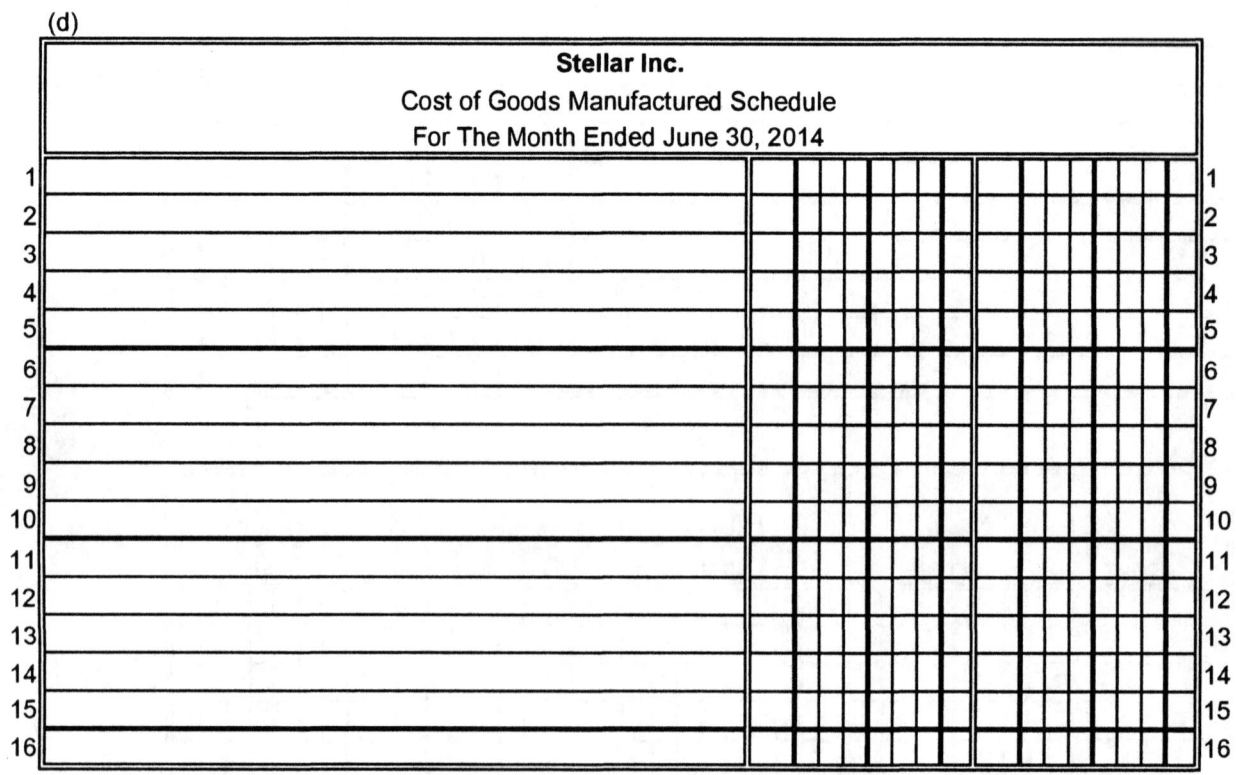

Stellar Inc.
Cost of Goods Manufactured Schedule
For The Month Ended June 30, 2014

(a)

Computation of predetermined overhead rate:

1 Department D:	1
2	2
3	3
4 Department E:	4
5	5
6	6
7 Department K:	7
8	8
9	9
10	10
11	11
12	12
13	13
14	14
15	15
16	16

(b)

Manufacturing Costs	Department		
	D	E	K
1			
2			
3			
4			
5			
6			

(c)

Manufacturing Overhead	Department		
	D	E	K
1			
2			
3			
4			
5			
6			

(a) - (f)

1	(a)		1
2			2
3			3
4			4
5			5
6	(b)		6
7			7
8			8
9			9
10			10
11	(c)		11
12			12
13			13
14			14
15	(d)		15
16			16
17			17
18	(e)		18
19			19
20			20
21			21
22			22
23	(f)		23
24			24
25			25
26			26
27			27
28			28
29			29
30			30
31			31
32			32
33			33
34			34
35			35
36			36
37			37
38			38
39			39
40			40

(g) - (m)

1	(g)		1
2			2
3	(h)		3
4			4
5	(i)		5
6			6
7			7
8			8
9			9
10	(j)		10
11			11
12	(k)		12
13			13
14	(l)		14
15			15
16			16
17			17
18			18
19	(m)		19
20			20
21			21
22			22
23			23
24			24
25			25
26			26
27			27
28			28
29			29
30			30
31			31
32			32
33			33
34			34
35			35
36			36
37			37
38			38
39			39
40			40

(a)

1	1
2	2
3	3
4	4
5	5
6	6
7	7
8	8
9	9
10	10
11	11
12	12
13	13
14	14
15	15
16	16
17	17
18	18
19	19
20	20
21	21
22	22
23	23
24	24
25	25
26	26
27	27
28	28
29	29
30	30
31	31
32	32
33	33
34	34
35	35
36	36
37	37
38	38
39	39
40	40

(b) and (e)

Job Cost Sheets

JOB NO. 25

Date	Direct Materials	Direct Labor	Manu-facturing Overhead

Cost of completed job

JOB NO. 26

Date	Direct Materials	Direct Labor	Manu-facturing Overhead

Cost of completed job

JOB NO. 27

Date	Direct Materials	Direct Labor	Manu-facturing Overhead

	Account Titles	Debit	Credit	
1	(c)			1
2				2
3				3
4				4
5				5
6				6
7				7
8				8
9				9
10				10
11				11
12				12
13				13
14	(d)			14
15				15
16				16
17				17
18				18
19				19
20				20
21				21
22				22
23	(e)			23
24				24
25				25
26				26
27	(f)			27
28				28
29				29
30				30
31				31
32				32
33				33
34				34
35				35
36				36
37				37
38				38
39				39
40				40

(g)

1		1
2	WORK IN PROCESS	2
3		3
4		4
5		5
6		6
7		7
8		8
9		9
10		10
11	Components of account balance:	11
12		12
13		13
14		14
15		15
16		16
17		17
18		18

(h)

1		1
2	MANUFACTURING OVERHEAD	2
3		3
4		4
5		5
6		6
7		7
8		8
9		9
10		10
11		11
12		12
13		13
14		14
15		15
16		16

(a)

1

2   WORK IN PROCESS INVENTORY

3

4

5

6

7

8

9

10 Supporting calculations for five postings to Work In Process Inventory:

11 (1)   (3)

12

13

14

15

16 (2)   (4)

17

18

19

20

21 (5)   (a)   Job 7650

22

23

24

25

26

27

28   (b)   Job 7651

29

30

31

32

33

34   (c)   Total cost of completed work

35

36

37

38

39

40

Name

Section

Date

Dosey Company

(a) (Continued)

Proof of ending Work In Process Inventory balance:

1		
2		
3		
4		
5		
6		
7		
8		
9		
10		
11	(b) Actual overhead costs	
12		
13		
14		
15		
16		
17		
18	Applied overhead costs	
19		
20		
21		
22		
23		
24		
25		
26		
27		
28		

	Date	Account Titles	Debit	Credit
29				
30				
31				
32				
33	(c)			
34				
35				
36				
37				
38				
39				
40				

(a)

	Account Titles	Debit	Credit
1	(i)		
2			
3			
4			
5			
6			
7			
8			
9			
10	(ii)		
11			
12			
13			
14			
15			
16			
17			
18			
19			
20			
21	(iii)		
22			
23			
24			
25			
26			
27			
28			
29			
30			

	Job	Direct Materials	Direct Labor	Manufacturing Overhead	Total Cost
1					
2					
3					
4					
5					

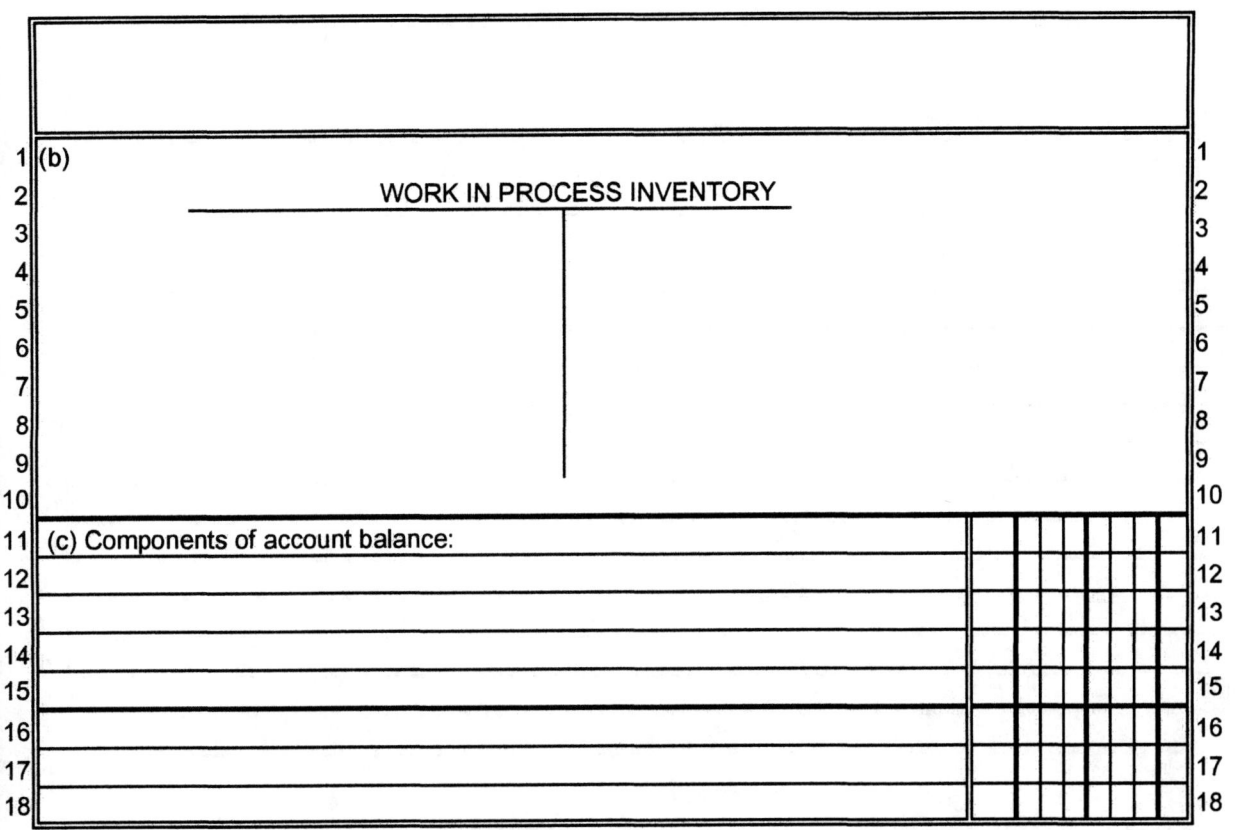

(b)

WORK IN PROCESS INVENTORY

(c) Components of account balance:

(d)

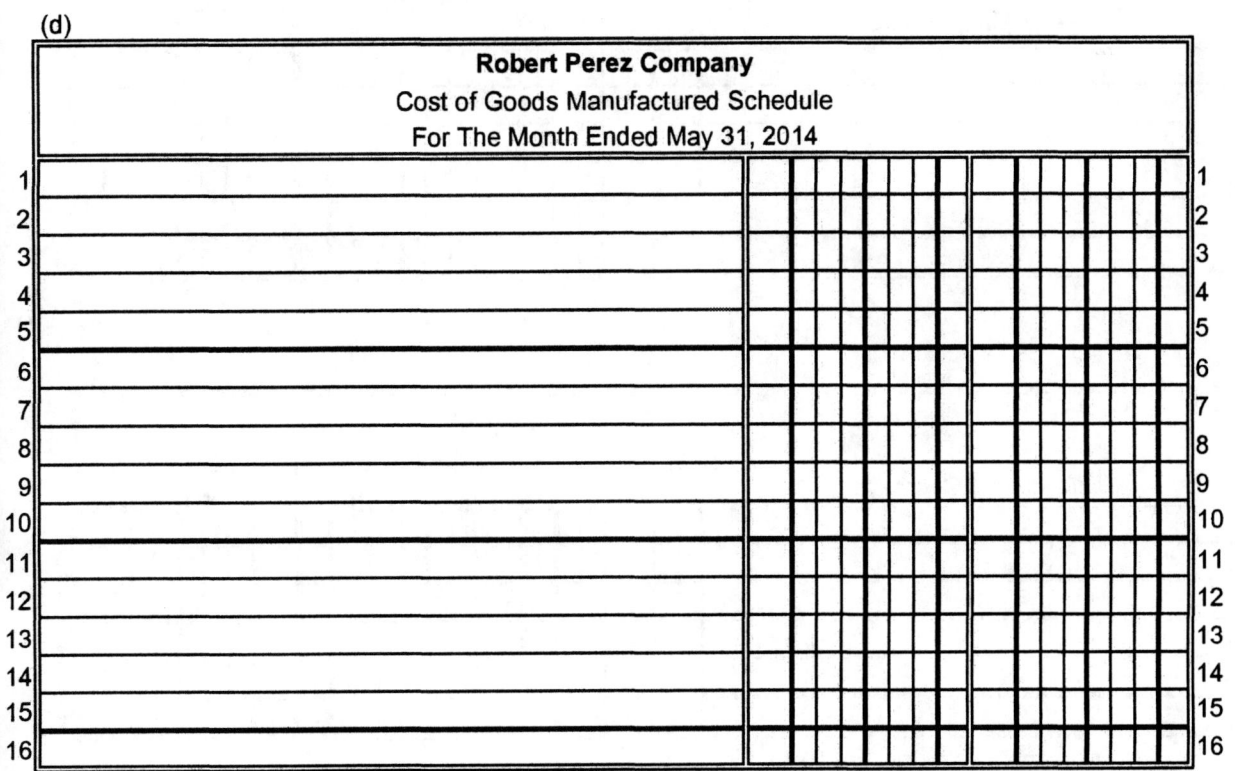

Robert Perez Company
Cost of Goods Manufactured Schedule
For The Month Ended May 31, 2014

(a)

Computation of predetermined overhead rates:	
Department A:	
Department B:	
Department C:	

(b)

Manufacturing Costs	Department		
	A	B	C

(c)

Manufacturing Overhead	Department		
	A	B	C

(a) - (g)

1	(a)								1
2									2
3									3
4									4
5	(b)								5
6									6
7									7
8									8
9									9
10	(c)								10
11									11
12									12
13	(e)								13
14									14
15	(f)								15
16									16
17									17
18									18
19									19
20									20
21	(g)								21
22									22
23									23
24									24
25									25
26									26
27									27
28									28
29									29
30									30
31									31
32									32
33									33
34									34
35									35
36									36
37									37
38									38
39									39
40									40

(h) - (n)

1	(h)				1
2					2
3	(i)				3
4					4
5	(j)				5
6					6
7					7
8					8
9					9
10	(k)				10
11					11
12	(l)				12
13					13
14					14
15	(m)				15
16					16
17	(n)				17
18					18
19					19
20					20
21					21
22					22
23					23
24					24
25					25
26					26
27					27
28					28
29					29
30					30
31					31
32					32
33					33
34					34
35					35
36					36
37					37
38					38
39					39
40					40

1	Cost for one kayak:		1
2			2
3			3
4			4
5			5
6			6
7			7
8			8
9			9
10			10
11			11
12			12
13			13
14			14
15			15
16			16
17			17
18			18
19			19
20			20
21			21
22			22
23			23
24			24
25			25
26			26
27			27
28			28
29			29
30			30
31			31
32			32
33			33
34			34
35			35
36			36
37			37
38			38
39			39
40			40

(a)

(b)

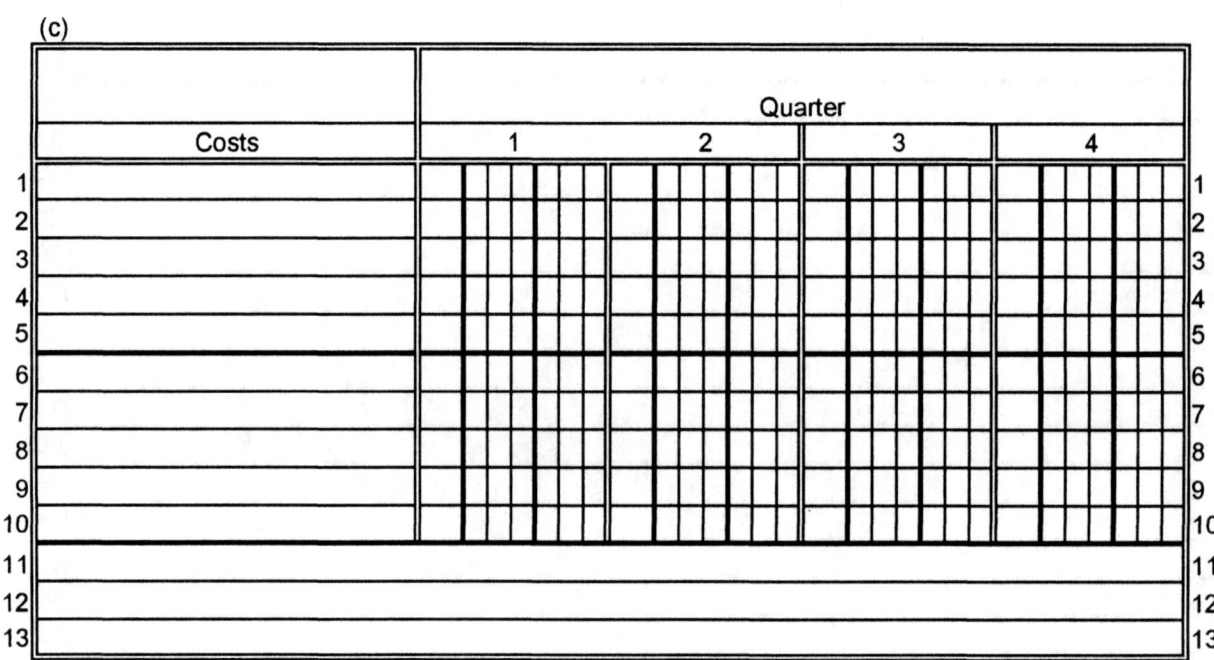

(c)

	Costs	Quarter			
		1	2	3	4

	Account Titles	Debit	Credit	
1	FIRST ENTRY			1
2	(a)			2
3				3
4				4
5				5
6	(b)			6
7				7
8				8
9				9
10				10
11	SECOND ENTRY			11
12	(a)			12
13				13
14				14
15				15
16	(b)			16
17				17
18				18
19				19
20				20
21	THIRD ENTRY			21
22	(a)			22
23				23
24				24
25				25
26	(b)			26
27				27
28				28
29				29
30				30
31	FOURTH ENTRY			31
32	(a)			32
33				33
34				34
35				35
36	(b)			36
37				37
38				38
39				39
40				40

BE17-1

	Date	Account Titles	Debit	Credit	
1	Mar 31				1
2					2
3					3
4					4
5					5
6	31				6
7					7
8					8
9	**BE17-2**				9
10	Mar 31				10
11					11
12					12
13					13
14	31				14
15					15
16					16
17					17
18	**BE17-3**				18
19	Mar 31				19
20					20
21					21
22					22
23					23
24					24
25					25
26					26
27					27
28					28
29					29
30					30
31					31
32					32
33					33
34					34
35					35
36					36
37					37
38					38
39					39
40					40

BE17-4

		Calculations	Materials	Conversion Costs	
1	Jan.				1
2					2
3	March				3
4					4
5	July				5
6					6
7					7

BE17-6	Equivalent Units	Unit Cost	Total Costs	
8	Assignment of Costs:				8
9					9
10					10
11					11
12					12
13					13
14					14
15					15
16					16
17					17
18					18
19					19
20					20
21					21
22					22
23					23
24					24
25					25
26					26
27					27
28					28
29					29
30					30
31					31
32					32
33					33
34					34
35					35
36					36
37					37
38					38
39					39
40					40

BE17-8

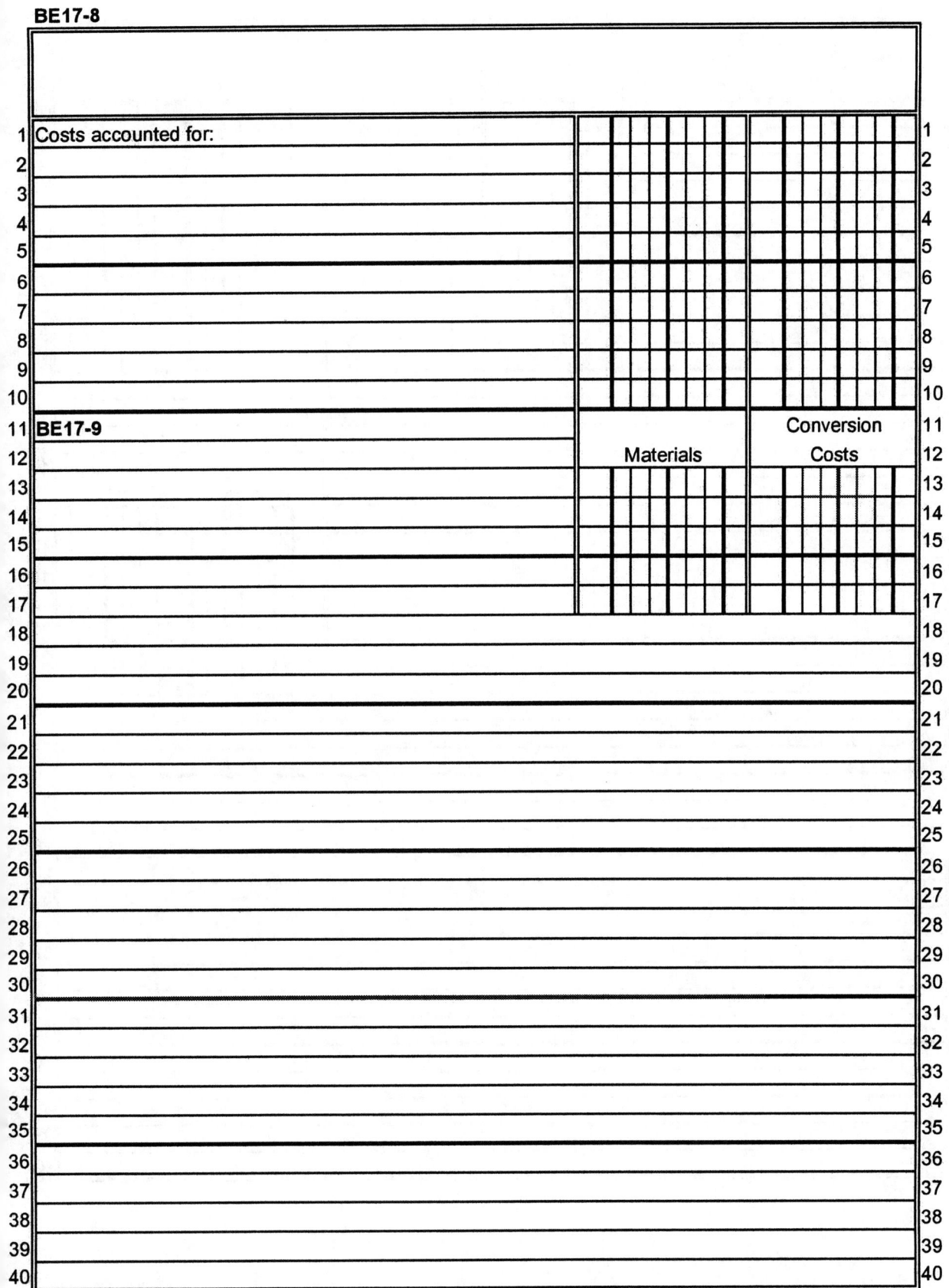

	Costs accounted for:			
1	Costs accounted for:			1
2				2
3				3
4				4
5				5
6				6
7				7
8				8
9				9
10				10
11	**BE17-9**	Materials	Conversion Costs	11

*BE17-10

	Costs to Be Assigned	Assignment of Costs	Equivalent Units	Unit Cost	Total Costs Assigned	
1						1
2						2
3						3
4						4
5						5
6						6
7						7
8						8
9						9
10						10

*BE17-11

		Equivalent Units	
		Materials	Conversion Costs
11				11
12				12
13				13
14				14
15				15
16	Units accounted for:			16
17				17
18				18
19				19
20				20
21				21
22				22
23				23
24				24
25				25
26				26
27				27
28				28
29				29
30				30
31				31
32				32
33				33
34				34
35				35
36				36
37				37
38				38
39				39
40				40

*BE17-11 (Continued)

COSTS	Materials	Conversion Costs	Total

Sanderson Company
(Partial) Production Cost Report
For the Month Ended March 31

		Account Titles	Debit	Credit	
1					1
2					2
3					3
4					4
5					5
6					6
7					7
8					8
9					9
10					10
11					11
12					12
13					13
14					14
15					15
16					16
17					17
18					18
19					19
20					20
21					21
22					22
23					23
24					24
25					25
26					26
27					27
28					28
29					29
30					30
31					31
32					32
33					33
34					34
35					35
36					36
37					37
38					38
39					39
40					40

DO IT! 17-3

	Equivalent Units	
	(a) Materials	(b) Conversion Costs
1		
2		
3		
4		
5		

6		
7		
8		
9		

DO IT! 17-4

		Equivalent Units
(a) Total units to be accounted for:		

(b)	Equivalent Units	
	Materials	Conversion Costs

(c) Cost reconciliation schedule

	Date	Account Titles	Debit	Credit	
1	Apr 30				1
2					2
3					3
4					4
5	30				5
6					6
7					7
8					8
9	30				9
10					10
11					11
12					12
13	30				13
14					14
15					15
16					16
17					17
18					18
19					19
20					20
21					21
22					22
23					23
24					24
25					25
26					26
27					27
28					28
29					29
30					30
31					31
32					32
33					33
34					34
35					35
36					36
37					37
38					38
39					39
40					40

Custer Company

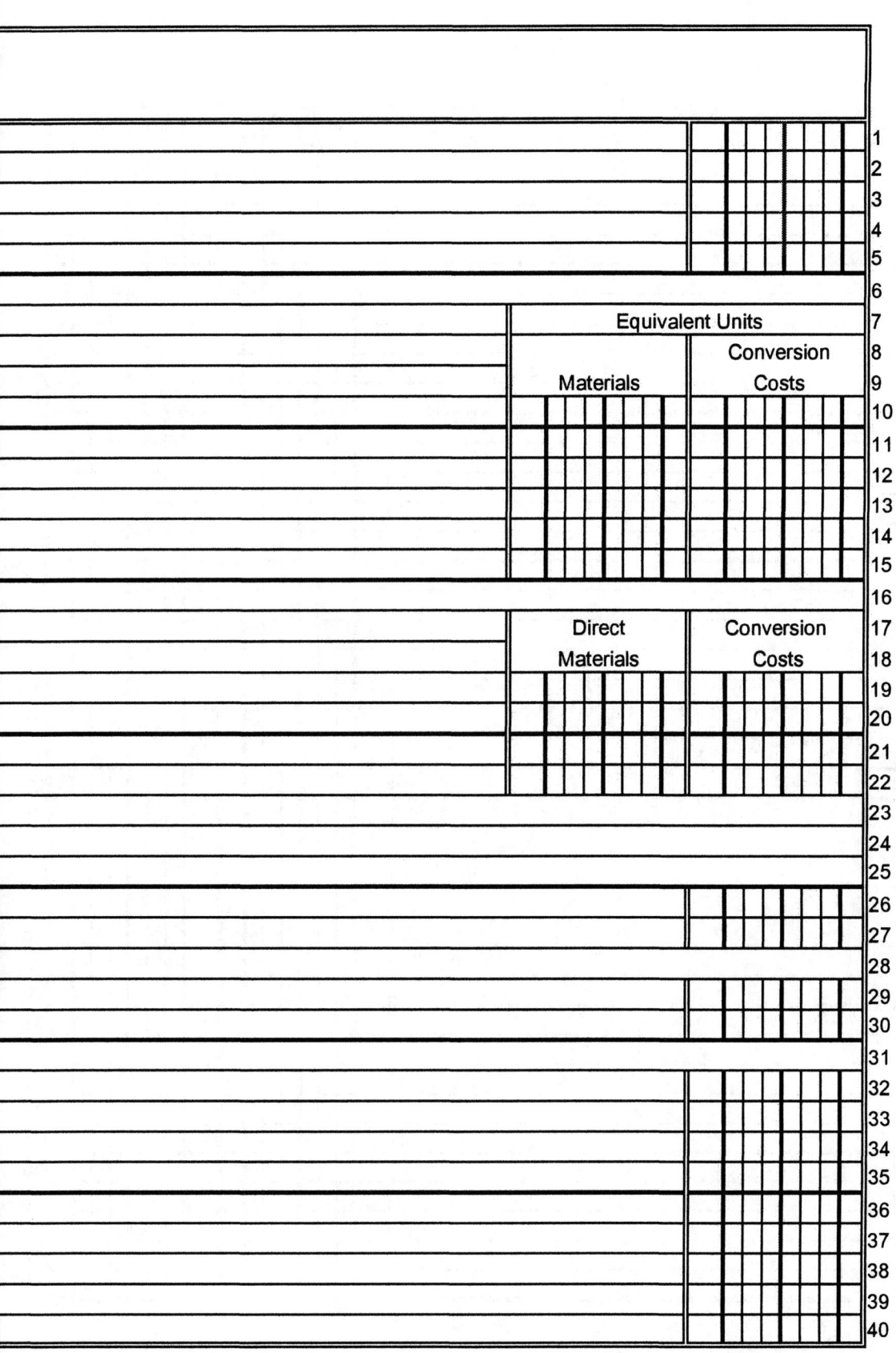

	Trans-action Number	Account Titles	Debit	Credit	
1	1.				1
2					2
3					3
4	2.				4
5					5
6					6
7	3.				7
8					8
9					9
10					10
11	4.				11
12					12
13					13
14					14
15	5.				15
16					16
17					17
18					18
19	6.				19
20					20
21					21
22					22
23	7.				23
24					24
25					25
26					26
27	8.				27
28					28
29					29
30					30
31	9.				31
32					32
33					33
34					34
35					35
36					36
37					37
38					38
39					39
40					40

E17-5

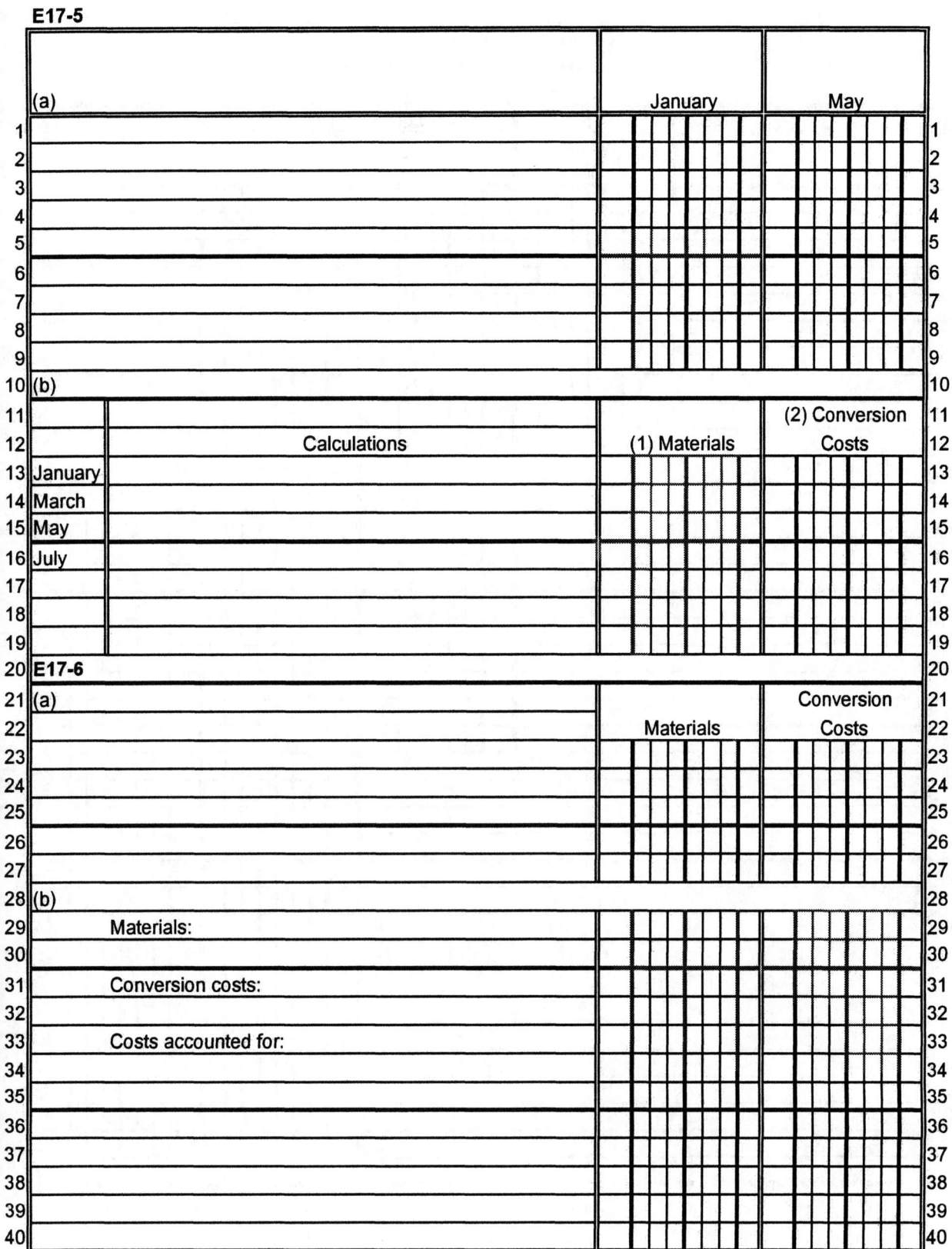

(a)		January	May	
1				1
2				2
3				3
4				4
5				5
6				6
7				7
8				8
9				9
10 (b)				10
11			(2) Conversion	11
12	Calculations	(1) Materials	Costs	12
13 January				13
14 March				14
15 May				15
16 July				16
17				17
18				18
19				19

E17-6

(a)		Materials	Conversion Costs	
21				21
22				22
23				23
24				24
25				25
26				26
27				27
28 (b)				28
29	Materials:			29
30				30
31	Conversion costs:			31
32				32
33	Costs accounted for:			33
34				34
35				35
36				36
37				37
38				38
39				39
40				40

Richards Furniture Company				
Production Cost Report - Sanding Department				
For The Month Ended March 31, 2014				
Quantities:	Physical Units	Equivalent Units		
		Materials	Conversion Costs	
1				
2				
3				
4				
5				
6				
7				
8				
9				
10				
Costs:		Materials	Conversion Costs	Total
12				
13				
14				
15				
16				
17				
18				
19				
20				
21				
22				
Cost Reconciliation Schedule:				
24				
25				
26				
27				
28				
29				
30				
31				
32				
33				
34				
35				
36				
37				

E17-8

(a)

	Materials	Conversion Costs
1		
2		
3		
4		
5		

(b)

	Materials	Conversion Costs	Total
7			
8			
9			
10			
11			
12			

(c)

	Materials	Conversion Costs
14		
15		
16		
17		
18		
19		
20		

E17-9

(a)   Materials:

Conversion costs:

(b)   Materials:

Conversion costs:

(c)   Units transferred out:

Units in ending work in process:

1	(a)　　　Materials:	1
2		2
3	Conversion costs:	3
4		4
5		5
6	(b)　　　Materials:	6
7		7
8	Conversion costs:	8
9		9
10		10
11	(c)　　　Units transferred out:	11
12		12
13	Units in ending work in process:	13
14		14
15		15
16		16
17		17
18		18
19		19
20		20
21		21
22		22
23		23
24		24
25		25
26		26
27		27
28		28
29		29
30		30
31		31
32		32
33		33
34		34
35		35
36		36
37		37
38		38
39		39
40		40

(a)	Physical Units	Equivalent Units		
		Materials	Conversion Costs	
1				
2				
3				
4				
5				
6				
7				
8				
9				
10				
11				
12				
13				
14				
15				

(b)	Materials	Conversion Costs	Total
16			
17			
18			
19			
20			
21			
22			
23			
24			
25			
26			
27			
28			
29			
30			
(c)			
31			
32			
33			
34			
35			
36			
37			
38			
39			
40			

Thorpe Company
Welding Department
Production Cost Report
For The Month Ended February 28, 2014

Quantities:	Physical Units	Equivalent Units		
		Materials	Conversion Costs	
1				
2				
3				
4				
5				
6				
7				
8				
9				
10				

Costs:		Materials	Conversion Costs	Total
13				
14				
15				
16				
17				
18				
19				
20				
21				
22				
23				

Cost Reconciliation Schedule:

E17-14

	(a) Physical Units	(b) Equivalent Units	
		Direct Materials	Conversion Costs
1			
2			
3			
4			
5			
6			
7			
8			
9			
10			

E17-15

	Equivalent Units	
(a)	Materials	Conversion Costs
1		
2		
3		
4		
5 (b)		
6 Materials		
7		
8 Conversion costs		
9		
10 Costs accounted for:		
11		
12		
13		
14		
15		
16		
17		
18		
19		
20		
21		
22		
23		
24		
25		

		Physical Units	Equivalent Units		
			Materials		Conversion Costs
(a)					
1 Applications completed:					
2					
3					
4					
5					
6					
7					
8 (b)					
9 Materials:					
10					
11 Conversion costs:					
12					
13					
14 Costs accounted for:					
15 Applications completed:					
16					
17					
18					
19					
20					
21					
22					
23					
24					
25					
26					
27					
28					
29					
30					
31					
32					
33					
34					
35					
36					
37					
38					
39					
40					

(a) (1) Materials:			
Production Data	Physical Units	Materials Added This Period	Equivalent Units
1			
2			
3			
4			
5			

(2) Conversion Costs:			
Production Data	Physical Units	Work Added This Period	Equivalent Units
9			
10			
11			
12			

(b) Unit costs are:	
Materials:	
Conversion Costs:	
Total	

Costs to Be Assigned	Assignment of Costs	Equivalent Units	Unit Cost	Total Costs Assigned
Tot. mfg. costs	Transferred out:			
	Work in process, August 31			

(a) (1)

Materials	Physical Units	Materials Added This Period	Equivalent Units

(2)

Conversion Costs	Physical Units	Work Added This Period	Equivalent Units

(b)   Unit costs are:

       Materials:

       Conversion Costs:

       Total

(c)

Costs to Be Assigned	Assignment of Costs	Equivalent Units	Unit Cost	Total Costs Assigned
Tot. mfg. costs	Transferred out:			
	Work in process, 9/30			

(a)

1	
2	
3	
4	
5	
6	

(b) Materials:

Production Data:

	Physical Units	Materials Added This Period	Equivalent Units

Unit cost

(c) Conversion costs:

Production Data:

	Physical Units	Work Added This Period	Equivalent Units

Unit cost

(d)

(e)

(f)

Majestic Company
Welding Department
Production Cost Report
For The Month Ended February 28, 2014

Quantities	Physical Units	Equivalent Units		Total
		Materials	Conversion Costs	
1 Units to be accounted for				
2				
3				
4				
5				
6 Units accounted for				
7				
8				
9				
10				
11				
12				
13				
14 Costs				
15 Unit costs				
16				
17				
18				
19				
20 Costs to be accounted for				
21				
22				
23				
24 Cost Reconciliation Schedule:				
25 Costs accounted for				
26				
27				
28				
29				
30				
31				
32				
33				
34				
35				
36				

Name _____

Section _____

Date _____   Conwell Company

		Account Titles	Debit	Credit	
1	1.				1
2					2
3					3
4	2.				4
5					5
6					6
7					7
8	3.				8
9					9
10					10
11	4.				11
12					12
13					13
14					14
15	5.				15
16					16
17					17
18	6.				18
19					19
20					20
21					21
22	7.				22
23					23
24					24
25	8.				25
26					26
27					27
28	9.				28
29					29
30					30
31					31
32					32
33					33
34					34
35					35
36					36
37					37
38					38
39					39
40					40

(a)

1 | Physical units:
2 |
3 |
4 |
5 |
6 |
7 |
8 |
9 |
10 |

(b) Equivalent units:

	Materials	Conversion Costs

(c) Unit costs:

	Materials	Conversion Costs	Total

(d) Costs accounted for:

	Equivalent Units	Unit Cost	Total Costs Assigned
Transferred out			
Work in process, June 30:			

(e)

	Rosenthal Company						
	Rosenthal Company						
	Production Cost Report - Molding Department						
	For The Month Ended June 30, 2014						
		Physical Units	Equivalent Units				
			Materials	Conversion Costs			
1	Quantities:						1
2	Units to be accounted for						2
3							3
4							4
5							5
6							6
7	Units accounted for						7
8							8
9							9
10							10
11							11
12	Costs:			Conversion			12
13	Unit costs:		Materials	Costs	Total		13
14							14
15							15
16							16
17							17
18	Costs to be accounted for						18
19							19
20							20
21							21
22							22
23							23
24	Cost reconciliation schedule:						24
25	Costs accounted for						25
26							26
27							27
28							28
29							29
30							30
31							31
32							32
33							33
34							34
35							35
36							36
37							37

(a)

	T12 Tables	C10 Chairs
(1) Physical units:		

(2) Equivalent units:	T12 Tables	
	Materials	Conversion Costs

	C10 Chairs	
	Materials	Conversion Costs

(3) Unit costs:	T12 Tables	C10 Chairs

(a) Continued

(4)	T12 Tables	
1 Costs accounted for:		1
2		2
3		3
4		4
5		5
6		6
7		7
8		8
9		9
10	C10 Chairs	10
11 Costs accounted for:		11
12		12
13		13
14		14
15		15
16		16
17		17
18		18
19		19
20		20
21		21
22		22
23		23
24		24
25		25
26		26
27		27
28		28
29		29
30		30
31		31
32		32
33		33
34		34
35		35
36		36
37		37
38		38
39		39
40		40

(b)

							Seagren Industries Inc. - Plant 1
				Production Cost Report - Cutting Department			
				For The Month Ended July 31, 2014			

		Physical Units	Equivalent Units		
			Materials	Conversion Costs	
1	Quantities:				1
2	Units to be accounted for				2
3					3
4					4
5					5
6					6
7	Units accounted for				7
8					8
9					9
10					10
11					11
12	Costs:			Conversion	12
13	Unit costs:		Materials	Costs	Total	13
14						14
15						15
16						16
17						17
18	Costs to be accounted for					18
19						19
20						20
21						21
22						22
23	Cost Reconciliation Schedule:					23
24	Costs accounted for					24
25						25
26						26
27						27
28						28
29						29
30						30
31						31
32						32
33						33
34						34
35						35
36						36
37						37

(a)	Physical Units	Equivalent Units	
		Materials	Conversion Costs
1 Units to be accounted for:			
2			
3			
4			
5			
6			
7 Units accounted for:			
8			
9			
10			
11			
12 Costs:			
13			
14			
15			
16			
17			
18 Cost per unit			
19			
20 (b)			
21 Costs accounted for:			
22			
23			
24			
25			
26			
27			
28			
29			
30			
31			
32			
33			
34			
35			
36			
37			
38			
39			
40			

(b)

Rivera Company
Assembly Department
Production Cost Report
For The Month Ended November 30, 2014

	Physical Units	Equivalent Units		
		Materials	Conversion Costs	
1 Quantities:				1
2 Units to be accounted for				2
3				3
4				4
5				5
6				6
7 Units accounted for				7
8				8
9				9
10				10
11				11

		Materials	Conversion Costs	Total	
12 Costs:					12
13 Unit costs:					13
14					14
15					15
16					16
17					17
18 Costs to be accounted for					18
19					19
20					20
21					21
22					22
23 Cost Reconciliation Schedule:					23
24 Costs accounted for					24
25					25
26					26
27					27
28					28
29					29
30					30
31					31
32					32
33					33
34					34
35					35
36					36

	Physical Units	Equivalent Units	
		Materials	Conversion Costs
(a) (1)			
1 Units to be accounted for:			
2			
3			
4			
5			
6			
7 Units accounted for:			
8			
9			
10			
11 (2)			
12 Costs:			
13			
14			
15			
16			
17			
18 Cost per unit			
19			
20 (3)			
21 Costs accounted for:			
22			
23			
24			
25			
26			
27			
28			
29			
30			
31			
32			
33			
34			
35			
36			
37			
38			
39			
40			

(b)

			Equivalent Units		
		Physical Units	Materials	Conversion Costs	
1	Quantities:				
2	Units to be accounted for				
3					
4					
5					
6					
7	Units accounted for				
8					
9					
10					
11					
12	Costs:			Conversion	
13	Unit costs:		Materials	Costs	Total
14					
15					
16					
17					
18	Costs to be accounted for				
19					
20					
21					
22					
23	Cost Reconciliation Schedule:				
24	Costs accounted for				
25					
26					
27					
28					
29					
30					
31					
32					
33					
34					
35					
36					

Morse Company
Basketball Department
Production Cost Report
For The Month Ended July 31, 2014

	Physical Units	Equivalent Units	
		Materials	Conversion Costs
1. (a) Computation of equivalent units:			
2.			
3.			
4.			
5.			
6.			
7.			
8.			
9.			
10.			
11.			
12. Computation of October unit costs:			
13.			
14.			
15.			
16.			
17.			
18.			
19.			
20.			
21. (b) Cost Reconciliation Schedule:			
22.			
23.			
24.			
25.			
26.			
27.			
28.			
29.			
30.			
31.			
32.			
33.			
34.			
35.			
36.			
37.			
38.			
39.			
40.			

(a) Bicycles (1) Equivalent units - Materials	Physical Units	% Added This Period	Equivalent Units	
1				1
2				2
3				3
4				4
5				5
6 Equivalent units - Conversion				6
7				7
8				8
9				9
10				10
11				11

12 (2) Unit Costs:		Materials	Conversion	
13				13
14				14
15				15
16				16
17				17
18				18

19 (3) Assignment of Costs:					
20 Costs 21 to Be 22 Assigned	Assignment of Costs	Equivalent Units	Unit Cost	Total Costs Assigned	
23					23
24					24
25					25
26					26
27					27
28					28
29					29
30					30
31					31
32					32
33					33
34					34
35					35

(a) Continued

Tricycles (1) Equivalent units - Materials	Physical Units	% Added This Period	Equivalent Units	
1				1
2				2
3				3
4				4
5				5

Equivalent units - Conversion				
6				6
7				7
8				8
9				9
10				10
11				11

(2) Unit Costs:	Materials	Conversion	
12			12
13			13
14			14
15			15
16			16
17			17
18			18

(3) Assignment of Costs:

Costs to Be Assigned	Assignment of Costs	Equivalent Units	Unit Cost	Total Costs Assigned	
20					20
21					21
22					22
23					23
24					24
25					25
26					26
27					27
28					28
29					29
30					30
31					31
32					32
33					33
34					34
35					35

(b)

Rondeli Company
Bicycles Department
Production Cost Report
For The Month Ended March 31

	Physical Units	Equivalent Units		
		Materials	Conversion Costs	
1 Quantities:				
2 Units to be accounted for				
3				
4				
5				
6				
7 Units accounted for				
8				
9				
10				
11				

	Materials	Conversion Costs	Total
12 Costs:			
13 Unit costs:			
14			
15			
16			
17			
18 Costs to be accounted for			
19			
20			
21			
22			
23 Cost Reconciliation Schedule:			
24 Costs accounted for			
25			
26			
27			
28			
29			
30			
31			
32			
33			
34			
35			
36			

	Trans- action	Account Titles	Debit	Credit	
1	1.				1
2					2
3					3
4	2.				4
5					5
6					6
7					7
8	3.				8
9					9
10					10
11	4.				11
12					12
13					13
14					14
15	5.				15
16					16
17					17
18	6.				18
19					19
20					20
21					21
22	7.				22
23					23
24					24
25	8.				25
26					26
27					27
28	9.				28
29					29
30					30
31					31
32					32
33					33
34					34
35					35
36					36
37					37
38					38
39					39
40					40

(a)

1 Physical units:

2

3

4

5

6

7

8

9

10

(b) Equivalent units:

	Materials	Conversion Costs

(c) Unit costs:

	Materials	Conversion Costs	Total

(d) Costs accounted for:

	Equivalent Units	Unit Cost	Total Costs Assigned
Transferred out			
Work in process, June 30:			

(e)

	Steiner Corporation				
	Production Cost Report - Molding Department				
	For The Month Ended January 31, 2014				
	Physical Units	Equivalent Units			
		Materials	Conversion Costs		
1 Quantities:					1
2 Units to be accounted for					2
3					3
4					4
5					5
6					6
7 Units accounted for					7
8					8
9					9
10					10
11					11
12 Costs:			Conversion		12
13 Unit costs:		Materials	Costs	Total	13
14					14
15					15
16					16
17					17
18 Costs to be accounted for					18
19					19
20					20
21					21
22					22
23					23
24 Cost reconciliation schedule:					24
25 Costs accounted for					25
26					26
27					27
28					28
29					29
30					30
31					31
32					32
33					33
34					34
35					35
36					36
37					37

(a)

	R12 Refrigerators	F24 Freezers
(1) Physical units:		

(2) Equivalent units:	R12 Refrigerators	
	Materials	Conversion Costs

	F24 Freezers	
	Materials	Conversion Costs

(3) Unit costs:	R12 Refrigerators	F24 Freezers

(a) Continued

(4)	R12 Refrigerators	
1 Costs accounted for:		1
2		2
3		3
4		4
5		5
6		6
7		7
8		8
9		9
10	F24 Freezers	10
11 Costs accounted for:		11
12		12
13		13
14		14
15		15
16		16
17		17
18		18
19		19
20		20
21		21
22		22
23		23
24		24
25		25
26		26
27		27
28		28
29		29
30		30
31		31
32		32
33		33
34		34
35		35
36		36
37		37
38		38
39		39
40		40

(b)

Borman Corporation - Plant A

Production Cost Report - Stamping Department

For The Month Ended June 30, 2014

	Physical Units	Equivalent Units		
		Materials	Conversion Costs	
1 Quantities:				
2 Units to be accounted for				
3				
4				
5				
6				
7 Units accounted for				
8				
9				
10				
11				
12 Costs:			Conversion	
13 Unit costs:		Materials	Costs	Total
14				
15				
16				
17				
18 Costs to be accounted for				
19				
20				
21				
22				
23 Cost Reconciliation Schedule:				
24 Costs accounted for				
25				
26				
27				
28				
29				
30				
31				
32				
33				
34				
35				
36				
37				

	Physical Units	Equivalent Units	
		Materials	Conversion Costs
(a)			
1 Units to be accounted for:			
2			
3			
4			
5			
6			
7 Units accounted for:			
8			
9			
10			
11			
12 Costs:			
13			
14			
15			
16			
17			
18 Cost per unit			
19			
20 (b)			
21 Costs accounted for:			
22			
23			
24			
25			
26			
27			
28			
29			
30			
31			
32			
33			
34			
35			
36			
37			
38			
39			
40			

(b)

Luxman Company
Assembly Department
Production Cost Report
For The Month Ended October 31, 2014

	Physical Units	Equivalent Units		
		Materials	Conversion Costs	
1 Quantities:				
2 Units to be accounted for				
3				
4				
5				
6				
7 Units accounted for				
8				
9				
10				
11				
12 Costs:			Conversion	
13 Unit costs:		Materials	Costs	Total
14				
15				
16				
17				
18 Costs to be accounted for				
19				
20				
21				
22				
23 Cost Reconciliation Schedule:				
24 Costs accounted for				
25				
26				
27				
28				
29				
30				
31				
32				
33				
34				
35				
36				

(a) (1)	Physical Units	Equivalent Units	
		Materials	Conversion Costs
Units to be accounted for:			
Units accounted for:			
(2)			
Costs:			
Cost per unit			
(3)			
Costs accounted for:			

(b)

		Swinn Company			
		Bicycle Department			
		Production Cost Report			
		For The Month Ended May 31, 2014			

		Physical Units	Equivalent Units		
			Materials	Conversion Costs	
1	Quantities:				
2	Units to be accounted for				
3					
4					
5					
6					
7	Units accounted for				
8					
9					
10					
11					
12	Costs:			Conversion	
13	Unit costs:		Materials	Costs	Total
14					
15					
16					
17					
18	Costs to be accounted for				
19					
20					
21					
22					
23	Cost Reconciliation Schedule:				
24	Costs accounted for				
25					
26					
27					
28					
29					
30					
31					
32					
33					
34					
35					
36					

	Physical Units	Equivalent Units	
		Materials	Conversion Costs
(a) Computation of equivalent units:			
Computation of March unit costs:			
(b) Cost Reconciliation Schedule:			

(a) Basketballs	Physical Units	% Added This Period	Equivalent Units
(1) Equivalent units - Materials			
Equivalent units - Conversion			

(2) Unit Costs:	Materials	Conversion

(3) Assignment of Costs:

Costs to Be Assigned	Assignment of Costs	Equivalent Units	Unit Cost	Total Costs Assigned

(a) Continued

Soccer balls (1) Equivalent units - Materials	Physical Units	% Added This Period	Equivalent Units
1			
2			
3			
4			
5			
6 Equivalent units - Conversion			
7			
8			
9			
10			
11			

(2) Unit Costs:	Materials	Conversion
13		
14		
15		
16		
17		
18		

(3) Assignment of Costs:

Costs to Be Assigned	Assignment of Costs	Equivalent Units	Unit Cost	Total Costs Assigned
23				
24				
25				
26				
27				
28				
29				
30				
31				
32				
33				
34				
35				

(b)

Holiday Company
Basketballs Department
Production Cost Report
For The Month Ended August 31

	Physical Units	Equivalent Units		
		Materials	Conversion Costs	
1 Quantities:				
2 Units to be accounted for				
3				
4				
5				
6				
7 Units accounted for				
8				
9				
10				
11				
12 Costs:			Conversion	
13 Unit costs:		Materials	Costs	Total
14				
15				
16				
17				
18 Costs to be accounted for				
19				
20				
21				
22				
23 Cost Reconciliation Schedule:				
24 Costs accounted for				
25				
26				
27				
28				
29				
30				
31				
32				
33				
34				
35				
36				

(b)

Current Designs
Fabrication Department
Production Cost Report
For The Month Ended April 30, 2014

	Physical Units	Equivalent Units		
		Materials	Conversion Costs	
1 Quantities:				
2 Units to be accounted for				
3				
4				
5				
6				
7 Units accounted for				
8				
9				
10				
11				
12 Costs:			Conversion	
13 Unit costs:		Materials	Costs	Total
14				
15				
16				
17				
18 Costs to be accounted for				
19				
20				
21				
22				
23 Cost Reconciliation Schedule:				
24 Costs accounted for				
25				
26				
27				
28				
29				
30				
31				
32				
33				
34				
35				
36				

1	(a)
2	
3	
4	
5	
6	
7	
8	
9	
10	
11	(b)
12	
13	
14	
15	
16	
17	
18	
19	
20	
21	
22	
23	
24	
25	
26	
27	
28	
29	
30	

(b)

Florida Beach Company Mixing Department Production Cost Report For The Month Ended July 31, 2014				
	Physical Units	Equivalent Units		
		Materials	Conversion Costs	
1 Quantities:				
2 Units to be accounted for				
3				
4				
5				
6				
7 Units accounted for				
8				
9				
10				
11				
12 Costs:			Conversion	
13 Unit costs:		Materials	Costs	Total
14				
15				
16				
17				
18 Costs to be accounted for				
19				
20				
21				
22				
23 Cost Reconciliation Schedule:				
24 Costs accounted for				
25				
26				
27				
28				
29				
30				
31				
32				
33				
34				
35				
36				

BE18-6

	Activity Cost Pool	Estimated Overhead		Expected Use of Cost Drivers per Activity	Activity-Based Overhead Rates		
1	Designing	$ 450000		12,000 Designer hours			1
2	Sizing and cutting	4000000		160,000 Machine hours			2
3	Stitching and trimming	1440000		80,000 Labor hours			3
4	Wrapping and packing	336000		32,000 Finished units			4
5							5

BE18-7

	Activity Cost Pool	Estimated Overhead		Expected Use of Cost Drivers per Activity	Activity-Based Overhead Rates		
7				Expected Use of Cost Drivers per Activity	Activity-Based Overhead Rates		7
8		Estimated Overhead					8
9	Activity Cost Pool						9
10		$ 90000					10
11	Ordering and receiving	480000		12,000 orders			11
12	Etching	1760000		60,000 Machine hours			12
13	Soldering			440,000 Labor hours			13
14							14

		Cost Drivers	Overhead Rates	Total Overhead Applied	
15					15
16		Cost Drivers	Rates	Applied	16
17		11,000 Orders			17
18		50,000 Machine hours			18
19		500,000 Labor hours			19
20					20

BE18-9

		Hours		
21				21
22	Value-added Activities	Hours		22
23				23
24				24
25				25
26				26
27				27
28	Non-value-added Activites	Hours		28
29				29
30				30
31				31
32				32
33				33
34				34
35				35
36				36
37				37
38				38
39				39
40				40

BE18-12

(a) Activity Cost Pool	Estimated Overhead	Expected Use of Cost Drivers per Activity	Activity-Based Overhead Rates	
1				1
2 Product design	$ 40000	10 changes		2
3 Machining	300000	150,000 Machine hours		3
4 Material handling	100000	100 set-ups		4
5				5

(b) Activity	Level of Activity	
Product design		9
Machining		10
Material handling		11

(a)   Computations of activity-based overhead rates per cost driver:

	Activity Cost Pool	Estimated Overhead		Expected Use of Cost Drivers per Activity	Activity-Based Overhead Rates	
1	Machine setup	$	16000	40 setups		1
2	Machining		110000	5,000 Machine hours		2
3	Packing		30000	500 orders		3
4		$	156000			4
5						5

6	(b) Assignment of each activity's overhead cost to products using ABC:		6
7			7
8	See next page		8
9			9
10	(c) Computation of overhead cost per unit:		10

		BC113	AD908	
11		BC113	AD908	11
12	Total costs assigned			12
13	Total units produced			13
14	Overhead cost per unit			14
15				15

16	(d)	16
17		17
18		18
19		19
20		20
21		21
22		22
23		23
24		24
25		25
26		26
27		27
28		28
29		29
30		30
31		31
32		32
33		33
34		34
35		35
36		36
37		37
38		38
39		39
40		40

(b)

Activity Cost Pools	BC113			AD908		
	Expected Use of Cost Drivers per Product	Activity-Based Overhead Rates	Cost Assigned	Expected Use of Cost Drivers per Product	Activity-Based Overhead Rates	Cost Assigned
1 Machine setup						
2 Machining						
3 Packing and shipping						
4 Total assigned costs						
5						
6						
7						
8						
9						
10						

	Estimated Overhead	Direct Labor Costs	Overhead Rate		
1 (a)					1
2					2
3					3
4					4
5					5
6 (b)		Expected Use of Cost Drivers per Activity		Activity-Based Overhead Rates	6
7	Estimated Overhead				7
8	Activity Cost Pool				8
9					9
10 Machining					10
11 Machine setup					11
12					12
13					13
14					14
15 (c) Traditional Costing		Standard		Custom	15
16					16
17					17
18					18
19					19
20 Activity-based costing		Standard		Custom	20
21 Machining:					21
22					22
23					23
24					24
25 Machine setup:					25
26					26
27					27
28					28
29					29
30					30
31					31
32					32
33					33
34					34
35					35
36					36
37					37
38					38
39					39
40					40

		Product 540X	Product 137Y	Product 249S	
1	(a) Traditional costing system:				1
2		Product 540X	Product 137Y	Product 249S	2
3					3
4	Sales				4
5	Costs				5
6	Operating income				6
7					7
8					8
9					9
10	(b) Activity-based costing system:				10
11		Product 540X	Product 137Y	Product 249S	11
12					12
13	Sales				13
14	Costs				14
15	Operating income				15
16					16
17					17
18					18
19					19
20	(c)				20
21	Product 540X:				21
22					22
23	Product 137Y:				23
24					24
25	Product 249S:				25
26					26
27					27
28					28
29					29
30	(d)				30
31					31
32					32
33					33
34					34
35					35
36					36
37					37
38					38
39					39
40					40

(a)

Activity Cost Pool	Estimated Overhead	Expected Use of Cost Drivers per Activity	Activity-Based Overhead Rates	
1				1
2				2
3				3
4				4
5				5

Activity-based costing		Wool		Cotton	
6					6
7 Cutting					7
8					8
9					9
10					10
11 Design					11
12					12
13					13
14					14
15					15
16					16

(b)

Estimated Overhead	Direct Labor Hours	Overhead Rate		
17				17
18				18
19				19
20				20
21				21
22				22
23				23

Traditional costing		Wool		Cotton	
24					24
25					25
26					26
27					27
28					28
29					29
30					30
31					31
32					32
33					33
34					34
35					35
36					36
37					37
38					38
39					39
40					40

(a)

1	Direct labor hours for car wheels				
2	Direct labor hours for truck wheels				
3	Total direct labor hours				

	Estimated Overhead	Direct Labor Hours	Overhead Rate

Overhead assigned:

	Car wheels	
	Truck wheels	
	Total overhead	

(b)

Activity Cost Pools	Estimated Overhead	Expected Use of Cost Drivers	ABC Overhead Rate
Machine setup			
Assembling			
Inspection			

(c) Car Wheels

Activiy Cost Pools	Expected Use of Cost Driver	Overhead Rate	Cost Assigned
Setting up machines			
Assembling			
Inspection			
Total costs assigned			

Truck Wheels

Setting up machines			
Assembling			
Inspection			
Total costs assigned			

(d)

(a) Activity Cost Pool	Estimated Overhead	Expected Use of Cost Drivers per Activity	Activity-Based Overhead Rates	
1 Scheduling and travel				1
2 Setup time				2
3 Supervision				3
4				4
5 Commercial				5
6 Cost Pools	Cost Drivers per	ABC OH Rate	OH Costs	6
7 Scheduling and travel				7
8 Setup time				8
9 Supervision				9
10 Total commercial overhead				10
11				11
12 Residential				12
13 Cost Pools	Cost Drivers	ABC OH Rate	OH Costs	13
14 Scheduling and travel				14
15 Setup time				15
16 Supervision				16
17 Total residential overhead				17
18				18
19				19
20 (b)	Commercial		Residential	20
21 Revenues				21
22 Direct material cost				22
23 Direct labor costs				23
24 Overhead cost				24
25 Operating income (loss)				25
26				26
27 (c)				27
28				28
29				29
30				30
31				31
32				32
33				33
34				34
35				35
36				36
37				37
38				38
39				39
40				40

		Traditional Costing	Activity-based Costing
1	(a) Traditional costing:		
2	Overhead rate =		
3			
4	(1) One mobile safe:		
5			
6			
7			
8	(2) One walk-in safe:		
9			
10			
11			
12	(b) Activity-based costing:		
13	(1) Material handing costs rate =		
14			
15	(a) One mobile safe:		
16			
17			
18			
19	(b) One walk-in safe:		
20			
21			
22			
23	(2) Purchasing activity costs rate =		
24			
25	(a) One mobile safe:		
26			
27			
28			
29	(b) One walk-in safe:		
30			
31			
32			
33	(c)	Traditional Costing	Activity-based Costing
34			
35			
36	Mobile safe		
37	Walk-in safe		
38			
39			
40			

Exercise 18-11

Major Instrument, Inc.

(a)

Activity	Overhead	Expected Use of Cost Drivers	Overhead Rate
1 Material handling			
2 Machine setups			
3 Quality inspections			
4			
5			

(b)

Cost Driver	Instruments		Gauges		Total
	Number	Cost	Number	Cost	Overhead
7 Requisitions					
8 Setups					
9					
10 Inspections					
11 Total costs					
12					
13 Total units					
14					
15 Cost per unit					
16					
17					
18					
19					
20					

(c)

1	1
2	2
3	3
4	4
5	5
6	6
7	7
8	8
9	9
10	10
11	11
12	12
13	13
14	14
15	15
16	16
17	17
18	18
19	19
20	20
21	21
22	22
23	23
24	24
25	25
26	26
27	27
28	28
29	29
30	30
31	31
32	32
33	33
34	34
35	35
36	36
37	37
38	38
39	39
40	40

(a)

(1)

	(2) Activity Cost Pool	Cost Drivers Used	Overhead Rate	Overhead Cost Assigned	
6	Sales commissions				
7	Advertising - TV/Radio				
8	Advertising - Newspaper				
9	Catalogs				
10	Cost of catalog sales				
11	Credit and collection				
12	Total assigned cost				
13	for March				

(b)

(c)

(a)

	(1)			
(2)	Cost Drivers Used	Overhead Rate	Overhead Cost Assigned	
Activity Cost Pool				
Inspections of material received				
In-process inspections				
FDA certification				
Total assigned cost				
for June				

(b)

(c)

(a) and (b)

(a)	Products			
	Home Model	Commercial Model		
Manufacturing Costs				

(b)

Activity Cost Pool	Estimated Overhead	Expected Use of Cost Driver		Activity- Based Overhead Rate	
		Number	Driver	Rate	Per
Receiving					
Forming					
Assembling					
Testing					
Painting					
Packing and shipping					
Total					

(c)

Activity Cost Pool	Home Model			Commercial Model		
	Expected Use of Drivers	Overhead Rate	Cost Assigned	Expected Use of Drivers	Overhead Rate	Cost Assigned
1 Receiving						
2 Forming						
3 Assembling						
4 Testing						
5 Painting						
6 Packing and shipping						
7 Total assigned cost						
8						
9						
10 Units produced						
11						
12 Overhead cost per unit						
13						
14						
15						
16						
17						
18						
19						
20						

(d)

	Products	
	Home Model	Commercial Model
1		
2		
3		
4		
5		
6		
7		

(e)

Activity	Value- vs Non-value-Added

(f) (1)

(2)

(a) Allocation of total manufacturing overhead using ABC-

	Overhead Rate	Royale				Majestic				Total Overhead
		Drivers Used		Cost Assigned		Drivers Used		Cost Assigned		
Purchase orders										
Machine setups										
Machine hours										
Inspections										
Total assigned costs										
Units produced										
Cost per unit										

(b) Per unit cost and gross profit under ABC costing were:

	Royale	Majestic

(c)

(a), (b), and (d)

1	(a) Predetermined overhead rate using machine hours:
2	
3	
4	
5	
6	(b) Manufacturing cost per stair under traditional costing:
7	
8	
9	
10	
11	
12	
13	
14	
15	
16	
17	
18	
19	
20	
21	(d)
22	
23	
24	
25	
26	
27	
28	
29	
30	
31	
32	
33	
34	
35	
36	
37	
38	
39	
40	

(c)

Manufacturing cost per stair under activity-based costing:					
Computation of Activity-based Overhead Rates					
Activity Cost Pool	Total Estimated Overhead	Expected Use of Cost Drivers per Activity		Activity-Based Overhead	
		Number	Driver	Rate	Per
Purchasing					
Handling materials					
Production					
Setting up machines					
Inspecting					
Inventory control					
Utilities					
Total					

Assignment of Overhead to Order of 250 Stairs					
		Expected Used of Driver		Activity Based Overhead	
Activity Cost Pool		Number	Driver	Rate	Cost Assigned
Purchasing					
Handling materials					
Production					
Setting up machines					
Inspecting					
Inventory control					
Utilities					
Total overhead assigned					

Total manufacturing cost per stair under ABC:	

Section

(a) and (b)

(a)   Computation of unit costs - traditional costing

Overhead cost per labor hour:

Manufacturing Costs	Products		
	CoolDay	LiteMist	

(b)

ty Cost Pool	Estimated Overhead	Expected Use of Cost Driver Number	Activity- Based Overhead	
			Rate	Per
Grape processing				
Aging				
Bottling and corking				
Labeling and boxing				
Maintain and inspect				
equipment				
Total				

(c)

Activity Cost Pool	CoolDay			LiteMist		
	Expected Use of Drivers	Overhead Rate	Cost Assigned	Expected Use of Drivers	Overhead Rate	Cost Assigned
1 Grape processing						
2 Aging						
3 Bottling and corking						
4 Labeling and boxing						
5 Maintain and inspect equipment						
6 Totals						
7						
8 Liters produced						
9						
10 Overhead cost per liter						
11						
12						
13						
14						
15						
16						
17						
18						
19						
20						

(d)

Manufacturing Costs	Products	
	CoolDay	LiteMist
1		
2		
3		
4		
5		

(e)

6	
7	
8	
9	
10	
11	
12	
13	
14	
15	
16	
17	
18	
19	
20	
21	
22	
23	
24	
25	
26	
27	
28	
29	
30	
31	
32	
33	
34	
35	
36	
37	
38	
39	
40	

(a), (c), and (d)

1 **(a)**	1
2 Overhead rate assigned to audit:	2
3	3
4 Overhead rate assigned to tax:	4
5	5
6	6
7	7
8	8
9	9
10	10

(c)			
11		Value-Added vs.	11
12	Activity	Nonvalue-Added	12
13			13
14			14
15			15
16			16
17			17
18			18
19			19
20			20
21			21
22			22
23			23
24			24
25			25

(d) Overhead assigned to the two service lines:	Audit	Tax	
26			26
27			27
28			28
29			29
30			30
31			31
32			32
33			33
34			34
35			35
36			36
37			37
38			38
39			39
40			40

(b) (1) Computation of activity-based overhead rates:

Activity Cost Pool	Estimated Overhead	Total Expected Use of Cost Drivers		Activity-Based Overhead		
		Amount	Driver	Rate	Per	
1 Employee training						1
2 Typing and secretarial						2
3 Computing						3
4 Facility rental						4
5 Travel						5
6 Total						6
7						7
8						8

(2) Assignment of overhead to audit and tax services:

Activity Cost Pool	Audit			Tax		
	Expected Use of Driver	Overhead Rate	Cost Assigned	Expected Use of Driver	Overhead Rate	Cost Assigned
1 Employee training						1
2 Typing and secretarial						2
3 Computing						3
4 Facility rental						4
5 Travel						5
6 Overhead asigned						6
7						7
8						8

(a) and (b)

	Products		
(a)	Deluxe Model	Standard Model	
1 Manufacturing Costs			
2			
3			
4			
5			
6			
7			
8			
9			
10			
11			
12			
13			
14			
15			

(b)	Estimated Overhead	Expected Use of Cost Driver		Activity-Based Overhead Rate	
Activity Cost Pool		Number	Driver	Rate	Per
20 Purchasing					
21 Receiving					
22 Assembling					
23 Testing					
24 Finishing					
25 Packing and shipping					
26 Total					

(c)

Activity Cost Pool	Deluxe Model			Standard Model		
	Expected Use of Drivers	Overhead Rate	Cost Assigned	Expected Use of Drivers	Overhead Rate	Cost Assigned
1 Purchasing						
2 Receiving						
3 Assembling						
4 Testing						
5 Finishing						
6 Packing and shipping						
7 Total assigned cost						
8						
9						
10 Units produced						
11						
12 Overhead cost per unit						
13						
14						
15						
16						
17						
18						
19						
20						

(d)

	Products	
	Deluxe Model	Standard Model
1		
2		
3		
4		
5		
6		
7		

(e)

Activity	Value- vs Non-value-Added

(f) (1)

(2)

	Elite		Preferred		Total
Overhead Rate	Drivers Used	Cost Assigned	Drivers Used	Cost Assigned	Overhead
(a) Allocation of total manufacturing overhead using ABC-					
Purchase orders					
Machine setups					
Machine hours					
Inspections					
Total assigned costs					
Units produced					
Cost per unit					

(b) and (c)

		Elite	Preferred	
1	(b) Per unit cost and gross profit under ABC costing were:			1
2				2
3				3
4				4
5				5
6				6
7				7
8				8
9				9
10				10
11				11
12				12
13				13
14				14
15	(c)			15
16				16
17				17
18				18
19				19
20				20
21				21
22				22
23				23
24				24
25				25
26				26
27				27
28				28
29				29
30				30
31				31
32				32
33				33
34				34
35				35
36				36
37				37
38				38
39				39
40				40

(a), (b), and (d)

1	(a) Predetermined overhead rate using materials cost:
2	
3	
4	
5	
6	(b) Manufacturing cost per armoire under traditional costing:
7	
8	
9	
10	
11	
12	
13	
14	
15	
16	
17	
18	
19	
20	
21	(d)
22	
23	
24	
25	
26	
27	
28	
29	
30	
31	
32	
33	
34	
35	
36	
37	
38	
39	
40	

(c)

	Manufacturing cost per armoire under activity-based costing:					
	Computation of Activity-based Overhead Rate					
	Activity Cost Pool	Total Estimated Overhead	Total Estimated Drivers		Activity-Based Overhead	
			Number	Driver	Rate	Per
4	Purchasing					
5	Handling materials					
6	Production					
7	Setting up machines					
8	Inspecting					
9	Inventory control					
10	Utilities					
11	Total					

	Assignment of Overhead to Order of 12 armoires				
	Activity Cost Pool	Expected Used of Driver		Activity Based Overhead Rate	Cost Assigned
		Number	Driver		
21	Purchasing				
22	Handling materials				
23	Production				
24	Setting up machines				
25	Inspecting				
26	Inventory control				
27	Utilities				
28	Total overhead assigned				

	Total manufacturing cost per armoire under ABC:	
33		
34		
35		
36		
37		
38		
39		

(a) and (b)

(a)   Computation of unit costs - traditional costing

1			
2	Overhead cost per labor hour:		
3			
4		Products		
5	Manufacturing Costs	Valley Fresh	Merando Valley	
6				
7				
8				
9				
10				
11				
12				
13				
14				
15				

(b)

Activity Cost Pool	Estimated Overhead	Expected Use of Cost Driver Number	Activity- Based Overhead	
			Rate	Per
Grape processing				
Aging				
Bottling and corking				
Labeling and boxing				
Maintain and inspect equipment				
Total				

(c)

Activity Cost Pool	Valley Fresh			Merando Valley		
	Expected Use of Drivers	Overhead Rate	Cost Assigned	Expected Use of Drivers	Overhead Rate	Cost Assigned
1 Grape processing						
2 Aging						
3 Bottling and corking						
4 Labeling and boxing						
5 Maintain and inspect equipment						
6 Totals						
7						
8 Gallons produced						
9						
10 Overhead cost per gallon						
11						
12						
13						
14						
15						
16						
17						
18						
19						
20						

(d)

Manufacturing Costs	Products	
	Valley Fresh	Merando Valley

(e)

(a), (c), and (d)

1	(a)	1
2	Computation of total overhead cost using direct labor hours:	2
3		3
4		4
5		5
6	Overhead assigned to corporate:	6
7	Overhead assigned to individual:	7
8		8
9		9
10		10

	(c) Activity	Value-Added vs. Nonvalue-Added	
11	(c)	Value-Added vs.	11
12	Activity	Nonvalue-Added	12
13			13
14			14
15			15
16			16
17			17
18			18
19			19
20			20
21			21
22			22
23			23
24			24
25			25

	(d) Overhead is assigned to the two service lines as follows:	Corporate	Individual	
26	(d) Overhead is assigned to the two service lines as follows:	Corporate	Individual	26
27				27
28	Traditional costing			28
29	ABC			29
30	Difference			30
31				31
32				32
33				33
34				34
35				35
36				36
37				37
38				38
39				39
40				40

(b) (1) Computation of activity-based overhead rates:

Activity Cost Pool	Estimated Overhead	Total Expected Use of Cost Drivers		Activity-Based Overhead Rates	
		Amount	Driver	Rate	Per
1 Employee training					1
2 Typing and secretarial					2
3 Computing					3
4 Facility rental					4
5 Travel					5
6 Total					6
7					7
8					8

(2) Assignment of overhead to corporate and individual services:

Activity Cost Pool	Corporate			Individual		
	Expected Use of Driver	Overhead Rate	Cost Assigned	Expected Use of Driver	Overhead Rate	Cost Assigned
1 Employee training						1
2 Typing and secretarial						2
3 Computing						3
4 Facility rental						4
5 Travel						5
6 Total overhead assigned						6
7						7
8						8

(a)		Composite	Rotomolded	
1				1
2				2
3				3
4				4
5				5
6				6
7				7
8 (b)		Composite	Rotomolded	8
9				9
10				10
11				11
12				12
13				13
14				14
15				15
16				16
17				17

(c)	Estimated Overhead	Expected Use of Cost Drivers	Activity-Based OH Rates	
18 Activity Cost Pools				18
19				19
20				20
21				21
22				22
23				23
24				24
25				25
26				26
27				27
28				28
29				29
30				30

31 (d)		31
32		32
33		33
34		34
35		35
36		36
37		37
38		38
39		39
40		40

Current Designs

(c)   (Continued)

| | Composite | | | Rotomolded | | |
Activity Cost Pool	Expected Use of Driver	Overhead Rate	Cost Assigned	Expected Use of Driver	Overhead Rate	Cost Assigned
1 Design						
2 Prototypes						
3 Molds						
4 Supervision						
5 Curing time						
6 Total amount allocated						
7 Directly assigned						
8 Total cost (a)						
9 Number of units (b)						
10 Cost assigned per unit (a) + (b)						
11						
12						
13						
14						
15						
16						
17						
18						
19						
20						

1	(a) Computation of activity-based overhead rate:						1

(a) Computation of activity-based overhead rate:

Activity Cost Pool	Total Estimated Overhead	Expected Used of Cost Driver		Activity-Based Overhead	
		Number	Driver	Rate	Per
Market analysis					
Product design					
Product development					
Prototype testing					

(b) Computation of charges to in-house manufacturing department-

Activity Cost Pool	Cost Drivers Used		Overhead Rate	Cost Assigned
	Amount	Driver		
Market analysis				
Product design				
Product development				
Prototype testing				
Total overhead assigned				

(c) Computation of charges to outside R&D contractor -

Activity Cost Pool	Cost Drivers Used		Overhead Rate	Cost Assigned
	Amount	Driver		
Market analysis				
Product design				
Product development				
Prototype testing				
Total overhead assigned				

(d)

BE19-4	High	Low	Difference	Variable Cost per Mile	
1					
2					
3					
4				High	Low
5					
6					
7					
8					
9					
10					
11					
12					
BE19-5	High	Low	Difference	Variable Cost per Unit	
14					
15					
16					
17				High	Low
18					
19					
20					
21					
22					
23					

BE19-7

Radial Inc.
CVP Income Statement
For the Quarter Ended March 31, 2014

(a)

	Maintenance Costs:	700 Machine Hours	300 Machine Hours	
1				1
2				2
3				3
4				4
5				5
6				6
7				7
8				8
9				9
10				10
11				11
12				12
13				13
14				14
15				15

(b)

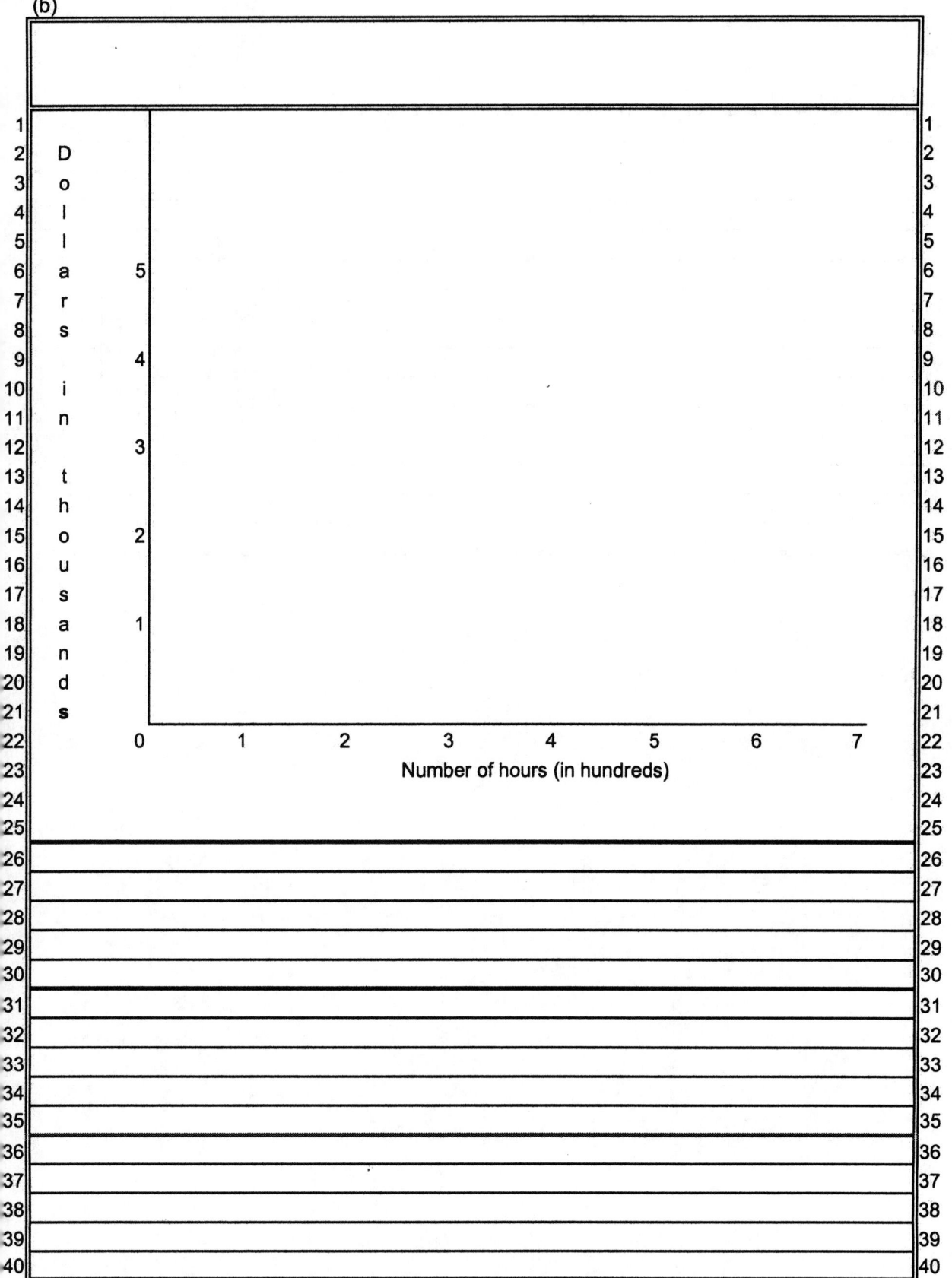

(a)

	Maintenance Costs:		Activity Level		
			High	Low	
1					1
2					2
3					3
4					4
5					5
6					6
7					7
8					8
9					9
10					10
11					11
12					12
13					13
14					14
15					15

(b)

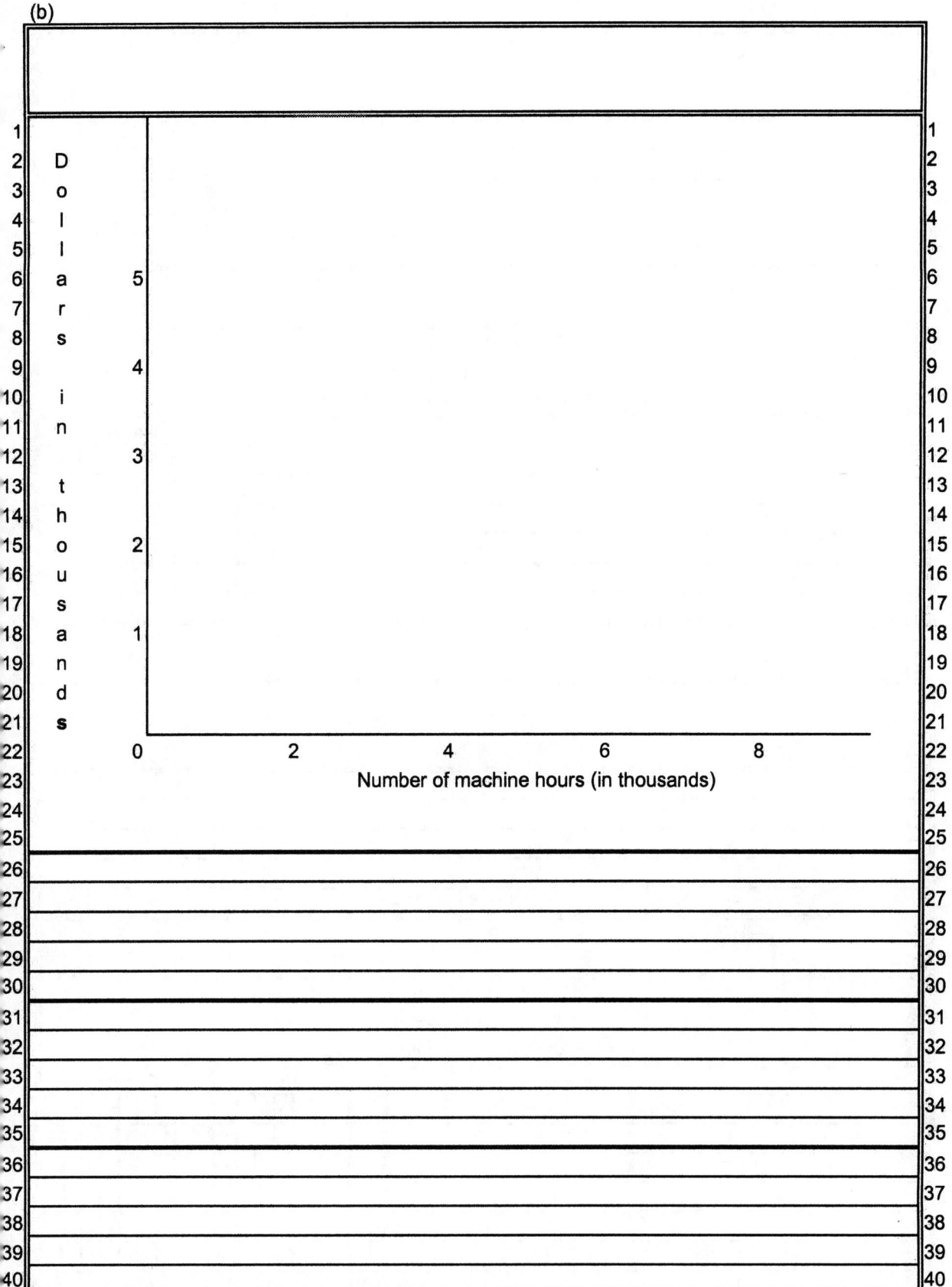

(a)

			1
1			1
2			2
3			3
4			4
5			5

(b)

Cannes Company

CVP Income Statement

For the Month Ended September 30, 2014

	Total	Per Unit	
1			1
2			2
3			3
4			4
5			5
6			6
7			7

(c)

		1
1		1
2		2
3		3
4		4
5		5

(d)

Cannes Company

CVP Income Statement

For the Month Ended September 30, 2014

	Total	Per Unit	
1			1
2			2
3			3
4			4
5			5
6			6
7			7
8			8

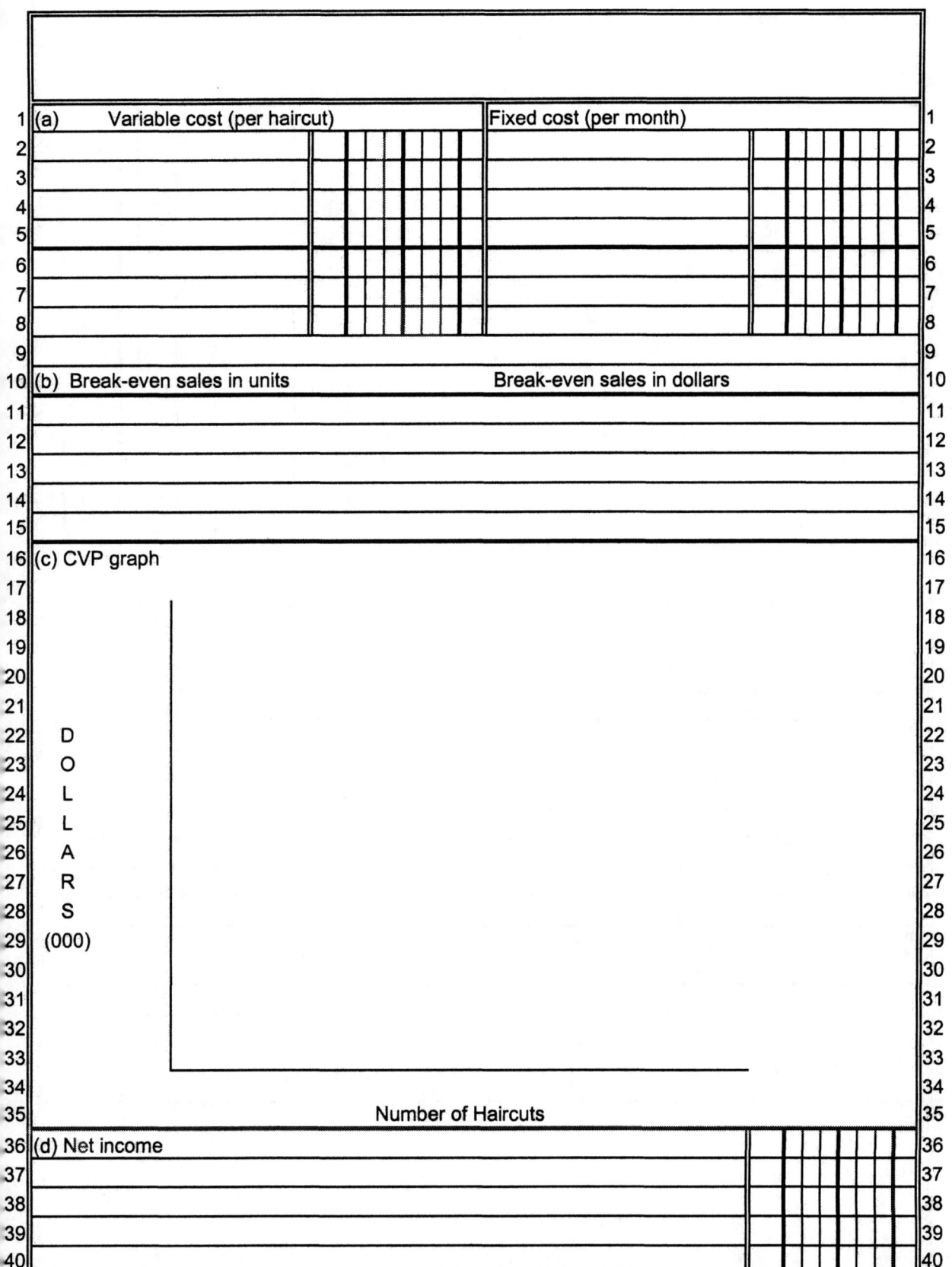

1	(a) Variable cost (per haircut)	Fixed cost (per month)	1
2			2
3			3
4			4
5			5
6			6
7			7
8			8
9			9
10	(b) Break-even sales in units Break-even sales in dollars	10
11		11
12		12
13		13
14		14
15		15
16	(c) CVP graph	16
17		17
18		18
19		19
20		20
21		21
22	D	22
23	O	23
24	L	24
25	L	25
26	A	26
27	R	27
28	S	28
29	(000)	29
30		30
31		31
32		32
33		33
34		34
35	Number of Haircuts	35
36	(d) Net income	36
37		37
38		38
39		39
40		40

(a)

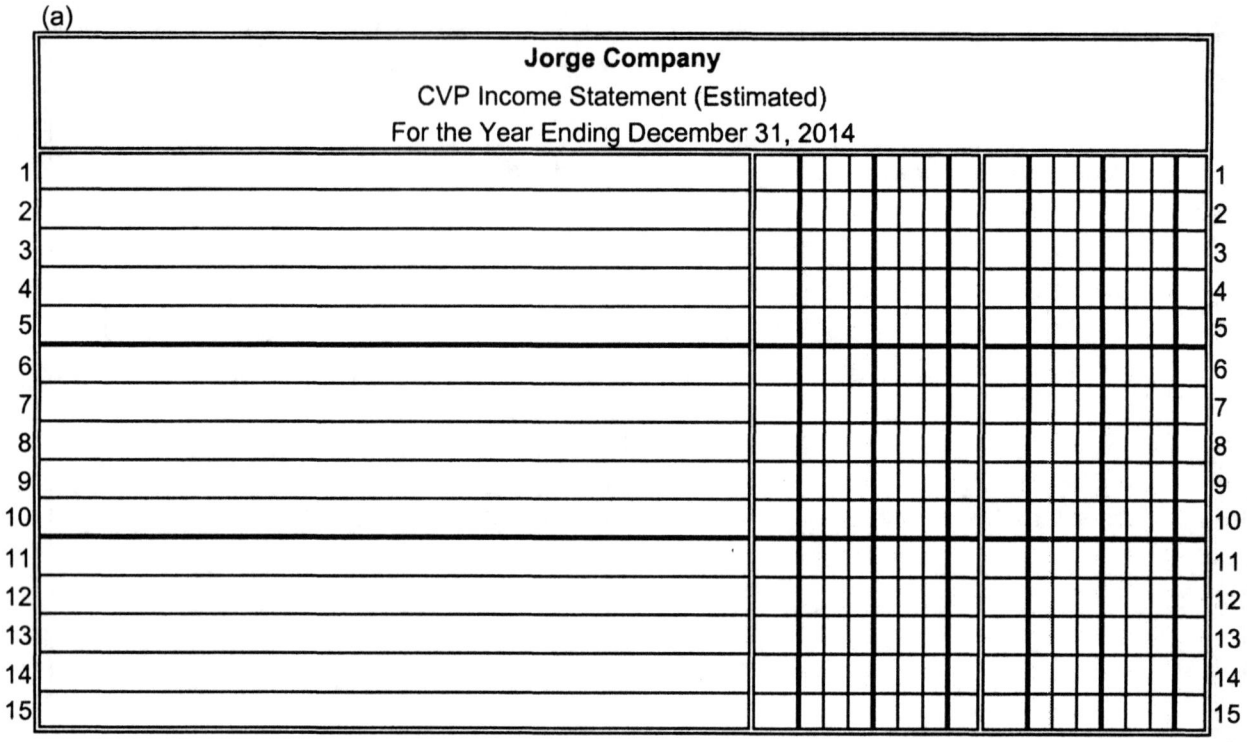

Jorge Company		
CVP Income Statement (Estimated)		
For the Year Ending December 31, 2014		
1		
2		
3		
4		
5		
6		
7		
8		
9		
10		
11		
12		
13		
14		
15		

(b), (c), and (d)

1 (b)

2

3

4 (1) Break-even sales in units   (2) Break-even sales in dollars

5

6

7

8

9 (c) Contribution margin ratio

10

11

12

13 Margin of safety ratio

14

15

16

17 (d) Required sales

18

19

20

21

(a) and (b)

1	(a) Current break-even point:
2	
3	
4	
5	
6	
7	
8	New break-even point:
9	
10	
11	
12	
13	(b) Current margin-of-safety ratio:
14	
15	
16	
17	
18	New margin-of-safety ratio:
19	
20	
21	
22	

(c)

Bargain Shoe Store
Comparative CVP Income Statement

	Current	New
1		
2		
3		
4		
5		
6		
7		
8		
9		
10		
11		
12		
13		

(a)

(1)	Current Year
1	
2	
3	
4	
5	
6	
7	
8	
9	
10	
11	
12	

	Current Year		Projected Year
13			
14			
15			
16			
17			
18			
19			
20			
21			
22			
23			
24			
25			
26			
27			

(2)	Current Year	Projected Year
Fixed costs:		

(b)

1	1
2	2
3	3
4	4
5	5
6	6
7	7
8	8
9	9
10	10
11	11
12 (c)	12
13	13
14	14
15	15
16	16
17	17
18	18
19	19
20 (d)	20
21	21
22	22
23	23
24	24
25	25
26	26
27	27
28	28
29	29
30	30
31	31
32	32
33	33
34	34
35	35
36	36
37	37
38	38
39	39
40	40

		(a) Variable cost (per haircut)			Fixed cost (per month)			
1	(a)	Variable cost (per haircut)			Fixed cost (per month)			1
2								2
3								3
4								4
5								5
6								6
7								7
8								8
9								9
10	(b) Break-even sales in units			Break-even sales in dollars				10
11								11
12								12
13								13
14								14
15								15

(c) CVP graph

D
O
L
L
A
R
S
(000)

Number of Haircuts

	(d) Net income			
36	(d) Net income			36
37				37
38				38
39				39
40				40

(a)

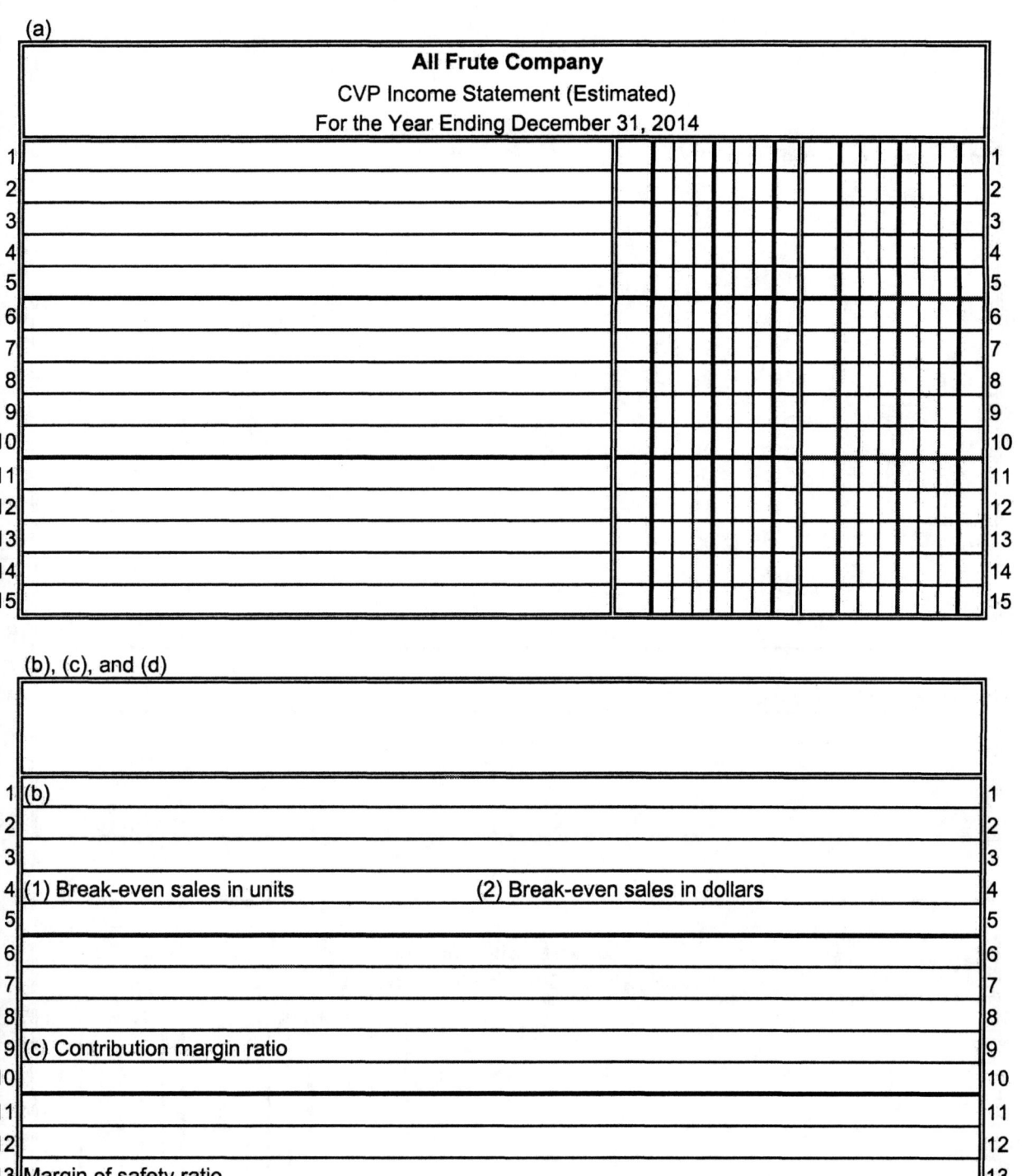

All Frute Company		
CVP Income Statement (Estimated)		
For the Year Ending December 31, 2014		
1		
2		
3		
4		
5		
6		
7		
8		
9		
10		
11		
12		
13		
14		
15		

(b), (c), and (d)

(b)

(1) Break-even sales in units   (2) Break-even sales in dollars

(c) Contribution margin ratio

Margin of safety ratio

(d) Required sales

(a) and (b)

1	(a) Current break-even point:
2	
3	
4	
5	
6	
7	
8	New break-even point:
9	
10	
11	
12	
13	(b) Current margin-of-safety ratio:
14	
15	
16	
17	
18	New margin-of-safety ratio:
19	
20	
21	
22	

(c)

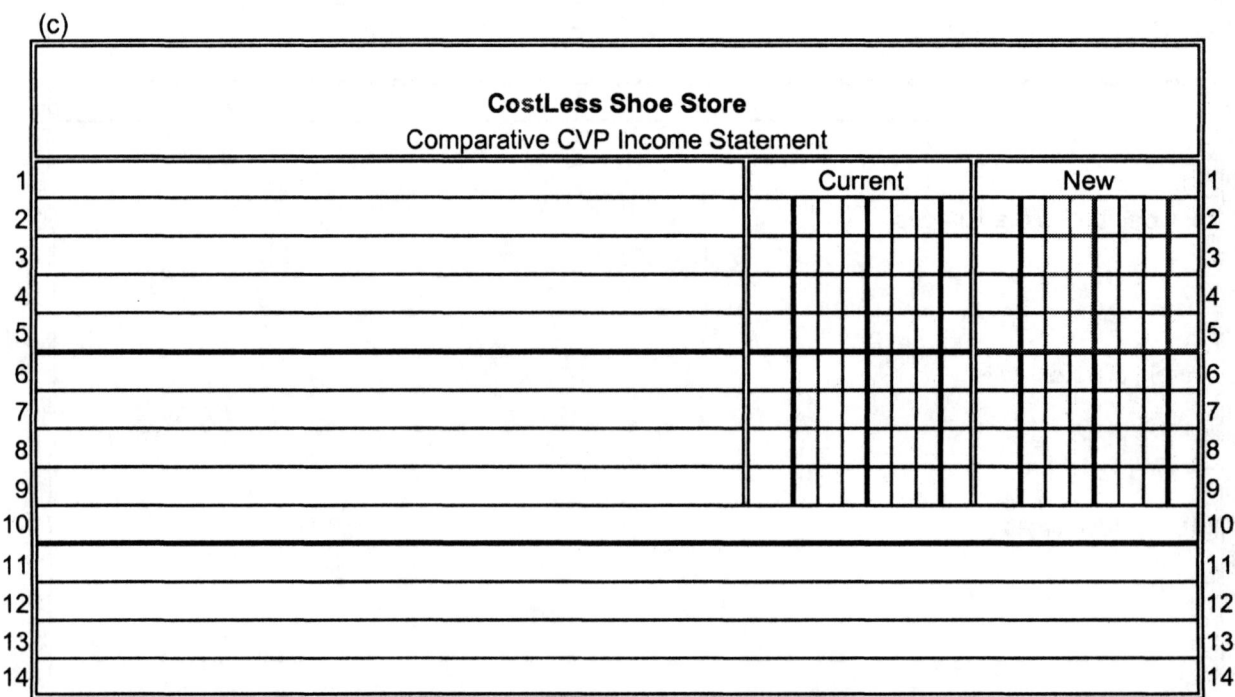

CostLess Shoe Store
Comparative CVP Income Statement

	Current	New

(a)

(1)	Current Year
1	
2	
3	
4	
5	
6	
7	
8	
9	
10	
11	
12	

	Current Year		Projected Year
13			
14			
15			
16			
17			
18			
19			
20			
21			
22			
23			
24			
25			
26			
27			

(2) Fixed costs:	Current Year	Projected Year
30		
31		
32		
33		
34		
35		
36		
37		
38		
39		
40		

(b)

(c)   Sales dollars required for

target net income =

(d)   Margin of safety ratio =

(e) (1)   Projected Year

(e) (Continued)

(2) Contribution margin ratio =	
(3) Break-even point in dollars =	

1 (a)   1
2   2
3   3
4   4
5   5
6   6
7   7
8 (b)   8
9   9
10   10
11   11
12 (c)   12
13   13
14   14
15 (d)   15
16   16
17   17
18   18
19 (e)   19
20   20
21   21
22   22
23   23
24   24
25   25
26   26
27   27
28   28
29   29
30   30
31   31
32   32
33   33
34   34
35   35
36   36
37   37
38   38
39   39
40   40

Name

Section

Date   Creative Ideas Company

	CAPITAL INTENSIVE		LABOR INTENSIVE	
(a) (1) Fixed costs:		(2) Fixed costs:		
1				
2				
3				
4				
5				
6 Unit contribution margin:		Unit contribution margin:		
7				
8				
9				
10				
11				
12				
13				
14				
15 Break-even Point in units:		Break-even Point in units:		
16				
17				
18 (b)				
19				
20				
21				
22				

(c)

1	1
2	2
3	3
4	4
5	5
6	6
7	7
8	8
9	9
10	10
11	11
12	12
13	13
14	14
15	15
16	16
17	17
18	18
19	19
20	20
21	21
22	22
23	23
24	24
25	25
26	26
27	27
28	28
29	29
30	30
31	31
32	32
33	33
34	34
35	35
36	36
37	37
38	38
39	39
40	40

(a) and (b)

1	(a) Variable costs per unit:	1
2		2
3		3
4		4
5		5
6		6
7	Fixed costs are:	7
8		8
9		9
10		10
11		11
12		12
13	The break-even points are:	13
14		14
15		15
16		16
17		17
18		18
19		19
20		20
21		21
22		22
23	(b)	23
24		24
25		25
26		26
27		27
28	Net income computation:	28
29		29
30		30
31		31
32		32
33		33
34		34
35		35
36		36
37		37
38		38
39		39
40		40
41		41

(b) (Continued), (c), and (d)

1	(b) (Continued) - New break-even point in dollars:	1
2		2
3		3
4		4
5		5
6		6
7		7
8	(c) Computations:	8
9		9
10		10
11		11
12		12
13		13
14	Net income calculation:	14
15		15
16		16
17		17
18		18
19		19
20		20
21		21
22		22
23		23
24		24
25		25
26		26
27		27
28		28
29		29
30		30
31	New break-even point in dollars:	31
32		32
33		33
34		34
35		35
36		36
37		37
38	(d)	38
39		39
40		40

BE20-2

Hamby Inc.
Income Statement
For the Quarter Ended March 31, 2014

1	
2	
3	
4	
5	
6	
7	
8	
9	
10	
11	
12	
13	
14	

BE20-7

Model	Sales Mix Percentage	Unit Contribution Margin	Weighted-Average Unit Contribution Margin
A12	60%		
B22	15%		
C124	25%		

BE20-8

Total break-even sales in units:

Units of A12 =

Units of B22 =

Units of C124 =

BE20-9

1	Weighted average contribution		1
2	margin ratio =		2
3			3
4			4
5	Total break-even point in dollars =		5
6			6
7			7
8	Birthday		8
9	Standard tapered		9
10	Large scented		10
11			11
12			12

BE20-11

		Product A	Product B	
13	**BE20-11**			13
14		Product A	Product B	14
15				15
16				16
17				17
18				18

BE20-13

		Break-even Point in Dollars		
19	**BE20-13**			19
20		Break-even Point in Dollars		20
21		Logan Co.	Morgan Co.	21
22				22
23				23
24				24
25				25
26				26
27				27
28				28
29				29

BE20-15

		Product 1	Product 2	
30	**BE20-15**			30
31		Product 1	Product 2	31
32				32
33				33
34				34
35				35
36				36
37				37
38				38
39				39
40				40

*BE20-16

	Variable Costing	
1		
2		
3		
4		
5		

*BE20-17

	Absorption Costing	
8		
9		
10		
11		
12		
13		

*BE20-18

(a) Absorption Costing:

(b) Variable Costing:

Amanda Inc.
Income Statement
For the Month Ended January 31, 2014

1		
2		
3		
4		
5		
6		
7		
8		
9		
10		
11		
12		
13		
14		
15 Contribution margin per unit:		
16		
17 Contribution margin ratio:		

DO IT! 20-3

			Basic	Basic Plus	Premium	
1	(a)	The sales mix percenatges as a function of units sold is:				1
2						2
3						3
4						4
5						5
6						6
7	(b)	The weighted-average unit contribution margin is:				7
8						8
9						9
10						10
11	(c)	The break-even point in units is:				11
12						12
13						13
14	(d)	The break-even units to produce for each product are:				14
15		Basic:					15
16		Basic Plus:					16
17		Premium:					17
18							18
19							19

DO IT! 20-4

			Good	Better	Best	
20							20
21	(a)						21
22							22
23							23
24							24
25	(b)	The contribution margin per unit of limited resource is:				25
26							26
27							27
28							28
29							29
30							30
31							31
32	(c)						32
33							33
34							34
35							35
36							36
37							37
38							38
39							39
40							40

E20-2

1	(a)	Contribution margin in dollars:		1
2				2
3				3
4				4
5				5
6		Contribution margin per unit:		6
7				7
8		Contribution margin ratio:		8
9				9
10	(b)	Break-even point in dollars:		10
11				11
12				12
13		Break-even point in units:		13
14				14
15				15
16	(c)	Margin of safety in dollars:		16
17				17
18				18
19		Margin of safety ratio:		19
20				20
21				21

E20-3

		August Results (Base Amounts)	Alternative 1 — Increase Selling Price by 10%	Alternative 2 — Decrease Variable Costs to 58% of Sales	Alternative 3 — Reduce Fixed Costs by $20,000	
32	Sales	$ 310000				32
33	Less: Variable Costs	210000				33
34	Fixed Costs	75000				34
35						35
36	Net Income	$ 25000				36
37						37
38						38
39						39
40						40

1	(a) (1)		1
2			2
3			3
4			4
5			5
6			6
7	(2)		7
8			8
9			9
10			10
11			11
12			12
13			13
14	(b)		14
15			15
16			16
17			17
18	(c)		18
19			19
20			20
21			21
22			22
23			23
24			24
25			25
26			26
27			27
28			28
29			29
30			30
31			31
32			32
33			33
34			34
35			35
36			36
37			37
38			38
39			39
40			40

E20-5 (a)

	Total	Per Unit
Hall Company		
CVP Income Statement (Current)		
For the Year Ended December 31, 2014		
1		
2		
3		
4		
5		
6		

(b)

	Total	Per Unit
Hall Company		
CVP Income Statement (With Changes)		
For the Year Ended December 31, 2014		
1		
2		
3		
4		
5		
6		
7		
8		

E20-6

	Sales Mix %	Contribution Margin Per Unit	Wtd.- Ave. Contribution Margin
1 Lawnmowers			
2 Weed-Trimmers			
3 Chainsaws			
4			
5			
6 Total break-even sales in units =			
7			
8			

	Sales Mix %	Total Break-even Sales in Units	Sales Units Needed Per Product
12 Lawnmowers			
13 Weed-trimmers			
14 Chainsaws			
15 Total units			
16			

(a)	Sales Mix %	Contribution Margin Ratio	Wtd. -Ave Contribution Margin Ratio	
1 Oil changes				1
2 Brake repair				2
3				3
4				4
5 Total break-even sales in dollars =				5
6				6
7				7

	Sales Mix %	Total Break-even Sales Dollars	Sales Dollars Needed Per Product	
8				8
9				9
10				10
11 Oil changes				11
12 Brake repair				12
13 Total sales				13
14				14
15 (b)				15
16 Sales to achieve target net income =				16
17				17
18				18

	Sales Mix %	Total Sales Needed	Sales Dollars Needed Per Product Per Store	
19				19
20				20
21				21
22				22
23 Oil changes				23
24 Brake repair				24
25				25
26				26
27				27
28				28
29				29
30				30
31				31
32				32
33				33
34				34
35				35
36				36
37				37
38				38
39				39
40				40

(a)

	Sales Mix %	Contribution Margin Ratio	Wtd.- Ave. Contribution Margin Ratio	
1 Mail pouches and				1
2 small boxes				2
3 Non-standard boxes				3
4				4
5				5
6 Total break-even sales in dollars =				6
7				7
8				8

	Sales Mix %	Total Break-even Sales Dollars	Sales Dollars Needed Per Product	
9				9
10				10
11				11
12 Mail pouches and				12
13 small boxes				13
14 Non-standard boxes				14
15 Total sales				15
16				16

(b)

	Sales Mix %	Contribution Margin Ratio	Wtd. Ave. Contribution Margin Ratio	
17				17
18				18
19				19
20				20
21 Mail pouches and				21
22 small boxes				22
23 Non-standard boxes				23
24				24
25				25
26 Total break-even sales in dollars =				26
27				27
28				28

	Sales Mix %	Sales in Dollars	Sales Dollars Per Product	
29				29
30				30
31 Mail pouches and				31
32 small boxes				32
33 Non-standard boxes				33
34 Total sales				34
35				35
36				36
37				37
38				38
39				39
40				40

(a)		
1	Weighted average unit	1
2	contribution margin =	2
3		3
4	Break-even point in units =	4
5		5
6	**(b)**	6
7	Shoes	7
8	Gloves	8
9	Range finders	9
10		10
11		11
12	**(c)**	12
13	Shoes	13
14	Gloves	14
15	Range finders	15
16	Total contribution margin	16
17	Fixed costs	17
18	Net income	18
19		19
20		20
21		21
22		22
23		23
24		24
25		25
26		26
27		27
28		28
29		29
30		30
31		31
32		32
33		33
34		34
35		35
36		36
37		37
38		38
39		39
40		40

E20-11

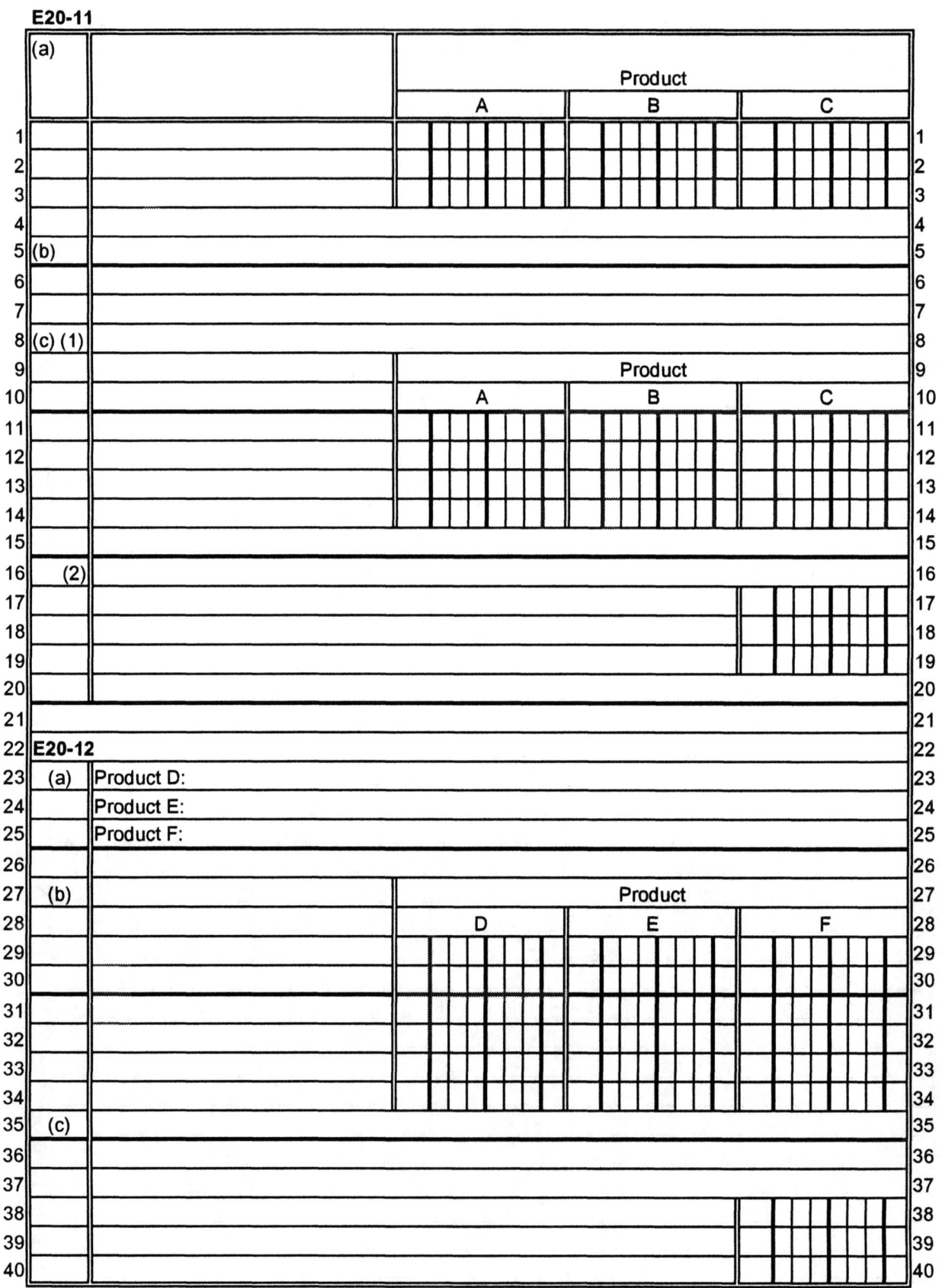

(a)		Product		
		A	B	C
1				
2				
3				
4				
5	(b)			
6				
7				
8	(c) (1)			
9		Product		
10		A	B	C
11				
12				
13				
14				
15				
16	(2)			
17				
18				
19				
20				
21				

E20-12

22					
23	(a)	Product D:			
24		Product E:			
25		Product F:			
26					
27	(b)		Product		
28			D	E	F
29					
30					
31					
32					
33					
34					
35	(c)				
36					
37					
38					
39					
40					

(a)		Product	
		Basic	Deluxe
1			
2			
3			
4			
5			
6			
7			

(b)	
8	
9	
10	

(c)

(1)		Basic	Deluxe	Total
12				
13				
14				
15				
16				
17				

(2)		Basic	Deluxe	Total
18				
19				
20				
21				
22				
23				

E20-14

(a)	Contribution Margin	Net Income	Degree of Operating Leverage	
1 Armstrong				1
2 Contador				2
3				3
4 Interpretation:				4
5				5
6				6
7				7

(b)	Armstrong Company	Contador Company	
8			8
9			9
10 Sales revenue			10
11 Variable costs			11
12 Contribution margin			12
13 Fixed costs			13
14 Net income			14
15			15

(c)		
16		16
17		17
18		18
19		19
20		20

E20-15

(a)	Contribution Margin	Net Income	Degree of Operating Leverage	
1 Manual system				1
2 Computerized system				2
3				3

(b)		
4		4
5		5
6		6
7		7
8		8

	Manual System	Computerized System	
9			9
10			10
11 Sales			11
12 Variable costs			12
13 Contribution margin			13
14 Fixed costs			14
15 Net income			15

E20-1! (Continued)

(c)	(Actual Sales -	Break-even Sales) +	Actual Sales =	Margin of Safety Ratio	
1 Manual system					1
2 Computerized system					2
3					3
4					4
5					5

E20-16

(a)	Contribution Margin +	Net Income =	Degree of Operating Leverage		
1 Traditional Yams					1
2 Auto-Yams					2
3					3
4					4
5					5
6					6
7					7
8					8
9					9
10					10
11					11
12					12

(b)	% Change in Sales x	Degree of Operating Leverage =	% Change in Net Income		
16 15% decrease:					16
17 Traditional Yams					17
18 Auto-Yams					18
19					19
20 10% incease:					20
21 Traditional Yams					21
22 Auto-Yams					22
23					23
24 (c)					24
25					25
26					26
27					27
28					28
29					29
30					30

(a)   Unit Cost

(b)

Felde Company
Income Statement - Variable Costing
For the Year Ended December 31, 2014

(c)

Unit Cost

(d)

Felde Company		
Income Statement - Absorption Costing		
For the Year Ended December 31, 2014		
1			1
2			2
3			3
4			4
5			5
6			6
7			7
8			8

*E20-18

(a)		
1 Finished goods inventory cost (variable costing):		1
2		2
3		3
4		4
5		5
6		6
7 Variable manufacturing cost per unit =		7
8		8
9 Finished goods inventory cost =		9
10		10
11 (b)		11
12		12
13		13
14		14
15		15
16		16
17		17
18		18
19		19
20		20
21		21
22		22
23		23
24		24
25		25
26		26
27		27

(a)

	Utility Expense									
1	Variable utilities:									1
2										2
3										3
4										4
5	Fixed utilities:									5
6										6
7										7
8										8
9	Variable Costing									9
10										10
11										11
12										12
13										13
14										14
15										15
16										16
17										17
18										18
19	(b)									19
20	Absorption Costing									20
21										21
22										22
23										23
24										24
25										25
26										26
27										27
28										28
29										29
30										30
31										31
32										32
33										33
34	(c)									34
35										35
36										36
37										37
38										38
39										39
40										40

(a)

(1)		Current Year
1		
2		
3		
4		
5		
6		
7		
8		
9		
10		
11		
12		

		Current Year		Projected Year
13				
14				
15				
16				
17				
18				
19				
20				
21				
22				
23				
24				
25				
26				
27				

(2)		Current Year	Projected Year
29	Fixed costs:		
30			
31			
32			
33			
34			
35			
36			
37			
38			
39			
40			

(b)

1		
2		
3		
4		
5		
6		
7		
8		
9		
10		
11		
12	(c)	Sales dollars required for
13		target net income =
14		
15		
16	(d)	Margin of safety ratio =
17		
18		
19		

			Current Year
20	(e) (1)		
21			
22			
23			
24			
25			
26			
27			
28			
29			
30			
31			
32			
33			
34			
35			
36			
37			
38	(2)	Contribution margin ratio =	
39			
40			

(e) (3)

1	Break-even point in dollars =	1
2		2
3		3
4		4
5	Comments:	5
6		6
7		7
8		8
9		9
10		10
11		11
12		12
13		13
14		14
15		15
16		16
17		17
18		18
19		19
20		20
21		21
22		22
23		23
24		24
25		25
26		26
27		27
28		28
29		29
30		30
31		31
32		32
33		33
34		34
35		35
36		36
37		37
38		38
39		39
40		40

(a)

		Product		
		Economy	Standard	Deluxe
1				
2				
3				
4				
5				
6				
7				
8				

(b)

		Product		
		Economy	Standard	Deluxe
10				
11				
12				
13				
14				
15				
16				
17				
18				
19				

(c)

(a)

	Sales Mix %	Contribution Margin Ratio	Wtd.- Ave. Contribution Margin Ratio	
1 Appetizers				1
2 Main entrees				2
3 Desserts				3
4 Beverages				4
5				5
6				6
7 Total sales required to				7
8 achieve target net income =				8
9				9
10				10

	Sales Mix %	Total Sales	Sales From Each Product	
11				11
12				12
13 Appetizers				13
14 Main entrees				14
15 Desserts				15
16 Beverages				16
17				17
18				18

(b)

	Sales Mix %	Contribution Margin Ratio	Wtd.- Ave. Contribution Margin Ratio	
1 Appetizers				1
2 Main entrees				2
3 Desserts				3
4 Beverages				4
5				5
6				6
7				7
8 Total sales required to				8
9 achieve target net income =				9
10				10

	Sales Mix %	Contribution Margin Ratio	Sales Dollars Per Product	
11				11
12				12
13 Appetizers				13
14 Main entrees				14
15 Desserts				15
16 Beverages				16
17				17

(c)

	Sales Mix %	Contribution Margin Ratio	Wtd.- Ave. Contribution Margin Ratio	
1 Appetizers				1
2 Main entrees				2
3 Desserts				3
4 Beverages				4
5				5
6				6
7 Total sales required to				7
8　achieve target net income =				8
9				9
10				10

	Sales Mix %	Total Sales	Sales From Each Product	
11				11
12				12
13 Appetizers				13
14 Main entrees				14
15 Desserts				15
16 Beverages				16
17				17
18				18
19				19
20				20
21				21
22				22
23				23
24				24
25				25
26				26
27				27
28				28
29				29
30				30
31				31
32				32
33				33
34				34
35				35
36				36
37				37
38				38
39				39
40				40

(a)

	Contribution Margin	Sales	Contribution Margin Ratio	
1 Viejo Company				1
2 Nuevo Company				2
3				3
4				4

	Fixed Costs	Contribution Margin Ratio	Break-even Point in Dollars	
5				5
6				6
7				7
8 Viejo Company				8
9 Nuevo Company				9
10				10
11				11

	Actual Sales	Break-even Sales	Actual Sales	Margin of Safety Ratio	
12					12
13					13
14 Viejo Company					14
15 Nuevo Company					15
16					16
17					17
18					18
19					19
20					20

(b)

	Contribution Margin	Net Income	Degree of Operating Leverage	
1 Viejo Company				1
2 Nuevo Company				2
3				3
4				4
5				5
6				6
7				7
8				8
9				9
10				10
11				11
12				12
13				13
14				14
15				15

(c)

	Viejo Company	Nuevo Company
1 Sales		
2 Variable costs		
3 Contribution margin		
4 Fixed costs		
5 Net income		
6		
7		
8		
9		
10		

(d)

	Viejo Company	Nuevo Company
1 Sales		
2 Variable costs		
3 Contribution margin		
4 Fixed costs		
5 Net income		
6		
7		
8		

(e)

1	1
2	2
3	3
4	4
5	5
6	6
7	7
8	8
9	9
10	10
11	11
12	12

(a)

		(All amounts are in $000s)	
1			
2			
3			
4			
5			
6			
7		Contribution margin ratio =	
8			
9		Break-even point =	
10			
11			
12	(b)		
13			
14			
15			
16			
17			
18		Contribution margin ratio =	
19			
20		Break-even point =	
21			
22			
23	(c)		
24	(1)	Current situation: from part (a)	
25			
26			
27	(2)	Proposed situation: from part (b)	
28			
29			
30			
31			
32			
33			
34			
35			
36			
37			
38			
39			
40			

(c) (Continued)

1		1
2		2
3		3
4		4
5		5
6		6
7		7
8		8
9		9
10		10
11		11
12		12
13		13
14	(d)	14
15		15
16		16
17		17
18		18
19		19
20		20
21		21
22		22
23		23
24		24
25		25
26		26
27		27
28		28
29		29
30		30
31		31
32		32
33		33
34		34
35		35
36		36
37		37
38		38
39		39
40		40

(a)

Gardner Company Income Statement - Variable Costing For the Year Ended December 31,	2013	2014
1		
2		
3		
4		
5		
6		
7		
8		
9		
10		
11		
12		
13		
14		
15		
16		
17		
18		
19		
20		
21		
22		
23		
24		
25		
26		
27		
28		
29		
30		

(b)

Gardner Company Income Statement - Absorption Costing For the Year Ended December 31,	2013	2014
1		
2		
3		
4		
5		
6		
7		
8		
9		
10		
11		
12		
13		
14		
15		

(c)

	2013	2014
1 Variable costing net inc.		
2 Fixed manufacturing OH		
3 expensed with variable		
4 costing		
5 Less: Fixed manufacturing		
6 overhead expensed with		
7 absorption costing		
8 Difference		
9 Absorption costing net inc.		
10		

(d)

1
2
3
4
5

(a)

Dilithium Batteries Division
Income Statement - Absorption Costing
For the Year Ended December 31, 2014

	60,000 Produced	90,000 Produced
1		
2		
3		
4		
5		
6		
7		
8		
9		
10		
11		
12		
13		
14		
15		

(b)

Dilithium Batteries Division
Income Statement - Variable Costing
For the Year Ended December 31, 2014

	60,000 Produced	90,000 Produced
1		
2		
3		
4		
5		
6		
7		
8		
9		
10		
11		
12		
13		
14		
15		
16		
17		
18		
19		
20		

(c)

1	Net income under absorption costing	1
2	Less: Fixed manufacturing cost included	2
3	in ending inventory	3
4	Net income under variable costing	4
5		5
6		6
7		7
8		8
9		9
10		10
11		11
12		12
13		13
14		14
15		15

(d)

1	1
2	2
3	3
4	4
5	5
6	6
7	7
8	8
9	9
10	10
11	11
12	12
13	13
14	14
15	15

(a)

	(1)		Current Year
1			
2			
3			
4			
5			
6			
7			
8			
9			
10			
11			
12			

			Current Year		Projected Year
13					
14					
15					
16					
17					
18					
19					
20					
21					
22					
23					
24					
25					
26					
27					

	(2)		Current Year	Projected Year
28				
29	Fixed costs:			
30				
31				
32				
33				
34				
35				
36				
37				
38				
39				
40				

(b)

1	1
2	2
3	3
4	4
5	5
6	6
7	7
8	8
9	9
10	10
11	11

(c)   Sales dollars required for
       target net income =

(d)   Margin of safety ratio =

(e) (1)   Current
                                                  Year

(2) Contribution margin ratio =

(e) (3)

1	Break-even point in dollars =	1
2		2
3		3
4		4
5	Comments:	5
6		6
7		7
8		8
9		9
10		10
11		11
12		12
13		13
14		14
15		15
16		16
17		17
18		18
19		19
20		20
21		21
22		22
23		23
24		24
25		25
26		26
27		27
28		28
29		29
30		30
31		31
32		32
33		33
34		34
35		35
36		36
37		37
38		38
39		39
40		40

(a)

		Product		
		Economy	Standard	Deluxe
1				
2				
3				
4				
5				
6				
7				
8				

(b)

		Product		
		Economy	Standard	Deluxe
9				
10				
11				
12				
13				
14				
15				
16				
17				
18				
19				

(c)

20	
21	
22	
23	
24	
25	
26	
27	
28	
29	
30	
31	
32	
33	
34	
35	
36	
37	
38	
39	
40	

(a)

	Sales Mix %	Contribution Margin Ratio	Wtd.- Ave. Contribution Margin Ratio	
1 Appetizers				1
2 Main entrees				2
3 Desserts				3
4 Beverages				4
5				5
6				6
7 Total sales required to				7
8 achieve target net income =				8
9				9
10				10

	Sales Mix %	Total Sales	Sales From Each Product	
11				11
12				12
13 Appetizers				13
14 Main entrees				14
15 Desserts				15
16 Beverages				16
17				17
18				18

(b)

	Sales Mix %	Contribution Margin Ratio	Wtd.- Ave. Contribution Margin Ratio	
1 Appetizers				1
2 Main entrees				2
3 Desserts				3
4 Beverages				4
5				5
6				6
7				7
8 Total sales required to				8
9 achieve target net income =				9
10				10

	Sales Mix %	Contribution Margin Ratio	Sales Dollars Per Product	
11				11
12				12
13 Appetizers				13
14 Main entrees				14
15 Desserts				15
16 Beverages				16
17				17

(c)

	Sales Mix %	Contribution Margin Ratio	Wtd.- Ave. Contribution Margin Ratio	
1 Appetizers				1
2 Main entrees				2
3 Desserts				3
4 Beverages				4
5				5
6				6
7 Total sales required to				7
8 achieve target net income =				8
9				9
10				10

	Sales Mix %	Total Sales	Sales From Each Product	
11				11
12				12
13 Appetizers				13
14 Main entrees				14
15 Desserts				15
16 Beverages				16
17				17
18				18
19				19
20				20
21				21
22				22
23				23
24				24
25				25
26				26
27				27
28				28
29				29
30				30
31				31
32				32
33				33
34				34
35				35
36				36
37				37
38				38
39				39
40				40

(a)

	Contribution Margin	Sales	Contribution Margin Ratio	
1 Lyte Company				1
2 Darke Company				2
3				3
4				4

	Fixed Costs	Contribution Margin Ratio	Break-even Point in Dollars	
5				5
6				6
7				7
8 Lyte Company				8
9 Darke Company				9
10				10
11				11

	Actual Sales	Break-even Sales	Actual Sales	Margin of Safety Ratio	
12					12
13					13
14 Lyte Company					14
15 Darke Company					15
16					16
17					17
18					18
19					19
20					20

(b)

	Contribution Margin	Net Income	Degree of Operating Leverage	
1 Lyte Company				1
2 Darke Company				2
3				3
4				4
5				5
6				6
7				7
8				8
9				9
10				10
11				11
12				12
13				13
14				14
15				15

(c)

	Lyte Company	Darke Company	
1 Sales			1
2 Variable costs			2
3 Contribution margin			3
4 Fixed costs			4
5 Net income			5
6			6
7			7
8			8
9			9
10			10

(d)

	Lyte Company	Darke Company	
1 Sales			1
2 Variable costs			2
3 Contribution margin			3
4 Fixed costs			4
5 Net income			5
6			6
7			7
8			8

(e)

1	1
2	2
3	3
4	4
5	5
6	6
7	7
8	8
9	9
10	10
11	11
12	12

ame

ection

ame   Peaches and Cream Corporation

(a)

	(All amounts are in $000s)		
1			1
2			2
3			3
4			4
5			5
6			6
7	Contribution margin ratio =		7
8			8
9	Break-even point =		9
10			10
11			11
12	(b)		12
13			13
14			14
15			15
16			16
17			17
18	Contribution margin ratio =		18
19			19
20	Break-even point =		20
21			21
22			22
23	(c)		23
24	(1) Current situation: from part (a)		24
25			25
26			26
27	(2) Proposed situation: from part (b)		27
28			28
29			29
30			30
31			31
32			32
33			33
34			34
35			35
36			36
37			37
38			38
39			39
40			40

(c) (Continued)

1		1
2		2
3		3
4		4
5		5
6		6
7		7
8		8
9		9
10		10
11		11
12		12
13		13
14	(d)	14
15		15
16		16
17		17
18		18
19		19
20		20
21		21
22		22
23		23
24		24
25		25
26		26
27		27
28		28
29		29
30		30
31		31
32		32
33		33
34		34
35		35
36		36
37		37
38		38
39		39
40		40

(a)

FAB Company Income Statement - Variable Costing For the Year Ended December 31,		
	2013	2014
1		
2		
3		
4		
5		
6		
7		
8		
9		
10		
11		
12		
13		
14		
15		
16		
17		
18		
19		
20		
21		
22		
23		
24		
25		
26		
27		
28		
29		
30		

(b)

	FAB Company	2013	2014
	Income Statement - Absorption Costing		
	For the Year Ended December 31,		
1			
2			
3			
4			
5			
6			
7			
8			
9			
10			
11			
12			
13			
14			
15			

(c)

		2013		2014	
1	Variable costing net inc.				
2	Fixed manufacturing OH				
3	expensed with variable				
4	costing				
5	Less: Fixed manufacturing				
6	overhead expensed with				
7	absorption costing				
8	Difference				
9	Abs. costing net inc.				
10					

(d)

1	
2	
3	
4	
5	

(a)

Electricoil Division		
Income Statement - Absorption Costing		
For the Year Ended December 31, 2014		
	200,000 Produced	250,000 Produced

(b)

Electricoil Division		
Income Statement - Variable Costing		
For the Year Ended December 31, 2014		
	200,000 Produced	250,000 Produced

(c)

1	Net income under absorption costing	
2	Less: Fixed manufacturing cost included	
3	in ending inventory	
4	Net income under variable costing	
5		
6		
7		
8		
9		
10		
11		
12		
13		
14		
15		

(d)

1	
2	
3	
4	
5	
6	
7	
8	
9	
10	
11	
12	
13	
14	
15	

1	(a)	Weighted-average unit
2		contribution margin:
3		
4		
5		
6	(b)	Break-even point in units:
7		
8		
9		Break-even sales distribution:
10		Rotomolded kayaks
11		Composite kayaks
12		
13		
14	(c)	Target net income in units:
15		
16		
17		
18		
19		
20		Break-even sales distribution:
21		Rotomolded kayaks
22		Composite kayaks
23		
24		
25		
26		
27		
28		
29		
30		

(d)

CVP Income Statement	Rotomolded	Composite
Degree of operating leverage		
Rotomolded kayaks		
Composite kayaks		

(a)

1	Sales	1
2	Less: Variable costs	2
3	Contribution margin	3
4	Less: Fixed costs	4
5	Net income	5

(b)

1	Contribution margin ratio =	1
2		2
3	Break-even point in dollars =	3
4		4
5	Margin of safety ratio =	5
6		6
7	Degree of operating leverage =	7
8		8

(c)

1	Sales	1
2	Less: Variable costs	2
3	Contribution margin	3
4	Less: Fixed costs	4
5	Net income	5

(d)

1	Contribution margin ratio =	1
2		2
3	Break-even point in dollars =	3
4		4
5	Margin of safety ratio =	5
6		6
7	Degree of operating leverage =	7

(e)

1	1
2	2
3	3
4	4
5	5
6	6
7	7
8	8
9	9
10	10
11	11
12	12
13	13
14	14
15	15
16	16
17	17
18	18
19	19
20	20
21	21
22	22
23	23
24	24
25	25
26	26
27	27
28	28
29	29
30	30
31	31
32	32
33	33
34	34
35	35
36	36
37	37
38	38
39	39
40	40

(a)

($ in millions)	Consumer Products	Pet Products	Soup and Infant Feeding Products	
1 Sales				1
2 Variable costs				2
3 Contribution margin				3
4				4
5 Contribution margin				5
6 ÷ Sales				6
7 Contribution margin ratio				7
8				8
9 Division sales				9
10 ÷ Total sales				10
11 Sales mix percentage				11
12				12

(b)

	Sales Mix %	Contribution Margin Ratio	Wtd.- Ave. Contribution Margin Ratio	
1 Consumer products				1
2 Pet products				2
3 Soup and infant feeding				3
4 products				4
5				5
6				6
7 Total sales required to				7
8 break-even (in millions)				8
9				9
10				10

	Sales Mix %	Total Sales	Sales From Each Product (in millions)	
				11
				12
				13
14 Consumer products				14
15 Pet products				15
16 Soup and infant feeding				16
17 products				17
18				18
19				19
20				20
21				21
22				22
23				23

(a)

1		1
2		2
3		3
4		4
5		5
6		6
7		7
8		8
9		9
10		10

(b)   (in millions of $)

FedEx Ground
Income Statement - Variable Costing
For the Year Ended May 31, 2008

1	Revenues	1
2	Variable costs:	2
3	Salaries and employee benefits	3
4	Purchased transportation	4
5	Fuel	5
6	Maintenance and repairs	6
7	Intercompany charges	7
8	Contribution margin	8
9	Fixed costs:	9
10	Rentals	10
11	Depreciation and amortization	11
12	Other	12
13	Net income	13
14		14
15		15
16	Contribution margin ratio =	16
17		17
18		18
19	Break-even point in dollars =	19
20		20
21		21
22		22
23		23
24		24
25		25

(c)

(i)	2008	2006
FedEx Express		
FedEx Ground		
FedEx Freight		
FedEx Services		
(ii)	2008	2006
FedEx Express		
FedEx Ground		
FedEx Freight		
FedEx Services		
(iii)		

ame

ection

ate

BE21-2

	Alternative A	Alternative B	Net Income Increase (Decrease)	
1				1
2				2
3				3
4				4
5				5
6				6
7				7

BE21-3

	Reject Order	Accept Order	Net Income Increase (Decrease)	
8				8
9				9
10				10
11				11
12				12
13				13
14				14
15				15
16				16
17				17

BE21-4

	Make	Buy	Net Income Increase (Decrease)	
18				18
19				19
20				20
21				21
22				22
23				23
24				24
25				25
26				26

BE21-5

	Sell	Process Further	Net Income Increase (Decrease)	
27				27
28				28
29				29
30				30
31				31
32				32
33				33
34				34
35				35
36				36
37				37
38				38
39				39
40				40

BE21-7

	Retain Equipment	Replace Equipment	Net 4 - Year Income Increase (Decrease)
1			
2			
3			
4			
5			
6			
7			

BE21-8

	Continue	Eliminate	Net Income Increase (Decrease)
9			
10			
11			
12			
13			
14			
15			
16			

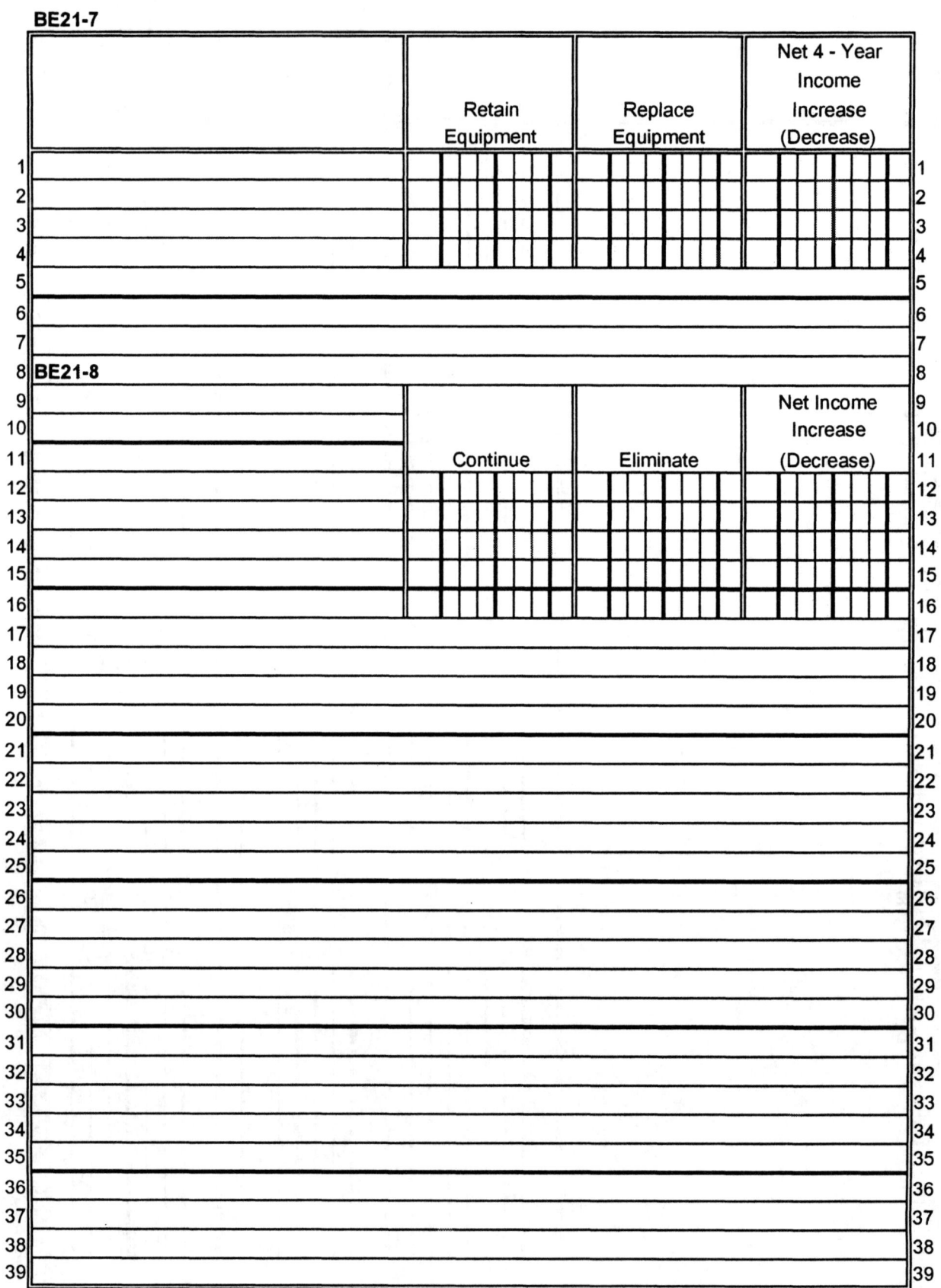

DO IT! 21-1

	Reject	Accept	Net Income Increase (Decrease)	
1				1
2				2
3				3
4				4
5				5
6				6
7				7

DO IT! 21-2

	Make	Buy	Net Income Increase (Decrease)	
8				8
9				9
10				10
(a) 11				11
12				12
13				13
14				14
15				15
16				16
17				17
18				18
19				19
20				20
21				21

	Make	Buy	Net Income Increase (Decrease)	
(b) 22				22
23				23
24				24
25				25
26				26
27				27
28				28
29				29
30				30
31				31
32				32
33				33
34				34
35				35
36				36
37				37
38				38
39				39
40				40

DO IT! 21-3

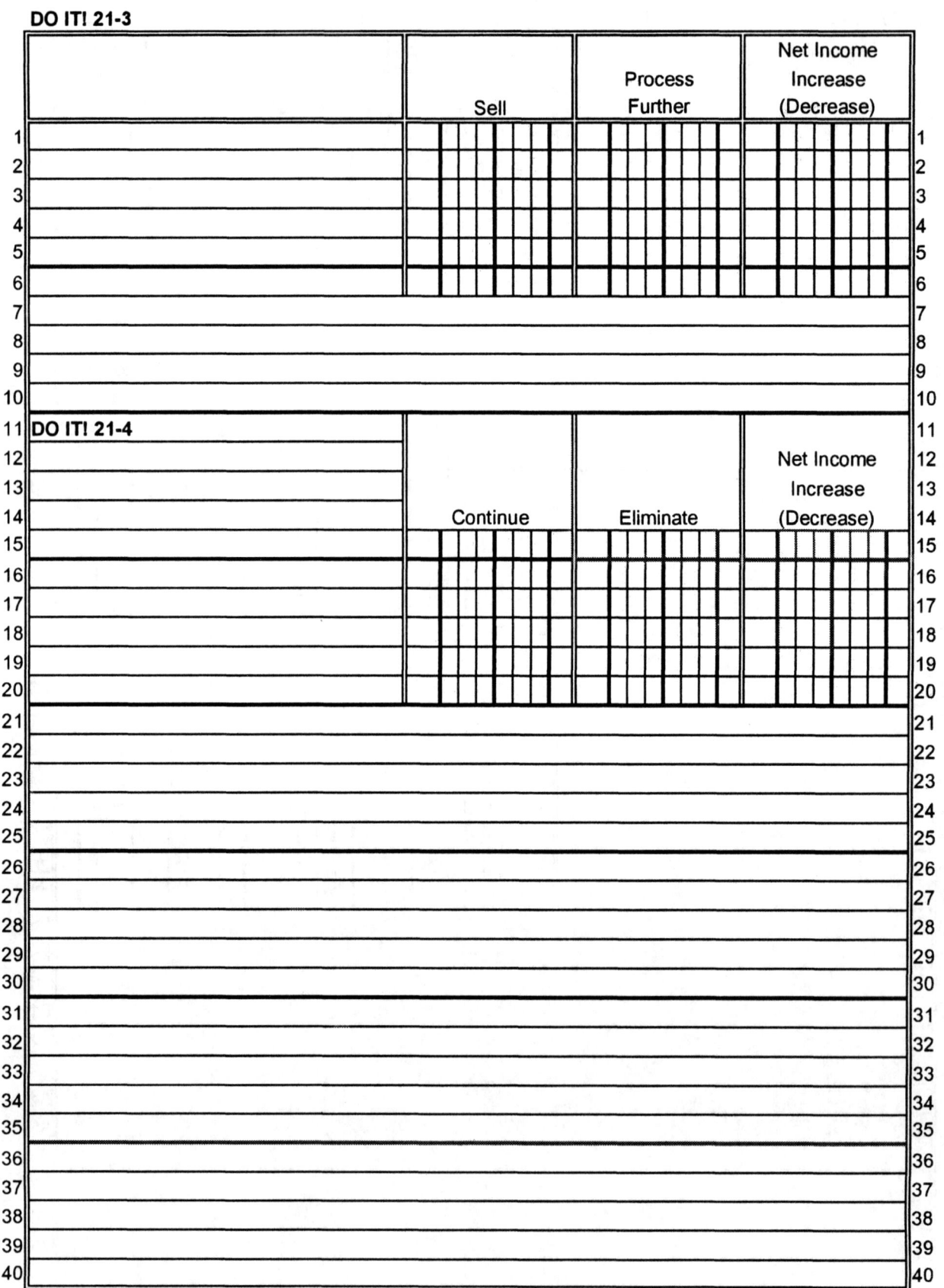

		Sell	Process Further	Net Income Increase (Decrease)	
1					1
2					2
3					3
4					4
5					5
6					6
7					7
8					8
9					9
10					10

DO IT! 21-4

		Continue	Eliminate	Net Income Increase (Decrease)	
11					11
12					12
13					13
14					14
15					15
16					16
17					17
18					18
19					19
20					20
21					21
22					22
23					23
24					24
25					25
26					26
27					27
28					28
29					29
30					30
31					31
32					32
33					33
34					34
35					35
36					36
37					37
38					38
39					39
40					40

(a)	Reject Order	Accept Order	Net Income Effect
1			
2			
3			
4			
5			
6			
7			
8			
9			
10			

(b)

(c)

E21-3

(a)	Reject Order	Accept Order	Net Income Increase (Decrease)
1			
2			
3			
4			
5			
6			
7			
8			
9			
10			
11			
12			
13			
14 (b)			
15			
16			
17			

E21-4

	Reject Order	Accept Order	Net Income Increase (Decrease)
1			
2			
3			
4			
5			
6			
7			
8			
9			
10			
11			
12			
13			
14			
15			
16			
17			
18			

E21-5

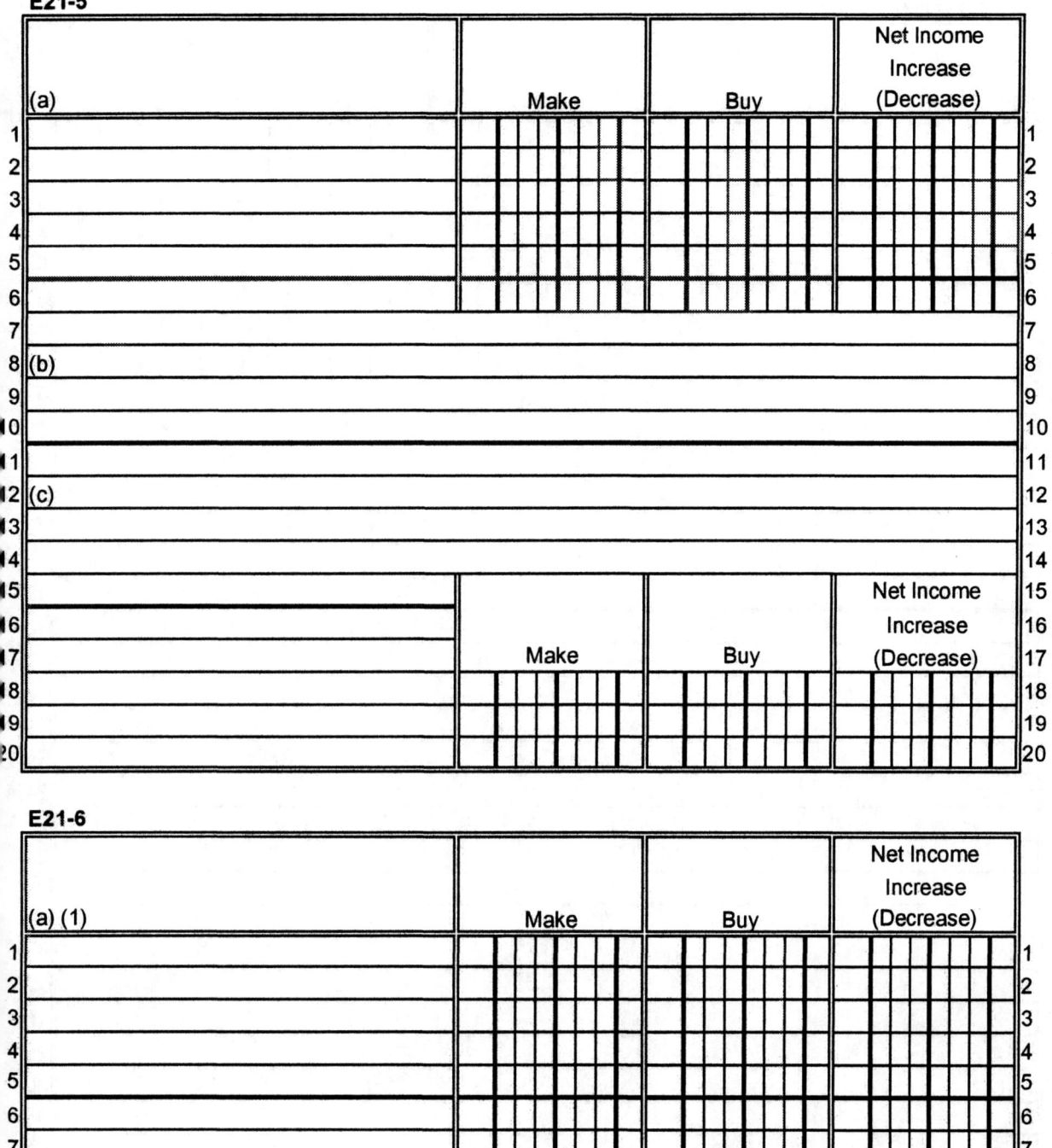

E21-6

(a) (Continued)

(a) (2)	Make	Buy	Net Income Increase (Decrease)
1			
2			
3			
4			
5			
6			
7			
8			
9			
10			

(b)

(a)	Make Sails	Buy Sails	Net Income Increase (Decrease)
1			
2			
3			
4			
5			

(b) (Based on 1,200 units)	Per Unit	Make	Buy	Net Income Increase (Decrease)

(c)

(a)

	Make IMC2	Buy IMC2	Net Income Increase (Decrease)
1			
2			
3			
4			
5			
6			
7			
8			
9			
10			
11			

(b)

(c)

	Sell Basic Kit			Process Further Stage 2 Kit			Net Income Increase (Decrease)		
1									
2									
3									
4									
5									
6									
7									
8									
9									
10									
11									
12									
13									
14									
15									
16									
17									
18									
19									
20									
21									
22									
23									
24									
25									
26									
27									
28									
29									
30									
31									
32									
33									
34									
35									
36									
37									
38									
39									
40									

(a)					
1	Sales				1
2	Joint costs				2
3	Net income				3
4					4
5	(b)				5
6	Sales				6
7	Joint costs				7
8	Additional costs				8
9	Net income				9
10					10

	(c)	Product 12	Product 14	Product 16	
11		Product 12	Product 14	Product 16	11
12	Incremental revenue				12
13	Incremental costs				13
14	Incremental profit (loss)				14
15					15
16					16
17					17
18					18

19	(d)		19
20	Sales		20
21	Joint costs		21
22	Additional costs		22
23	Net income		23
24			24
25			25
26			26
27			27
28			28
29			29
30			30

E21-11

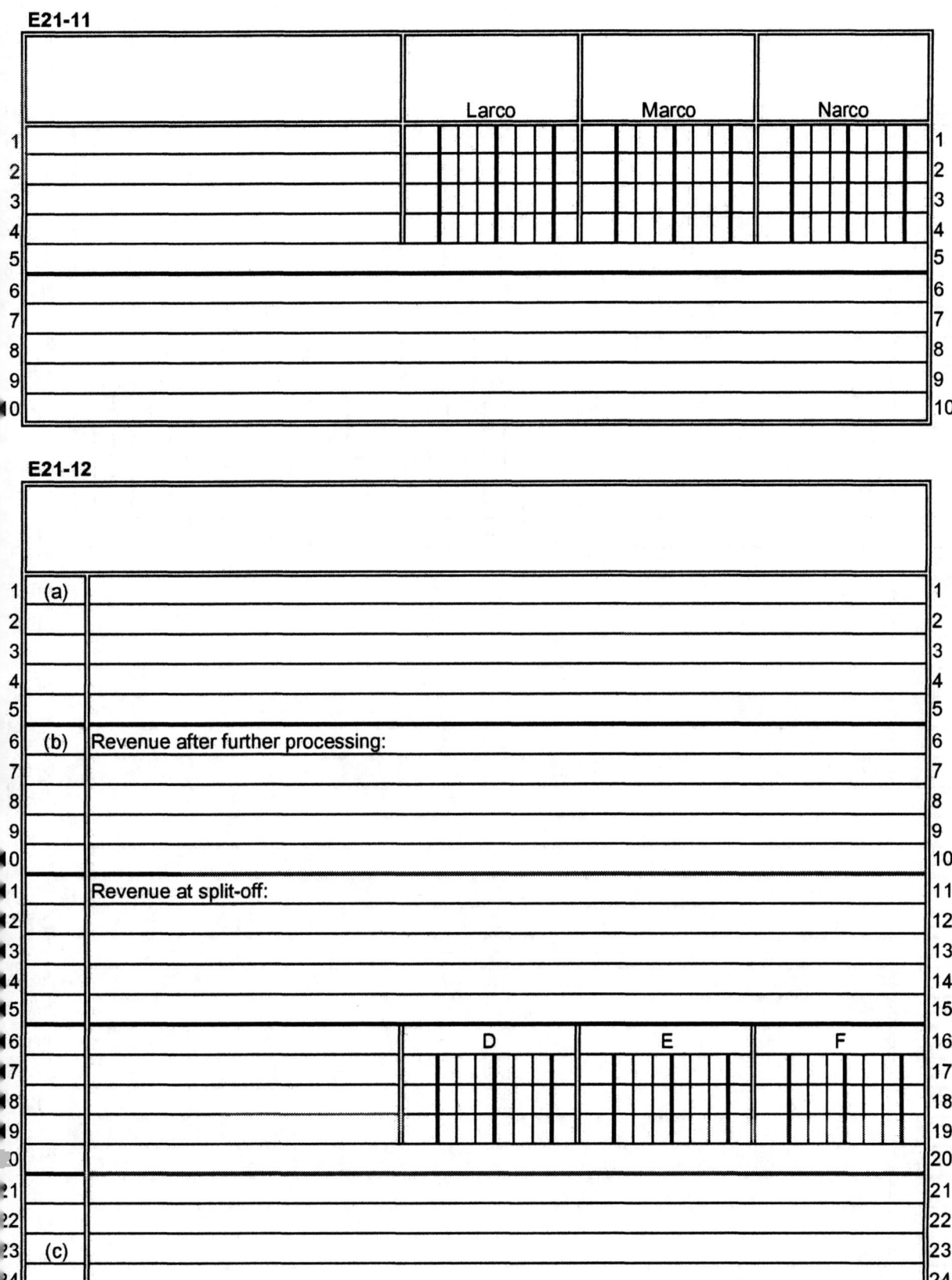

		Larco	Marco	Narco	
1					1
2					2
3					3
4					4
5					5
6					6
7					7
8					8
9					9
10					10

E21-12

1	(a)					1
2						2
3						3
4						4
5						5
6	(b)	Revenue after further processing:				6
7						7
8						8
9						9
10						10
11		Revenue at split-off:				11
12						12
13						13
14						14
15						15
16			D	E	F	16
17						17
18						18
19						19
20						20
21						21
22						22
23	(c)					23
24						24
25						25

	(a)					
1						1
2						2
3						3
4						4
5						5
6						6
7	(b)		Retain Scanner	Replace Scanner	Net Income Increase (Decrease)	7
8						8
9						9
10						10
11						11
12						12
13						13
14						14
15						15
16						16
17						17
18						18
19	(c)					19
20						20
21						21
22						22
23						23
24						24
25						25
26						26
27						27
28						28
29						29
30						30
31						31
32						32
33						33
34						34
35						35
36						36
37						37
38						38
39						39
40						40

E21-14

	Retain Machine	Replace Machine	Net Income Increase (Decrease)	
1				1
2				2
3				3
4				4
5				5
6				6
7				7
8				8
9				9
10				10

E21-15

	Continue	Eliminate	Net Income Increase (Decrease)	
1				1
2				2
3				3
4				4
5				5
6				6
7				7
8				8
9				9
10				10
11				11
12				12
13				13
14				14
15				15
16				16
17				17
18				18
19				19
20				20
21				21
22				22
23				23
24				24
25				25

			Tingler	Shocker	Total	
1	(a)					1
2						2
3						3
4	(b)					4
5						5
6						6
7						7
8						8
9						9
10						10
11						11
12						12
13						13
14	(c)					14
15						15
16						16
17						17
18						18
19						19
20						20
21						21
22						22
23						23
24						24
25						25
26						26
27						27
28						28
29						29
30						30
31						31
32						32
33						33
34						34
35						35
36						36
37						37
38						38
39						39
40						40

ame

ection

ate

	C	D	E	
Calculation of contribution margin per unit:				
1				1
2				2
3				3
4				4
5 Fixed costs =				5
6				6
7				7

	C	D	Total	
8 Company profit with Products A and B:				8
9				9
10				10
11				11
12				12
13				13
14				14
15				15
16				16
17				17

	C	E	Total	
18 Company profit with Product A and C:				18
19				19
20				20
21				21
22				22
23				23
24				24
25				25
26				26
27				27
28				28
29				29
30				30
31				31
32				32
33				33
34				34
35				35
36				36
37				37
38				38
39				39
40				40

(a)

	Reject Order	Accept Order	Net Income Increase (Decrease)
1			
2			
3			
4			
5			
6			
7			
8			
9			
10			
11			
12			
13			
14			
15			
16			
17			
18			
19			
20			
21			
22			
23			
24			
25			
26 (b)			
27			
28			
29			
30			
31 (c)			
32			
33			
34			
35			
36 (d)			
37			
38			
39			
40			

Name

Section

Date   Shatner Manufacturing Company

(a)

		Make CISCO	Buy CISCO	Net Income Increase (Decrease)	
1					1
2					2
3					3
4					4
5					5
6					6
7					7
8					8
9					9
10					10
11					11
12					12

(b)

13		13
14		14
15		15
16		16
17		17
18		18

(c)

19		19
20		20
21		21
22		22

		Make CISCO	Buy CISCO	Net Income Increase (Decrease)	
23					23
24					24
25					25
26					26
27					27
28					28
29					29
30					30

31		31
32		32
33		33
34		34

(d)

35		35
36		36
37		37
38		38
39		39
40		40

(a)

	(1)	Table Cleaner Not Processed Further			
1					1
2					2
3					3
4					4
5					5
6					6
7					7
8					8
9					9
10					10
11	(2)	Table Cleaner Processed Further			11
12					12
13					13
14					14
15					15
16					16
17					17
18					18
19					19
20					20
21					21
22					22
23					23
24					24
25	(3)				25
26					26
27					27
28					28
29	(b)		Don't Process Table Cleaner Further	Process Table Cleaner Further	Net Income Increase (Decrease)	29
30						30
31						31
32						32
33						33
34						34
35						35
36						36
37						37
38						38
39						39
40						40

(a)

1			1
2			2
3			3
4			4
5			5
6			6
7			7

(b) (1)

	Retain Old Elevator	
8		8
9		9
10		10
11		11
12		12
13		13
14		14
15		15
16		16
17		17

(2)

	Replace Old Elevator	
18		18
19		19
20		20
21		21
22		22
23		23
24		24
25		25
26		26
27		27
28		28
29		29

(c)

	Retain Old Elevator	Replace Old Elevator	Net Income Increase (Decrease)	
30				30
31				31
32				32
33				33
34				34
35				35
36				36
37				37
38				38
39				39
40				40

(d)

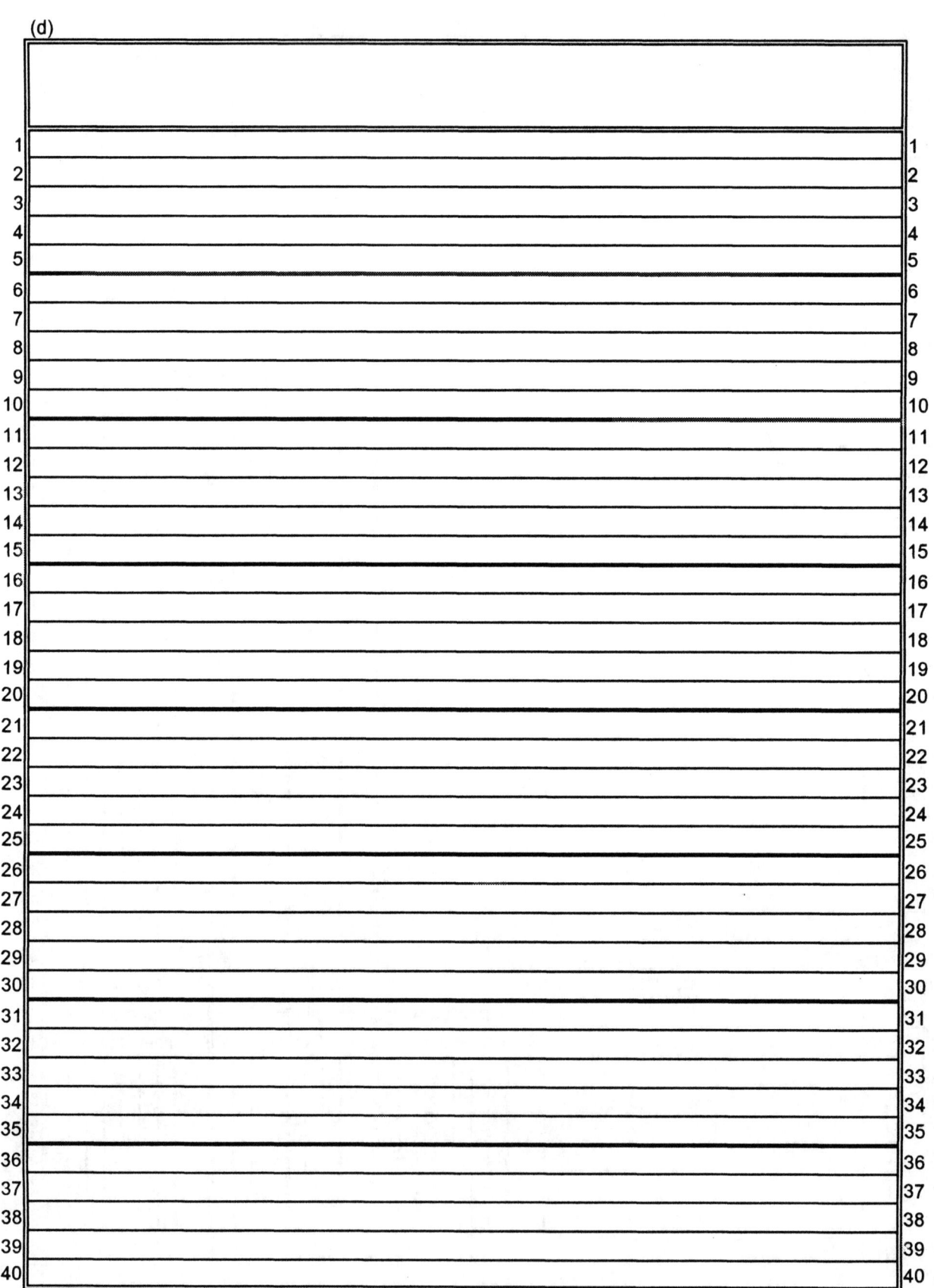

(a)

		Division I	Division II
1			
2			
3			
4			
5			
6			
7			

(b)

(1) Division I	Continue	Eliminate	Net Income Increase (Decrease)
1			
2			
3			
4			
5			
6			
7			
8			
9			
10 (2) Division II			
11			
12			
13			
14			
15			
16			
17			
18			
19			
20			
21			
22			
23			
24			
25			
26			
27			
28			

(c)

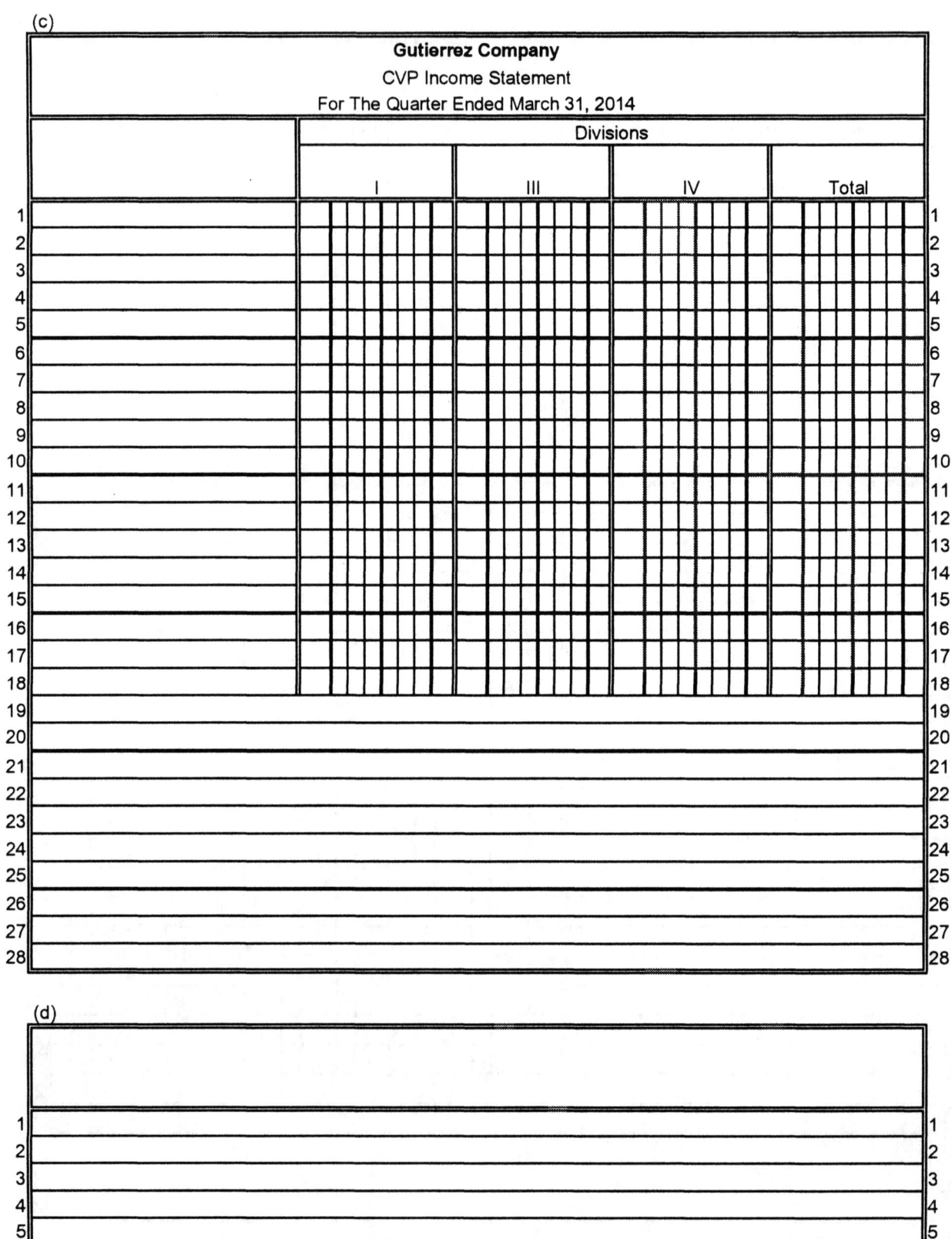

Gutierrez Company

CVP Income Statement

For The Quarter Ended March 31, 2014

	Divisions			
	I	III	IV	Total
1				
2				
3				
4				
5				
6				
7				
8				
9				
10				
11				
12				
13				
14				
15				
16				
17				
18				
19				
20				
21				
22				
23				
24				
25				
26				
27				
28				

(d)

1	
2	
3	
4	
5	

(a)

	Reject Order	Accept Order	Net Income Increase (Decrease)	
1				1
2				2
3				3
4				4
5				5
6				6
7				7
8				8
9				9
10				10
11				11
12				12
13				13
14				14
15				15

(b), (c), and (d)

1	(b)	1
2		2
3		3
4	(c)	4
5		5
6		6
7		7
8	(d)	8
9		9
10		10
11		11
12		12
13		13
14		14
15		15
16		16
17		17
18		18
19		19
20		20

(a)

		Make FIZBE	Buy FIZBE	Net Income Increase (Decrease)
1				
2				
3				
4				
5				
6				
7				
8				
9				
10				
11				
12				

(b)

13	
14	
15	
16	
17	
18	

(c)

		Make FIZBE	Buy FIZBE	Net Income Increase (Decrease)
19				
20				
21				
22				
23				
24				
25				

26	
27	
28	
29	
30	
31	
32	
33	

(d)

34	
35	
36	
37	
38	
39	
40	

(a)

(1)	Cleaner Not Processed Further

1			
2			
3			
4			
5			
6			
7			
8			
9			
10			

(2)	General-Purpose Cleaner Processed Further

12			
13			
14			
15			
16			
17			
18			
19			
20			
21			
22			
23			
24			

(3)

(b)

		Don't Process G-P Cleaner Further	Process G-P Cleaner Further	Net Income Increase (Decrease)

(a)

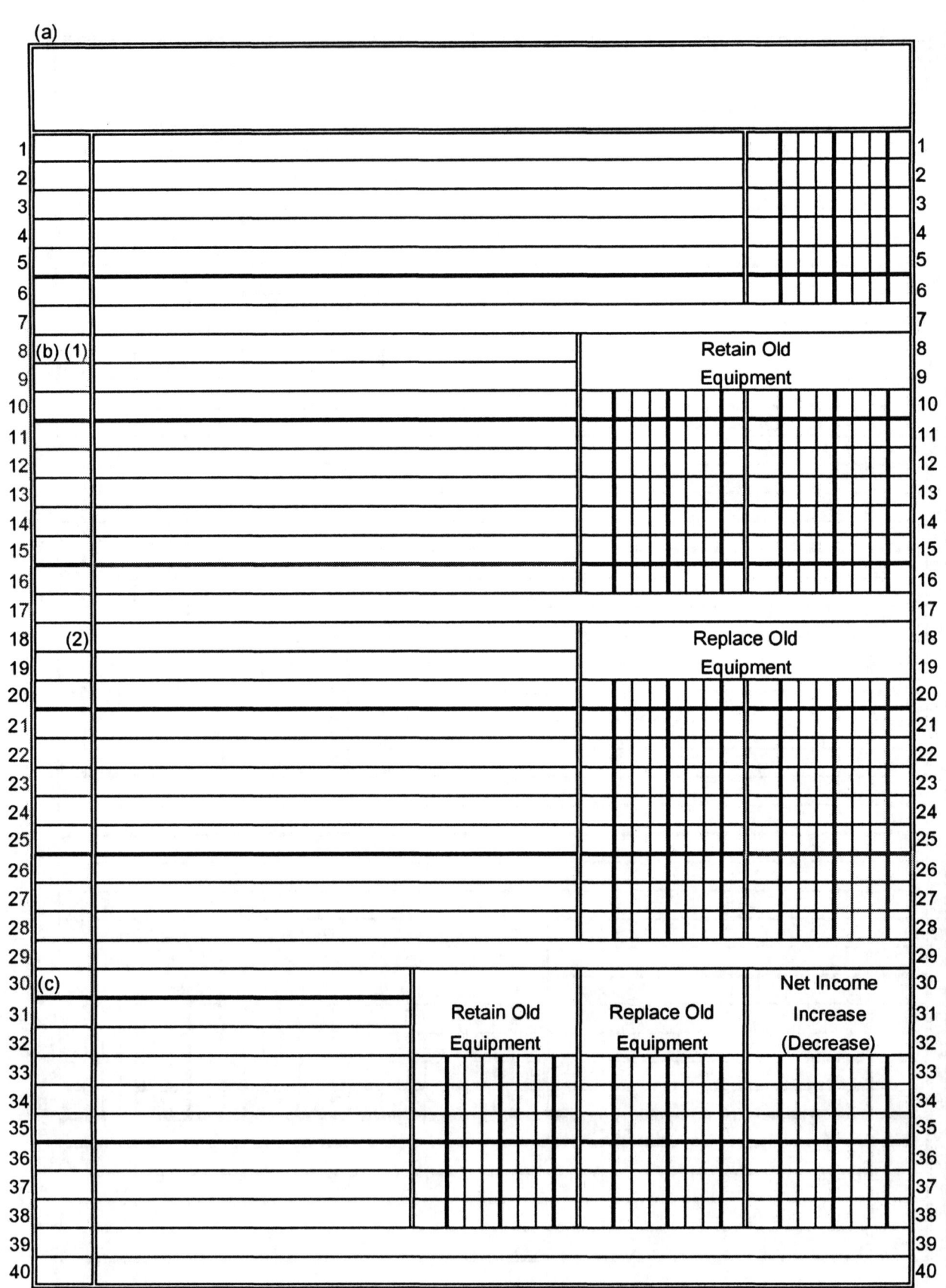

	1
	2
	3
	4
	5
	6
	7

(b) (1)

	Retain Old Equipment

(2)

	Replace Old Equipment

(c)

	Retain Old Equipment	Replace Old Equipment	Net Income Increase (Decrease)

(d)

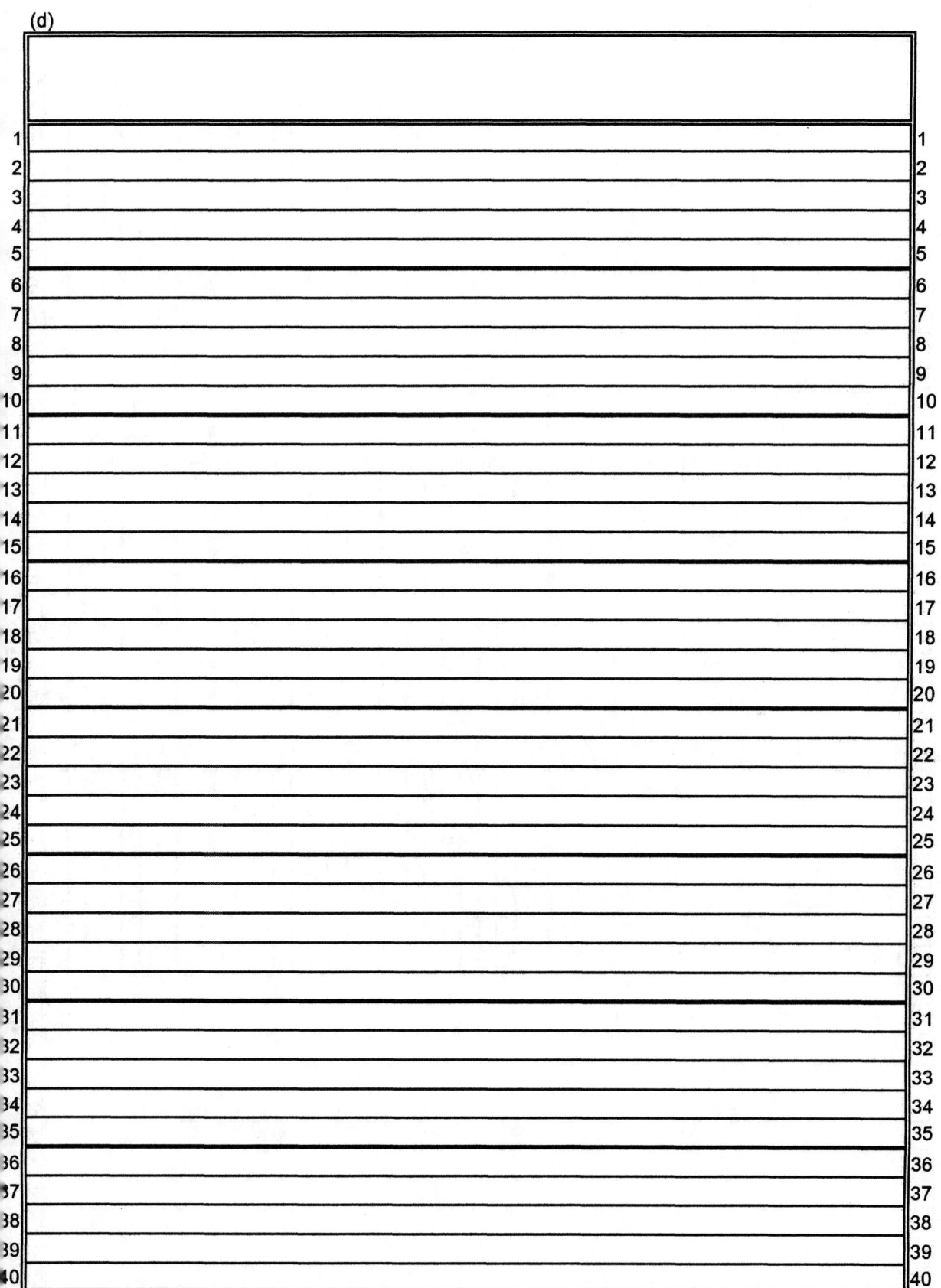

(a)

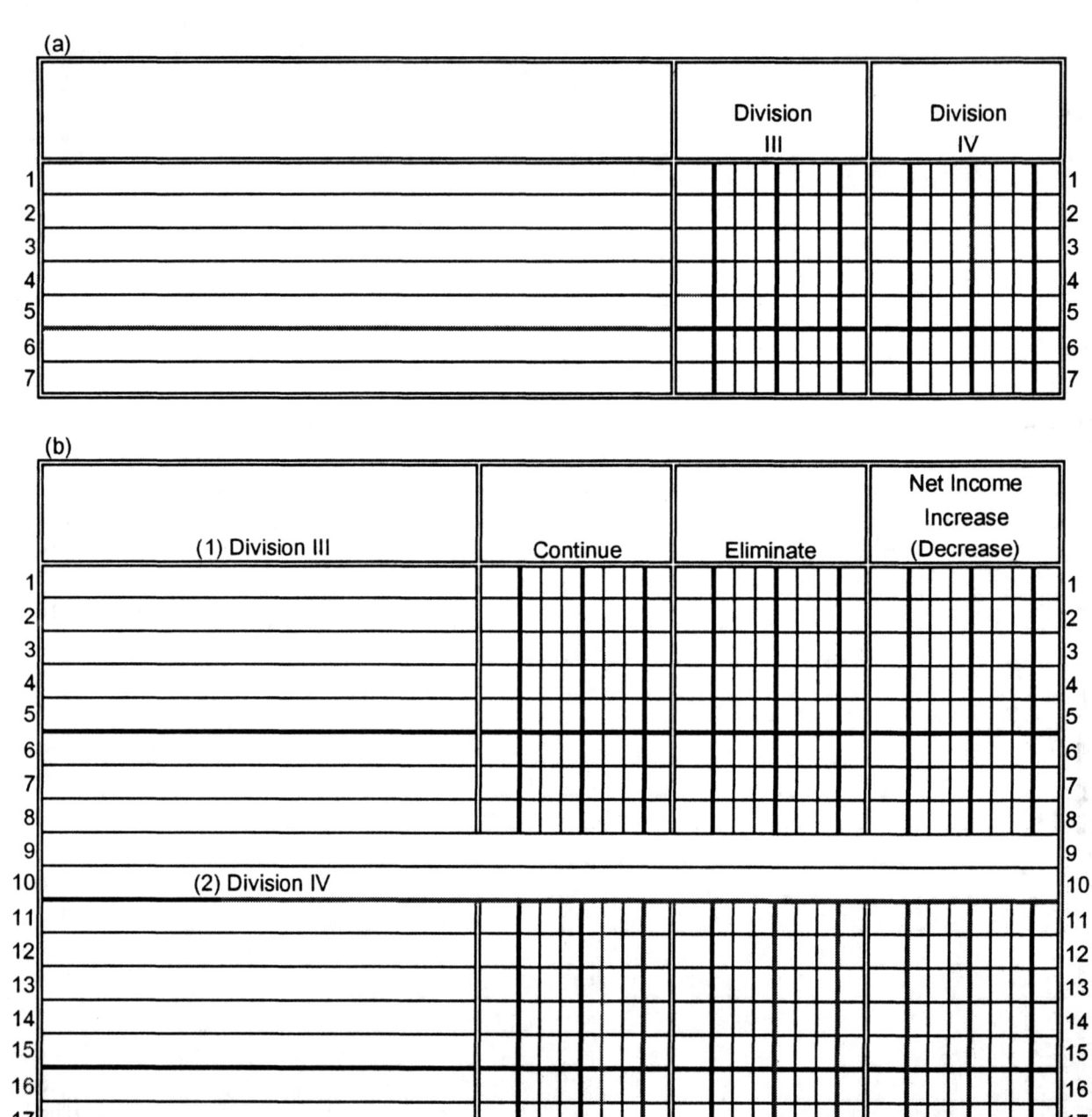

	Division III	Division IV
1		
2		
3		
4		
5		
6		
7		

(b)

(1) Division III	Continue	Eliminate	Net Income Increase (Decrease)
1			
2			
3			
4			
5			
6			
7			
8			
9			
(2) Division IV			
11			
12			
13			
14			
15			
16			
17			
18			
19			
20			
21			
22			
23			
24			
25			
26			
27			
28			

ame

ection

ate   Panda Corporation

(c)

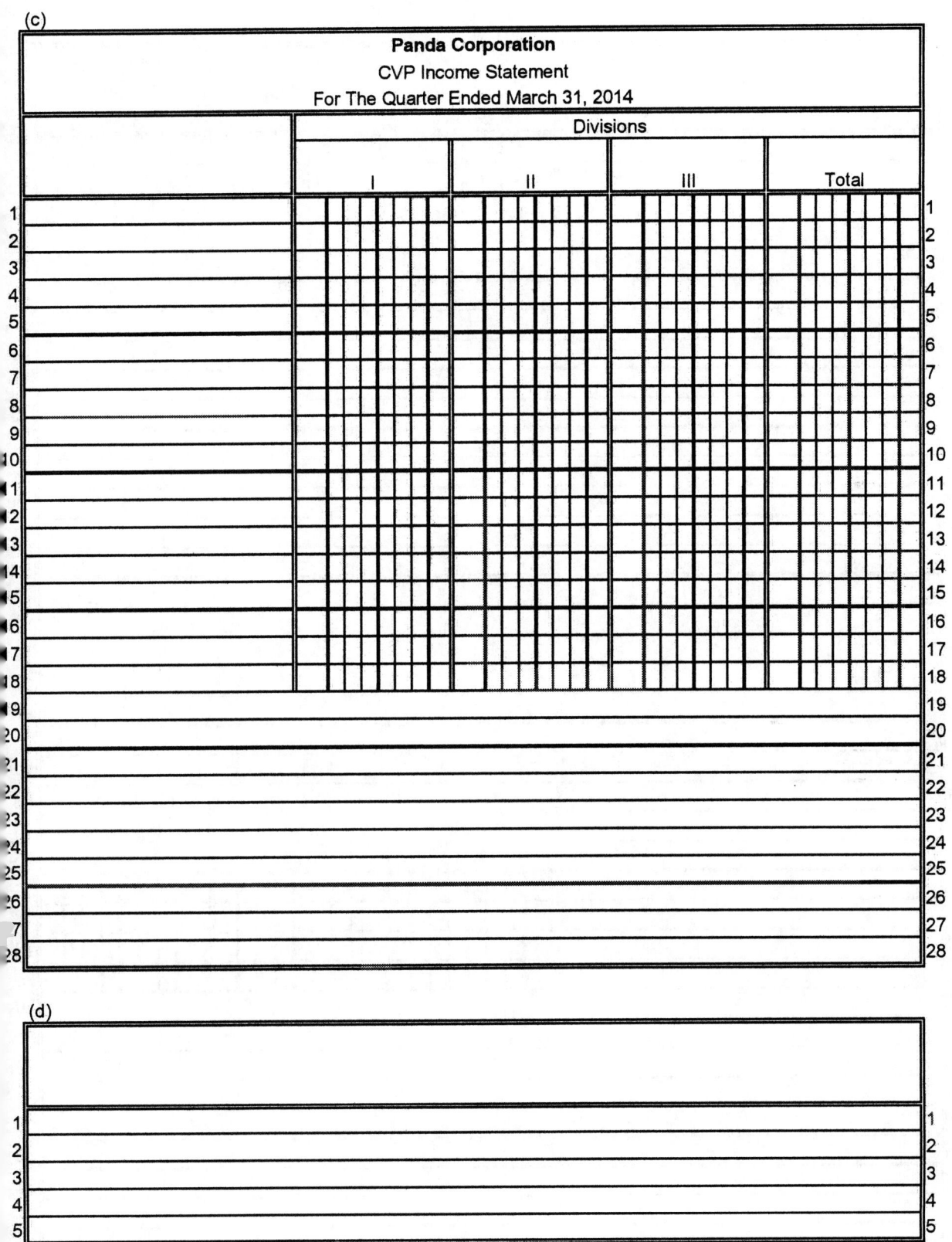

		Divisions			
		I	II	III	Total
1					
2					
3					
4					
5					
6					
7					
8					
9					
10					
11					
12					
13					
14					
15					
16					
17					
18					
19					
20					
21					
22					
23					
24					
25					
26					
27					
28					

Panda Corporation
CVP Income Statement
For The Quarter Ended March 31, 2014

(d)

1	
2	
3	
4	
5	

(a)   Situtaion #1

		Reject Order	Accept Order	Net Income Increase (Decrease)
1				
2				
3				
4				
5				
6				
7				

(b)

Situation #2

(a)

		Retain Oven	Replace Oven	Net Income Increase (Decrease)

(b)

(b) (Continued)

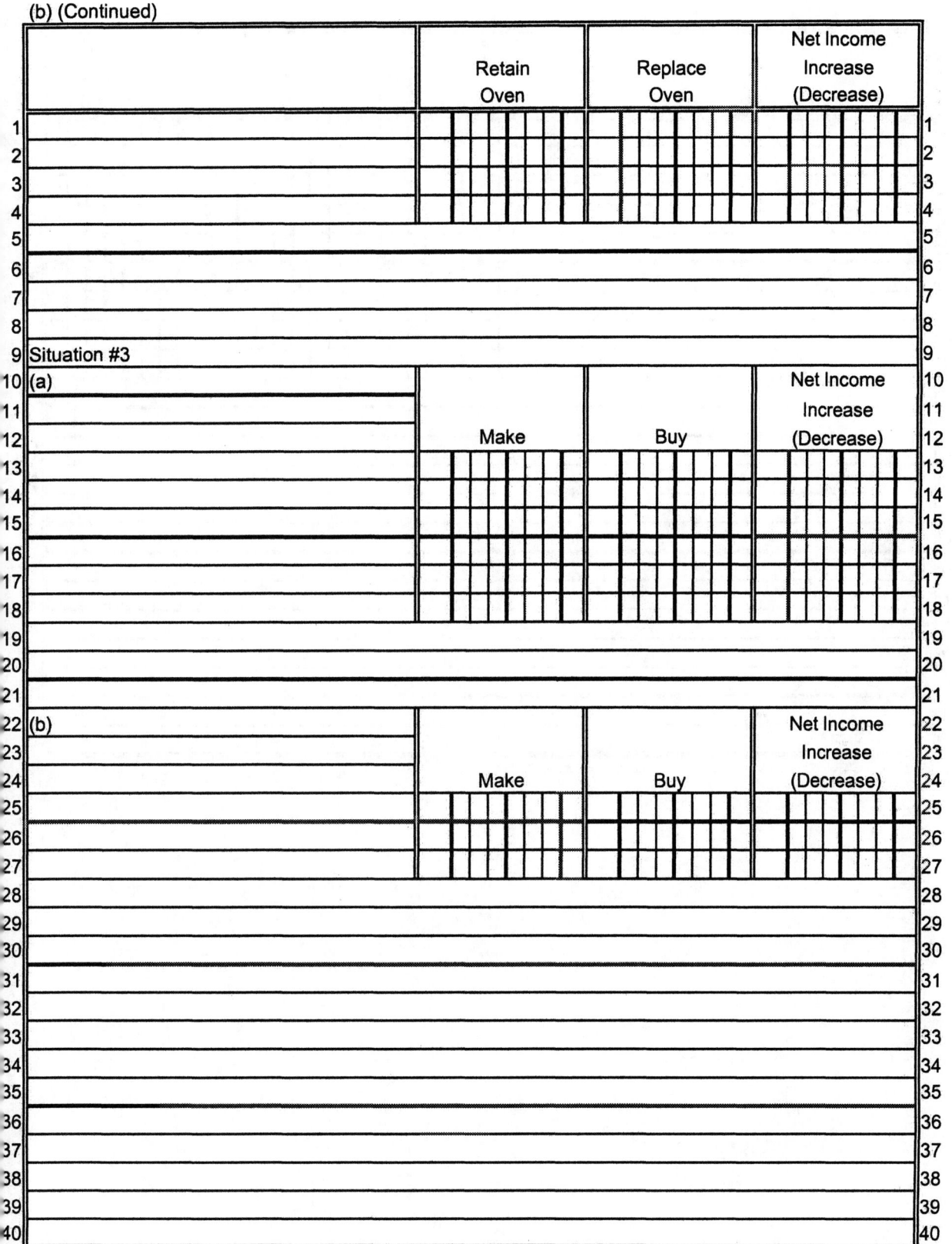

	Retain Oven	Replace Oven	Net Income Increase (Decrease)
1			
2			
3			
4			
5			
6			
7			
8			

Situation #3

(a)

	Make	Buy	Net Income Increase (Decrease)
13			
14			
15			
16			
17			
18			

(b)

	Make	Buy	Net Income Increase (Decrease)
25			
26			
27			

	Retain Old Machine	Purchase New Machine	Net Income Increase (Decrease)
1			
2			
3			
4			
5			
6			
7			
8			
9			
10			
11			
12			
13			
14			
15			
16			
17			
18			
19			
20			
21			
22			

(a)

		Make	Buy Trans-Tech	Buy Omega
1				
2				
3				
4				
5				
6				
7				
8				
9				
10				
11				
12				
13				
14				
15				
16				
17				
18				
19				
20				
21				
22				
23				
24				
25	(b)			
26				
27				
28				
29				
30				
31				
32				
33				
34				
35				
36				
37				
38				
39				
40				

(c)

	1
1	
2	2
3	3
4	4
5	5
6	6
7	7
8	8
9	9
10	10

ame   Chapter 22 Brief Exercises

ection

ate

BE22-2

		1	2	3	4	5	6	7		
1										1
2										2
3										3
4										4
5										5
6										6
7										7
8										8
9										9
10										10
11										11
12										12
13										13
14										14
15										15
16										16
17										17
18										18
19										19
20										20
21										21
22										22
23										23
24										24
25										25
26										26
27										27
28										28
29										29
30										30
31										31
32										32
33										33
34										34
35										35
36										36
37										37
38										38
39										39
40										40

DO IT! 22-2

1			1
2			2
3			3
4			4
5			5
6			6
7			7
8			8
9	Target selling price =		9
10			10
11			11

DO IT! 22-3

		Total Cost /	Total Hours =	Per Hour Charge	
13					13
14					14
15					15
16					16
17					17
18					18
19					19
20					20
21					21
22					22
23					23
24					24
25					25
26					26
27	Cost of dishwasher repair:				27
28					28
29					29
30					30
31					31
32					32
33					33
34					34
35					35
36					36
37					37
38					38
39					39
40					40

	(a)							
1	Market price							
2	Less: Desired profit							
3	Target cost							
4								
5	(b)							

E22-4

		(a) Total cost per unit:	Per Unit	
1				1
2				2
3				3
4				4
5				5
6				6
7				7
8				8
9		(b) Target selling price =		9
10				10
11				11

E22-5

		(a) Total cost per unit:	Per Unit	
12				12
13				13
14				14
15				15
16				16
17				17
18				18
19				19
20				20
21				21
22				22
23		(b) Desired ROI per unit =		23
24				24
25				25
26				26
27				27
28		(c) Markup percentage		28
29		using toatl cost per unit =		29
30				30
31				31
32				32
33				33
34		(d) Target selling price =		34
35				35
36				36
37				37
38				38
39				39
40				40

E22-6

			Per Session	
1	(a)	Total cost per session:		1
2				2
3				3
4				4
5				5
6				6
7				7
8				8
9				9
10	(b)	Desired ROI per session =		10
11				11
12				12
13				13
14	(c)	Markup percenatge on		14
15		Total cost per session:		15
16				16
17				17
18	(d)	Target price per session =		18
19				19
20				20

E22-7

	(a)	
1	Fixed manufacturing overhead per unit =	1
2		2
3	Fixed selling and administrative expenses per unit =	3
4		4
5	(b) Desired ROI per unit =	5
6		6
7		7
8		8
9		9
10		10
11		11
12		12
13		13
14		14
15		15

E22-7 (Continued)

	(c)	Target selling price:	Per Unit	
1				1
2				2
3				3
4				4
5				5
6				6
7				7
8				8
9				9
10				10

E22-8

	(a)	Total Cost /	Total Hours =	Per Hour Charge	
1	Hourly rate for repairs:				1
2					2
3	Overhead costs:				3
4					4
5					5
6					6
7					7
8	Profit margin			.	8
9	Rate charged per hour of labor				9
10					10

	(b)	Material Loading Charges /	Total Invoice Cost, Parts and Materials =	Material Loading Percentage	
11					11
12					12
13					13
14					14
15	Overhead costs:				15
16					16
17					17
18					18
19					19
20					20
21					21
22	Profit margin				22
23	Material loading percentage				23
24					24
25					25

E22-8 (Continued)

(c)   Job: Pace Corporation - Rebuild spot welder

1	Labor charges:
2	
3	Material charges:
4	
5	
6	Total price of labor and material
7	

E22-9

(a)	Total Cost /	Total Hours =	Per Hour Charge	
1 Hourly labor rate for repairs:				
2				
3 Overhead costs:				
4				
5				
6				
7				
8 Profit margin				
9 Rate charged per hour of labor				

(b)	Material Loading Charges /	Total Invoice Cost, Parts and Materials =	Material Loading Percentage	
16 Overhead costs:				
17				
18				
19				
20				
21				
22				
23 Profit margin				
24 Material loading percentage				

E22-9 Continued)

	(c)			
1	Job: Bull Builders			1
2	Labor charges			2
3				3
4	Material charges:			4
5				5
6				6
7	Total price of labor and material			7
8				8
9				9
10				10

E22-10

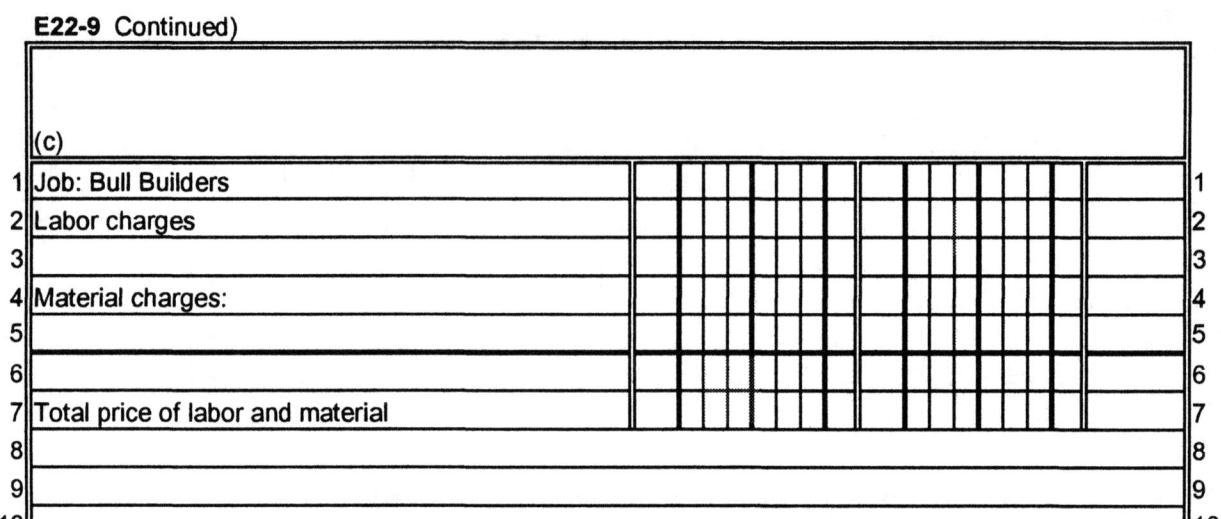

		Total Cost /	Total Hours =	Hourly Charge		
1	Hourly labor rate:					1
2						2
3	Overhead costs:					3
4						4
5						5
6	Total hourly cost					6
7						7
8	Profit margin =					8
9						9
10	(b)	Material Loading Charges /	Total Invoice Costs, Parts & Materials =	Material Loading Percentage		10
11						11
12						12
13	Overhead costs:					13
14						14
15						15
16						16
17						17
18						18
19	Other overhead costs					19
20	Total					20
21						21
22	Material loading charge (with profit)					22
23	Material loading charge (without profit)					23
24	Profit margin on materials					24
25						25

E22-1((Continued)

	(c)		
1	Labor charges:		1
2			2
3	Material charges:		3
4			4
5			5
6	Total price of labor and materials		6
7			7
8			8
9			9
10			10

E22-13

	(a)		
1	Minimum transfer price =		1
2			2
3			3
4	(b) The lost contribution margin per unit is:		4
5			5
6			6
7			7
8			8
9	Total lost contribution margin =		9
10			10
11			11
12	(c)		12
13			13
14			14
15			15
16			16
17			17
18			18
19			19
20			20

(a)

(1) The effect on Cycle Division is:

	Present Situation	Purchase from FrameBody
Selling price		
Variable cost of goods sold:		
Body frame		
Other variable costs		
Contribution margin		

(2) The effect on FrameBody is:

Selling price to Cycle Division	
Variable cost of goods sold:	

(3) The effect on Ayala's net income is:

(b)

(1) The effect on Cycle Division is:

(2) The effect on FrameBody is:

Selling price lost	
Selling price to Cycle Division	
Lost contribution margin per cycle	
Number of cycles	
Lost contribution margin	

(3) The effect on Ayala's net income is:

Cycle Division gain	
FrameBody loss	
Overall loss	

(a)		Division A	Division B	Total Company	
1					1
2					2
3					3
4					4
5					5
6					6
7					7
8	(b)				8
9					9
10					10
11					11
12	(c) (i)				12
13					13
14					14
15	(ii)				15
16					16
17					17
18	(iii)				18
19					19
20					20
21					21
22					22
23					23
24					24
25					25
26					26
27					27
28					28
29					29
30					30
31					31
32					32
33					33
34					34
35					35
36					36
37					37
38					38
39					39
40					40

	(a)		Per Unit
1			
2			
3			
4			
5			
6			
7			
8			
9			
10	(b)	Desired ROI per unit =	
11			
12			
13	(c)	Absorption cost pricing	
14		markup percentage =	
15			
16			
17	(d)	Variable cost pricing	
18		markup percentage =	
19			
20			
21			
22			
23			
24			
25			
26			
27			
28			
29			
30			
31			
32			
33			
34			
35			
36			
37			
38			
39			
40			

(a)					Variable Cost Per Unit	
1						1
2						2
3						3
4						4
5						5
6						6
7		Total Costs /		Budgeted Volume =	Cost Per Unit	7
8						8
9						9
10						10
11						11
12						12
13						13
14	Variable cost per unit					14
15	Fixed cost per unit					15
16	Total cost per unit					16
17						17
18	(b) Totl cost per unit					18
19	Markup					19
20	Desired ROI per unit					20
21						21
22						22
23	(c) Total cost per unit					23
24	Desired ROI per unit					24
25	Target selling price					25
26						26
27						27
28	(d) Variable cost per unit					28
29	Fixed cost per unit					29
30	Total cost per unit					30
31						31
32						32
33						33
34						34
35						35
36						36
37						37
38						38
39						39
40						40

(a)			Variable Cost Per Unit
1			
2			
3			
4			
5			
6			
7			
8			
9		Total Costs /	Budgeted Volume =	Cost Per Unit
10				
11				
12				
13				
14				
15				
16				
17	Variable cost per unit			
18	Fixed cost per unit			
19	Total cost per unit			
20				
21				
22	Desired ROI per unit =			
23				
24				
25	Markup percentage =			
26				
27				
28	Total cost per unit			
29	Desired ROI per unit			
30	Target selling price			
31				
32				
33				
34				
35				
36				
37				
38				
39				
40				

(b)			Variable Cost Per Unit	
1				
2				
3				
4				
5				
6				
7				
8				
9		Total Costs /	Budgeted Volume =	Cost Per Unit
10				
11				
12				
13				
14				
15				
16				
17				
18	Variable cost per unit			
19	Fixed cost per unit			
20	Total cost per unit			
21				
22				
23	Desired ROI per unit =			
24				
25				
26				
27	Markup percentage =			
28				
29				
30				
31	Total cost per unit			
32	Desired ROI per unit			
33	Target selling price			
34				
35				
36				
37				
38				
39				
40				

	(a) Computation of time charge rate:	Total Cost /	Total Hours =	Per Hour Charge	
1	Hourly labor rate for repairs:				1
2					2
3	Overhead costs:				3
4					4
5					5
6					6
7					7
8	Rate charged per labor hour				8
9					9
10					10
11	(b)	Material Loading	Total Invoice Cost, Parts	Material Loading	11
12					12
13	Computation of material loading charge:	Charges /	and Materials =	Percentage	13
14	Overhead costs:				14
15					15
16					16
17					17
18					18
19					19
20					20
21	Total				21
22					22
23	Material loading percentage				23
24					24
25	(c) Price quotation for time and material:				25
26					26
27	**Jose's Electronic Repair Shop**				27
28	Time and Material Price Quotation				28
29	January 5, 2014				29
30	Job: Rebuild big screen TV set:				30
31					31
32	Labor charges:				32
33					33
34	Material charges:				34
35					35
36					36
37	Total price of labor and material				37
38					38
39					39
40					40

1	(a)	1
2		2
3		3
4		4
5		5
6		6
7	(b)	7
8		8
9		9
10		10
11		11
12		12
13		13
14		14
15		15
16		16
17	(c)	17
18		18
19		19
20		20
21		21
22		22
23		23
24		24
25		25
26		26
27	(d)	27
28	The printing operation would lose:	28
29		29
30		30
31	Business Books would save:	31
32		32
33	Overall loss to the company as a whole	33
34		34
35		35
36		36
37		37
38		38
39		39
40		40

(a)

(b)

Lost contribution margin by Board Division:

Total lost contribution margin

Lost contribution margin by Chip Division:

Total lost contribution margin

Overall lost contribution margin for the company

1	(a) Absorption cost pricing:	
2		
3	Computation of unit manufacturing cost and target selling price	
4		
5		
6		
7		
8		
9		
10		
11		
12		
13		
14		
15		
16		
17		
18		
19		
20	(b) Variable cost pricing:	
21		
22	Computation of total variable cost and target selling price	
23		
24		
25		
26		
27		
28		
29		
30		
31		
32		
33		
34		
35		
36		
37		
38		
39		
40		

	Absorption Cost Pricing		Per Unit
1	(a) Computation of unit manufacturing cost:		
2			
3			
4			
5			
6			
7			
8			
9			
10			
11	Computation of markup percentage to provide a 25% ROI:		
12			
13	Markup		
14	Percentage =		
15			
16			
17	(b) Computation of target price:		
18			
19	Target price =		
20			
21	Proof of 25% ROI under absorption cost approach:		
22	**Anderson Windows Inc.**		
23	Budgeted Absorption Cost Approach Income Statement		
24	(Tinted Window)		
25			
26			
27			
28			
29			
30			
31			
32			
33	Desired ROI =		
34			
35			
36	Markup percenatge =		
37			
38			
39			
40			

	Variable Cost Pricing		
1	(c) Computation of unit variable cost:		
2			
3			Per Unit
4			
5			
6			
7			
8			
9			
10			
11			
12	Computation of markup percentage to provide a 25% ROI:		
13			
14	Markup		
15	Percentage =		
16			
17			
18	(d) Computation of target price:		
19			
20	Target price =		
21			
22	Proof of 25% ROI under variable cost pricing:		
23	**Anderson Windows Inc.**		
24	Budgeted Contribution Cost Approach Income Statement		
25	(Tinted Window)		
26			
27			
28			
29			
30			
31			
32			
33			
34			
35	Desired ROI =		
36			
37			
38	Markup percentage =		
39			
40			

	(e)		
1			1
2			2
3			3
4			4
5			5
6			6
7			7
8			8
9			9
10			10
11			11
12			12
13			13
14			14
15			15
16			16
17			17
18			18
19			19
20			20
21			21
22			22
23			23
24			24
25			25
26			26
27			27
28			28
29			29
30			30
31			31
32			32
33			33
34			34
35			35
36			36
37			37
38			38
39			39
40			40

(a)	Variable Cost Per Unit
1	
2	
3	
4	
5	
6	

	Total Costs /	Budgeted Volume =	Cost Per Unit
7			
8			
9			
10			
11			
12			
13			

		Variable Cost Per Unit
14	Variable cost per unit	
15	Fixed cost per unit	
16	Total cost per unit	
17		
18	(b) Total cost per unit	
19	Markup	
20	Desired ROI per unit	
21		
22		
23	(c) Total cost per unit	
24	Desired ROI per unit	
25	Target selling price	
26		
27		

28	(d) Variable cost per unit		
29	Fixed cost per unit		
30	Total cost per unit		

(a)	Variable Cost Per Unit
1	
2	
3	
4	
5	
6	
7	
8	

	Total Costs /	Budgeted Volume =	Cost Per Unit
9			
10			
11			
12			
13			
14			
15			
16			

17 Variable cost per unit	
18 Fixed cost per unit	
19 Total cost per unit	
20	
21	
22 Desired ROI per unit =	
23	
24	
25 Markup percentage =	
26	
27	
28 Total cost per unit	
29 Desired ROI per unit	
30 Target selling price	
31	
32	
33	
34	
35	
36	
37	
38	
39	
40	

				Variable Cost Per Unit	
(b)					
1					1
2					2
3					3
4					4
5					5
6					6
7					7
8					8

	Total Costs /	Budgeted Volume =	Cost Per Unit	
9				9
10				10
11				11
12				12
13				13
14				14
15				15
16				16
17				17
18 Variable cost per unit				18
19 Fixed cost per unit				19
20 Total cost per unit				20
21				21
22				22
23 Desired ROI per unit =				23
24				24
25				25
26				26
27 Markup percentage =				27
28				28
29				29
30				30
31 Total cost per unit				31
32 Desired ROI per unit				32
33 Target selling price				33
34				34
35				35
36				36
37				37
38				38
39				39
40				40

(a) Computation of time charge rate:	Total Cost /	Total Hours =	Per Hour Charge	
1	Hourly labor rate for repairs:				1
2					2
3	Overhead costs:				3
4					4
5					5
6					6
7					7
8	Rate charged per hour of labor				8
9					9
10					10

(b)	Material Loading Charges	Total Invoice Cost, Parts and Materials	Material Loading Percentage	
11					11
12					12
13	Computation of material loading charge:				13
14	Overhead costs:				14
15					15
16					16
17					17
18					18
19					19
20					20
21	Total				21
22					22
23	Material loading percentage				23
24					24
25	(c) Price quotation for time and material:				25
26					26

	Armstrong Bike Repair Shop Time and Material Price Quotation January 5, 2014		
27			27
28			28
29			29
30	Job: Fix Superior Mountain bike		30
31			31
32	Labor charges:		32
33			33
34	Material charges:		34
35			35
36			36
37	Total price of labor and material		37
38			38
39			39
40			40

1	(a)	1
2		2
3		3
4		4
5		5
6		6
7	(b)	7
8		8
9		9
10		10
11		11
12		12
13		13
14		14
15		15
16		16
17	(c)	17
18		18
19		19
20		20
21		21
22		22
23		23
24		24
25		25
26		26
27	(d)	27
28	The printing operation would lose:	28
29		29
30		30
31	Winner! would save:	31
32		32
33	Overall loss to the company as a whole	33
34		34
35		35
36		36
37		37
38		38
39		39
40		40

(a)

(b)

Lost contribution margin by Alto Division:

Total lost contribution margin

Lost contribution margin by Peg Division:

Total lost contribution margin

Overall lost contribution margin for the company

(a)	Absorption cost pricing:	
	Computation of unit manufacturing cost and target selling price	
(b)	Variable cost pricing:	
	Computation of total variable cost and target selling price	

	Absorption Cost Pricing		
1	(a) Computation of unit manufacturing cost:		1
2			2
3		Per Unit	3
4			4
5			5
6			6
7			7
8			8
9			9
10			10
11	Computation of markup percentage to provide a 25% ROI:		11
12			12
13	Markup		13
14	Percentage =		14
15			15
16			16
17	(b) Computation of target price:		17
18			18
19	Target price =		19
20			20
21	Proof of 25% ROI under absorption cost approach:		21
22	Georgia Gould Bikes Inc.		22
23	Budgeted Absorption-Cost Income Statement		23
24	(Mountain Bike)		24
25			25
26			26
27			27
28			28
29			29
30			30
31			31
32			32
33	Desired ROI =		33
34			34
35			35
36	Markup percenatge =		36
37			37
38			38
39			39
40			40

	Variable Cost Pricing			
1	(c) Computation of unit variable cost:			1
2				2
3			Per Unit	3
4				4
5				5
6				6
7				7
8				8
9				9
10				10
11				11
12	Computation of mark up percentage to provide a 25% ROI:			12
13				13
14	Markup			14
15	Percentage =			15
16				16
17				17
18	(d) Computation of target price:			18
19				19
20	Target price =			20
21				21
22	Proof of 25% ROI under variable cost pricing:			22
23	**Georgia Gould Bikes Inc.**			23
24	Budgeted Variable-Cost Income Statement			24
25	(Mountain Bike)			25
26				26
27				27
28				28
29				29
30				30
31				31
32				32
33				33
34				34
35	Desired ROI =			35
36				36
37				37
38	Markup percentage =			38
39				39
40				40

	(e)		
1			1
2			2
3			3
4			4
5			5
6			6
7			7
8			8
9			9
10			10
11			11
12			12
13			13
14			14
15			15
16			16
17			17
18			18
19			19
20			20
21			21
22			22
23			23
24			24
25			25
26			26
27			27
28			28
29			29
30			30
31			31
32			32
33			33
34			34
35			35
36			36
37			37
38			38
39			39
40			40

	Total Cost	Total Hours	Per Hour Charge
1			
2			
3			
4			
5 Profit margin			
6 Rate charge per hour of labor			
7			
8			
9 Job: Composite kayak repair:			
10			
11			
12			
13			
14			
15			
16			
17			
18			
19			
20			
21			
22			
23			
24			
25			
26			
27			
28			
29			
30			
31			
32			
33			
34			
35			
36			
37			
38			
39			
40			

	(a)				
1					
2					
3					
4					
5					
6					
7					
8					
9					
10					
11					
12					
13					
14					
15					
16					
17					
18					

(b)	Variable cost per unit:	Basic Wash	Deluxe Wash	Premium Wash

	Fixed cost per unit:	Total Costs /	Budgeted Volume =	Cost Unit

Computation of selling price (45,000 units):	Basic	Deluxe	Premium

1	(c)	Revenues:			1
2					2
3					3
4					4
5					5
6		Variable expenses:			6
7					7
8					8
9					9
10					10
11		Fixed expenses			11
12		Net income			12
13					13
14					14
15		ROI =			15
16					16
17					17
18					18
19					19
20	(d)				20
21					21
22					22
23					23
24					24
25					25
26					26
27					27
28					28
29					29
30					30
31					31
32					32
33					33
34					34
35					35
36					36
37					37
38					38
39					39
40					40

BE23-2

Palermo Company
Sales Budget
For the Year Ending December 31, 2014

	Quarter				Year
	1	2	3	4	
1					
2					
3					
4					
5					
6					
7					
8					
9					
10					

BE23-3

Palermo Company
Production Budget
For the First Six Months Ending June 30, 2014

	Quarter		Six Months
	1	2	
11			
12			
13			
14			
15			
16			
17			
18			
19			
20			
21			
22			
23			

BE23-4

Perine Company		
Direct Materials Budget		
For the Month Ending January 31, 2014		
1		
2		
3		
4		
5		
6		
7		
8		
9		
10		
11		
12		
13		
14		

BE23-5

Mize Company				
Direct Labor Budget				
For the Six Months Ending June 30, 2014				
	Quarter		Six	
	1	2	Months	

Name

Section

Date

BE23-6

Roche Inc.

Manufacturing Overhead Budget

For the Year Ending December 31, 2014

	Quarter				Year
	1	2	3	4	
1					
2					
3					
4					
5					
6					
7					

BE23-7

Noble Company

Selling and Administrative Expense Budget

For the Year Ending December 31, 2014

	Quarter				Year
	1	2	3	4	
8					
9					
10					
11					
12					
13					
14					
15					
16					
17					
18					
19					
20					
21					
22					
23					

Name

Section

Date

BE23-8

North Company
Budgeted Income Statement
For the Year Ending December 31,2014

BE23-9

Credit Sales	Collections from Customers January	February	March
$200,000			
260,000			
300,000			

BE23-10

DO IT! 23-2

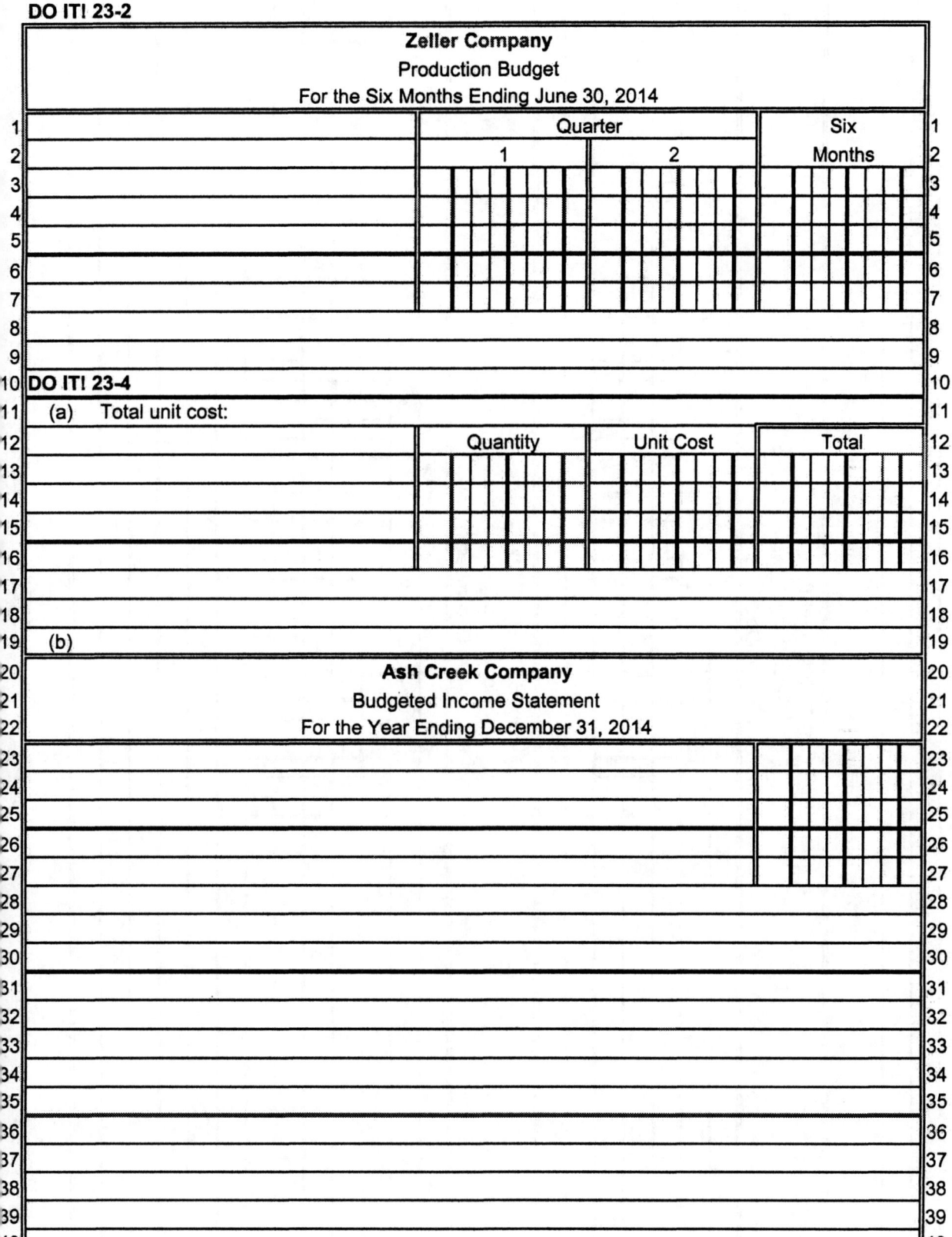

Zeller Company			
Production Budget			
For the Six Months Ending June 30, 2014			
	Quarter		Six
	1	2	Months

DO IT! 23-4

(a)   Total unit cost:

	Quantity	Unit Cost	Total

(b)

Ash Creek Company	
Budgeted Income Statement	
For the Year Ending December 31, 2014	

Name

Section

Date

Ash Creek Company

Ash Creek Company
Sales Budget
For the Year Ending December 31, 2014

	Quarter				Year
	1	2	3	4	
1					
2					
3					
4					
5					
6					
7					

Ash Creek Company
Production Budget
For the Year Ending December 31, 2014

	Quarter				Year
	1	2	3	4	
8					
9					
10					
11					
12					
13					
14					
15					
16					
17					
18					
19					
20					
21					
22					
23					

Ash Creek Company
Direct Materials Budget
For the Year Ending December 31, 2014

	Quarter				Year
	1	2	3	4	
8					
9					
10					
11					
12					
13					
14					
15					
16					
17					
18					
19					
20					
21					
22					
23					

Batista Company								
Cash Budget								
April								

You will find this working paper at the end of this booklet.

You will find this working paper at the end of this booklet.

Name

Section

Date

TurneyCompany

TurneyCompany
Production Budget
For the Year Ending December 31, 2014

Product HD-240

		Quarter					Year
		1	2	3	4		

	1						
	2						
	3						
	4						
	5						
	6						
	7						
	8						
	9						
	10						
	11						
	12						
	13						
	14						
	15						

E23-5

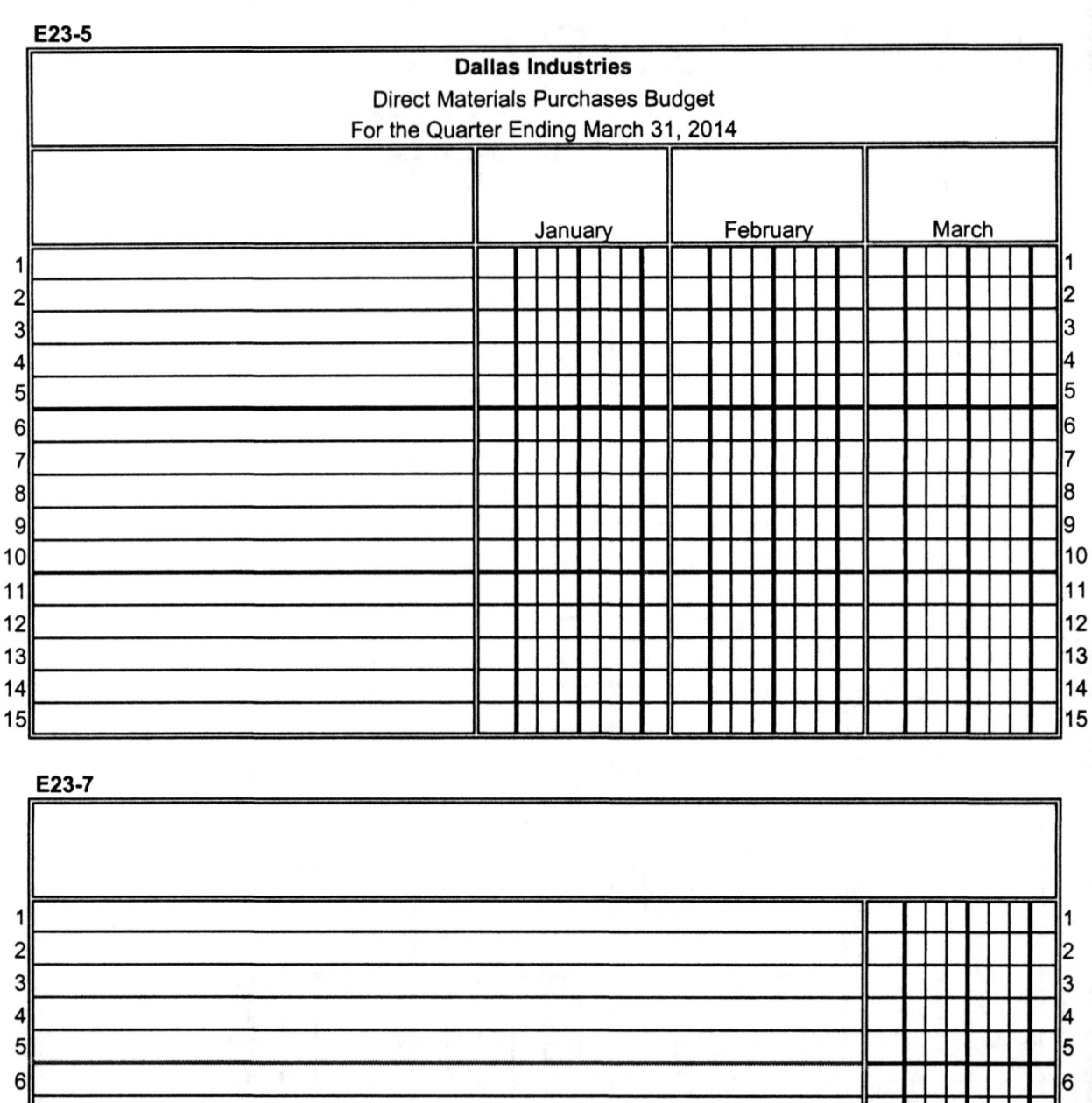

Dallas Industries

Direct Materials Purchases Budget

For the Quarter Ending March 31, 2014

	January	February	March
1			
2			
3			
4			
5			
6			
7			
8			
9			
10			
11			
12			
13			
14			
15			

E23-7

1	
2	
3	
4	
5	
6	
7	
8	
9	
10	
11	
12	
13	
14	
15	
16	
17	

(a)

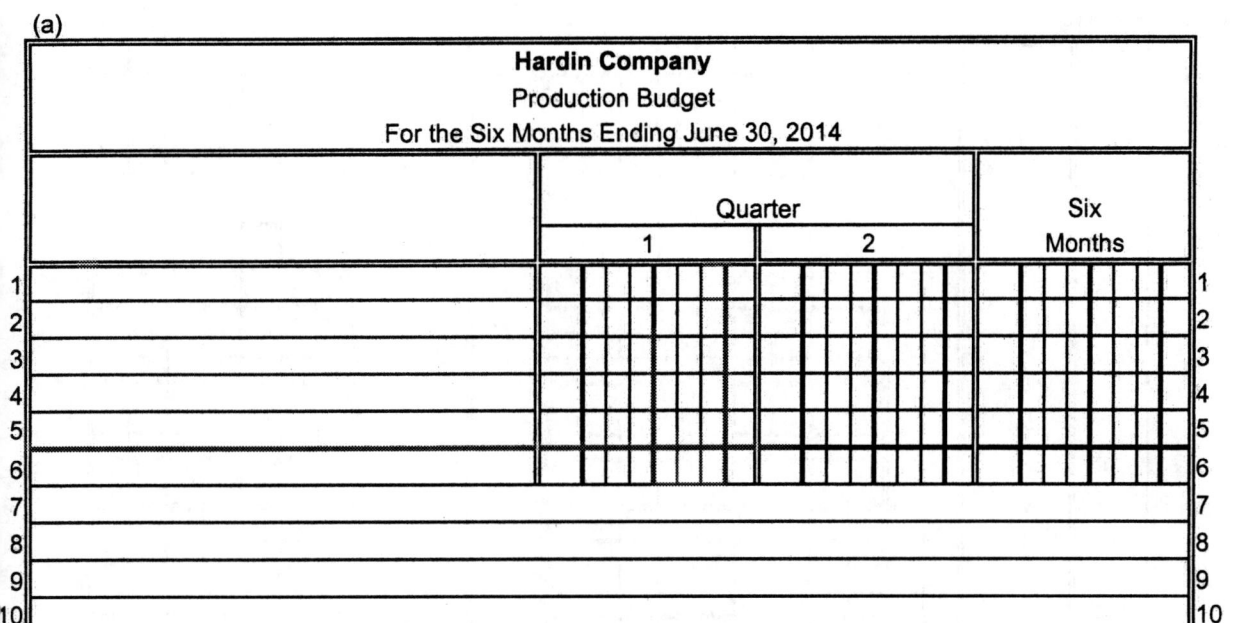

Hardin Company Production Budget For the Six Months Ending June 30, 2014			
	Quarter		Six Months
	1	2	
1			
2			
3			
4			
5			
6			
7			
8			
9			
10			

(b)

Hardin Company Direct Materials Budget For the Six Months Ending June 30, 2014			
	Quarter		Six Months
	1	2	
1			
2			
3			
4			
5			
6			
7			
8			
9			
10			
11			
12			
13			
14			
15			
16			

E23-8

Rodriquez, Inc.
Direct Labor Budget
For the Year Ending December 31, 2011

	Quarter				Year
	1	2	3	4	
1					
2					
3					
4					
5					
6					
7					
8					
9					

E23-9

Donnegal Company
Production Budget
For the Quarter Ending March 31, 2014

	Jan	Feb	Mar	Total
1				
2				
3				
4				
5				
6				
8				

Section

Date   Donnegal Company

E23-9   (Concluded)

Donnegal Company
Direct Labor Budget
For the Quarter Ending March 31, 2014

	Jan	Feb	Mar	Total	
1					1
2					2
3					3
4					4
5					5
6					6
7					7
8					8

Exercise 23-10

Atlanta Company

Atlanta Company
Manufacturing Overhead Budget
For the Year Ending December 31, 2011

	Variable Overhead per DLH	Quarter 1	Quarter 2	Quarter 3	Quarter 4	Year	
Variable Costs							1
Indirect materials							2
Indirect labor							3
Maintenance							4
Total variable							5
							6
							7
Fixed costs							8
Supervisory salaries							9
Depreciation							10
Maintenance							11
Total fixed							12
Total manufacturing overhead							13
							14
Direct labor hours							15
Manufacturing overhead rate							16
per direct labor hour							17
							18

	Quarter		Six Months
	1	**2**	

Duncan Company
Selling and Administrative Expense Budget
For the Six Months Ending June 30, 2014

	1	2	3	4	5	6	7	8	9	10	11	12	13	14	15	16	17	18	19	20	21	22	23	24	25	26	27	28	29	30

(a)

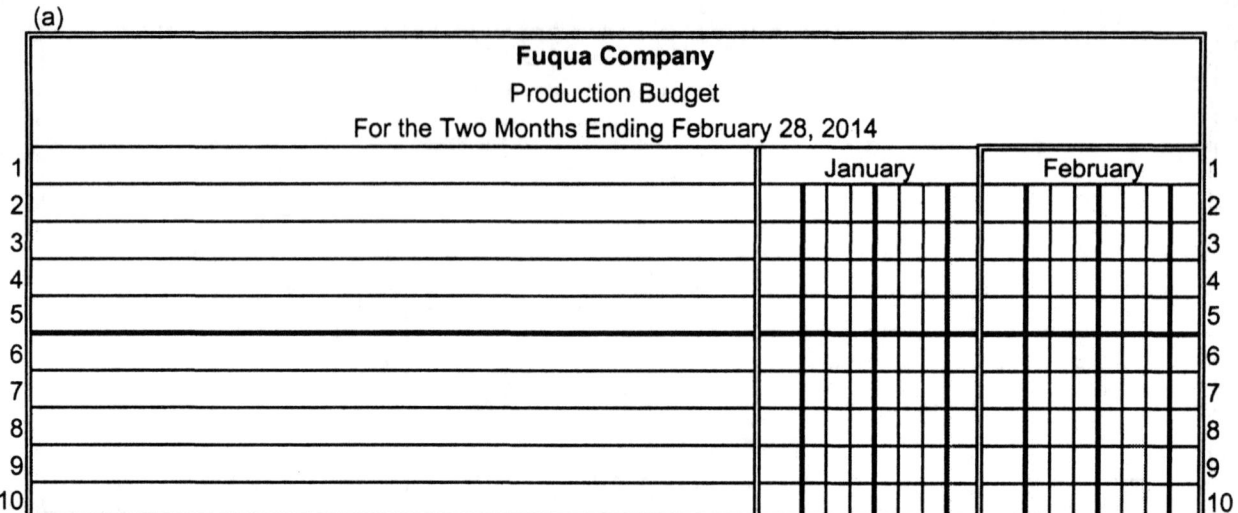

Fuqua Company
Production Budget
For the Two Months Ending February 28, 2014

	January	February
1		
2		
3		
4		
5		
6		
7		
8		
9		
10		

(b)

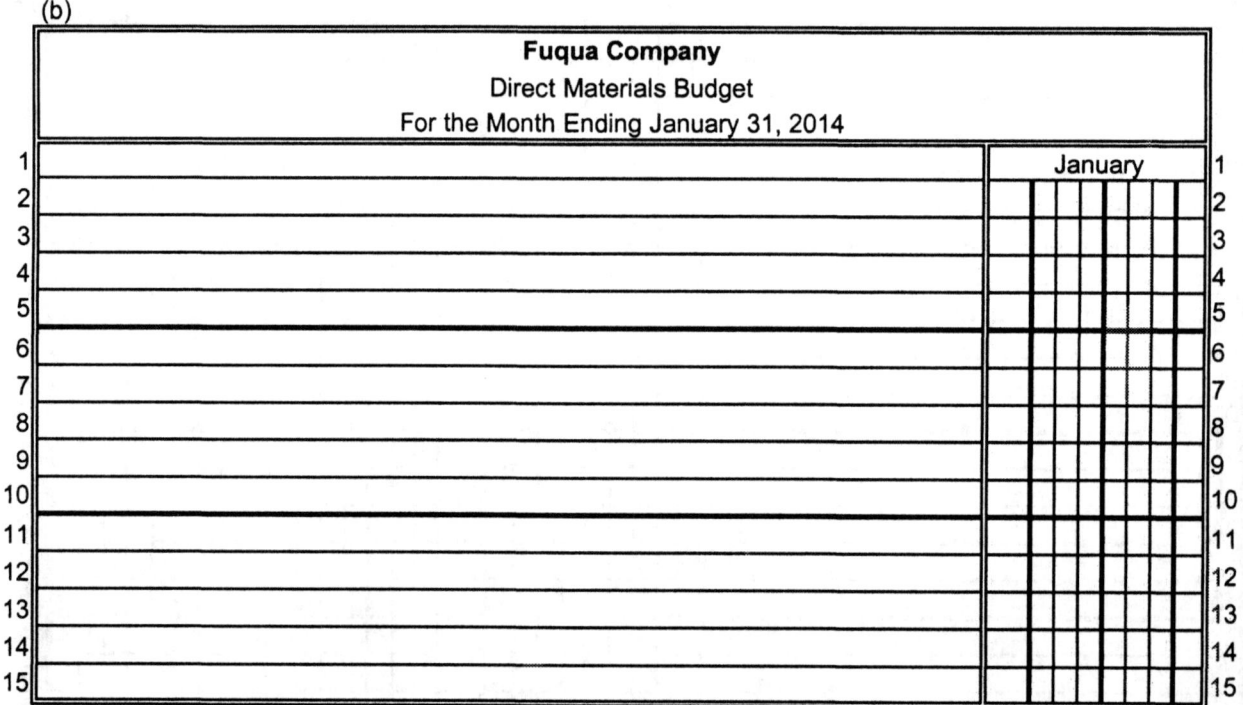

Fuqua Company
Direct Materials Budget
For the Month Ending January 31, 2014

	January
1	
2	
3	
4	
5	
6	
7	
8	
9	
10	
11	
12	
13	
14	
15	

(a)

Dalby Company				
Computation of Cost of Goods Sold				
For the Year Ending December 31, 2014				
1				1
2				2
3				3
4				4
5				5
6				6
7				7
8				8
9				9
10				10

(b)

Dalby Company				
Budgeted Income Statement				
For the Year Ending December 31, 2014				
1				1
2				2
3				3
4				4
5				5
6				6
7				7
8				8
9				9
10				10

Danner Company

Cash Budget

For the Two Months Ending February 28, 2014

	January	Februrary
Beginning Cash Balance	$ 45000	

Aaron Corporation Cash Budget For the Quarter Endingd March 31, 2014							
1	Beginning cash balance	$		3	0	0	0	0	1
2								2
3								3
4								4
5								5
6								6
7								7
8								8
9								9
10								10
11								11
12								12
13								13
14								14
15								15
16								16
17								17
18								18
19								19
20								20
21								21
22								22
23								23
24								24
25								25
26								26
27								27
28								28
29								29
30								30

(a)

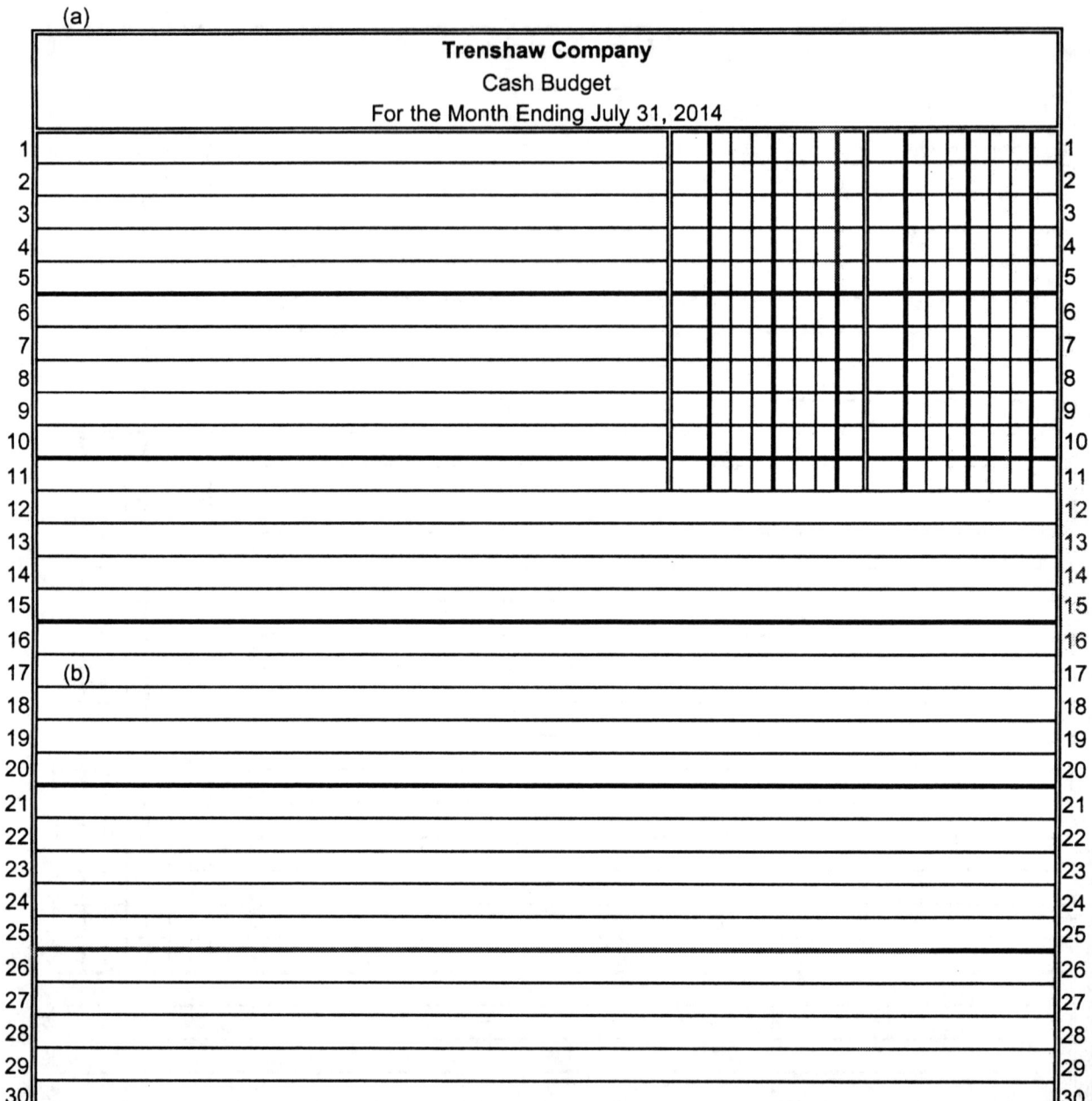

Trenshaw Company		
Cash Budget		
For the Month Ending July 31, 2014		

(b)

(a)

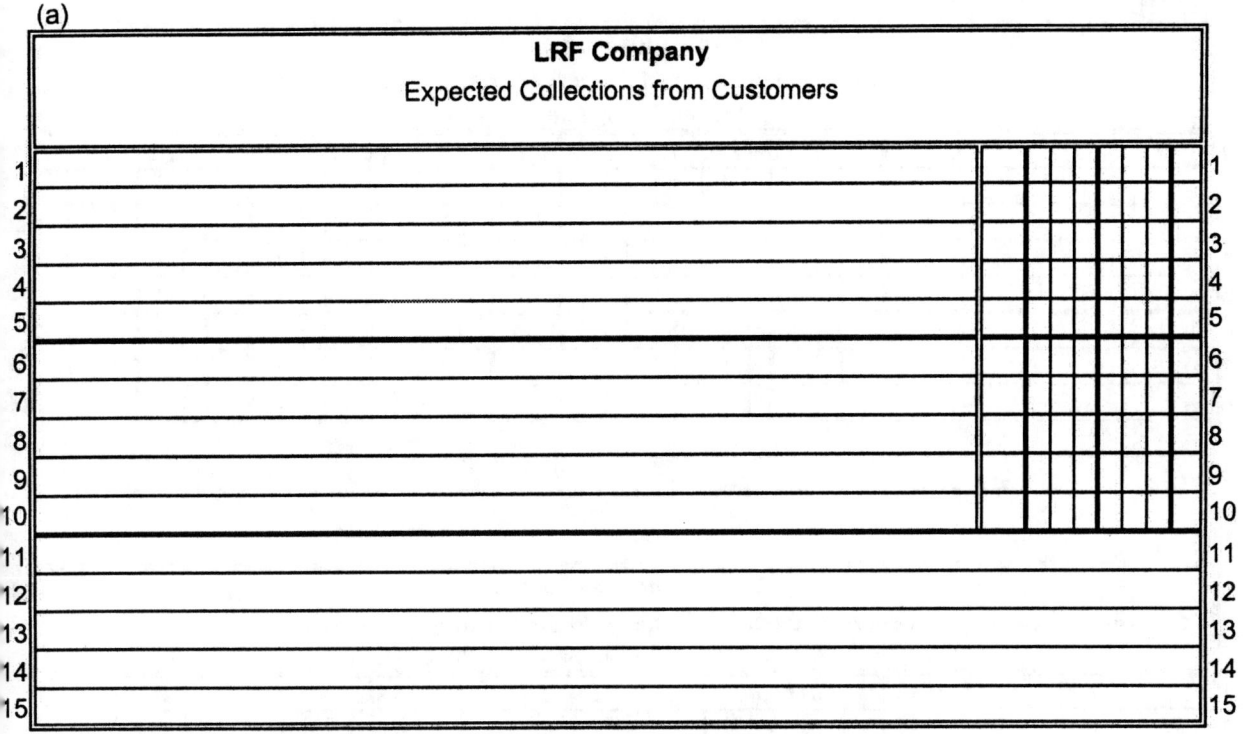

(b)

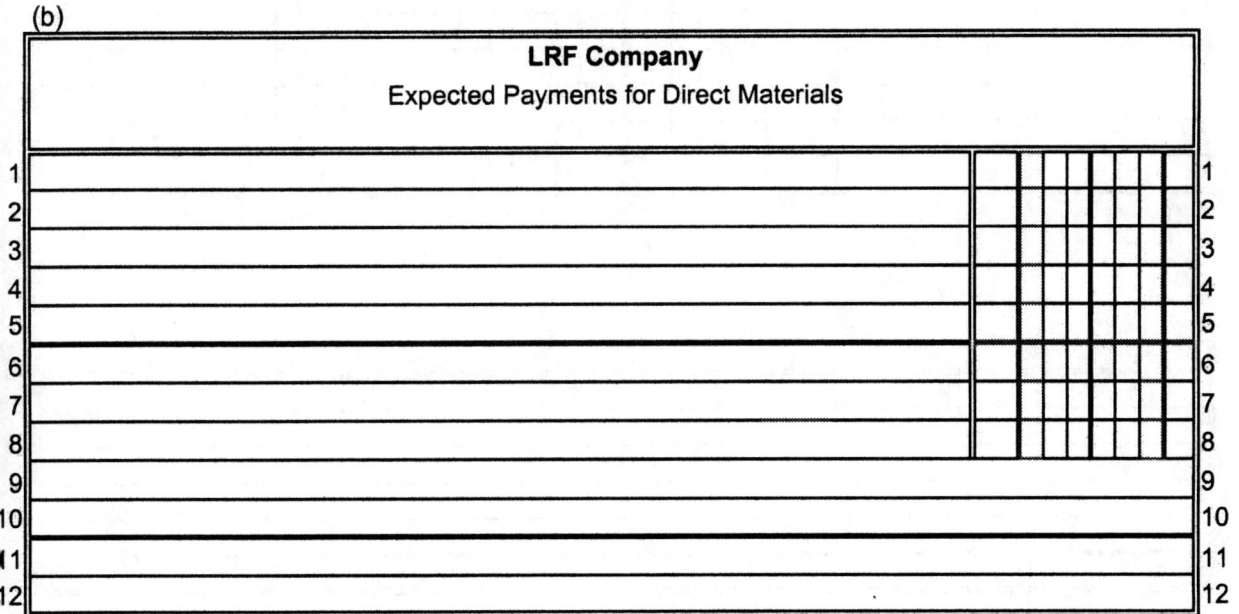

(a) (1)

Green Landscaping Inc.

Schedule of Expected Collections from Clients

For the Quarter Ending March 31, 2014

	January	February	March	Quarter

(2)

Green Landscaping Inc.

Schedule of Expected Payments for Landscaping Supplies

For the Quarter Ending March 31, 2014

	January	February	March	Quarter

(b)

(1)	
(2)	

Lager Dental Clinic Cash Budget For the Two Quarters Ending June 30, 2014	1st Quarter	2nd Quarter	
1			1
2 Beginning Cash Balance	$ 30000		2
3			3
4			4
5			5
6			6
7			7
8			8
9			9
10			10
11			11
12			12
13			13
14			14
15			15
16			16
17			17
18			18
19			19
20			20
21			21
22			22
23			23
24			24
25			25
26			26
27			27
28			28
29			29
30			30

(a)

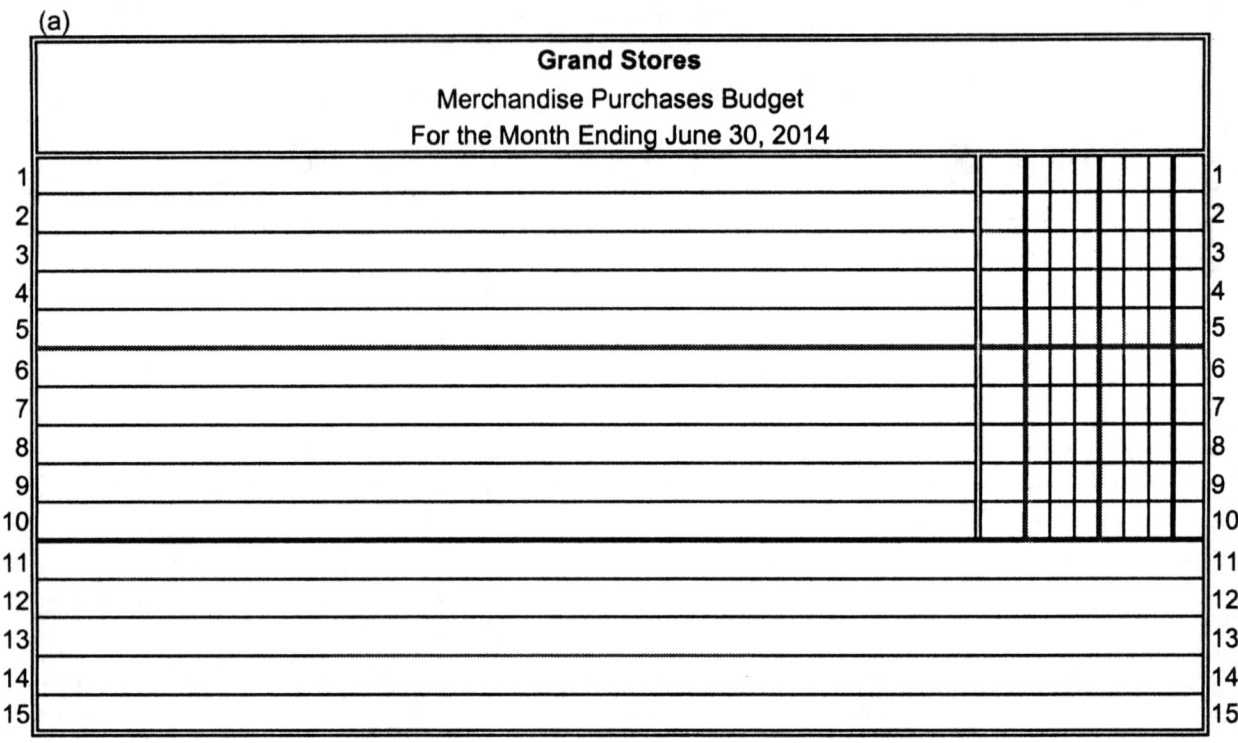

Grand Stores

Merchandise Purchases Budget

For the Month Ending June 30, 2014

(b)

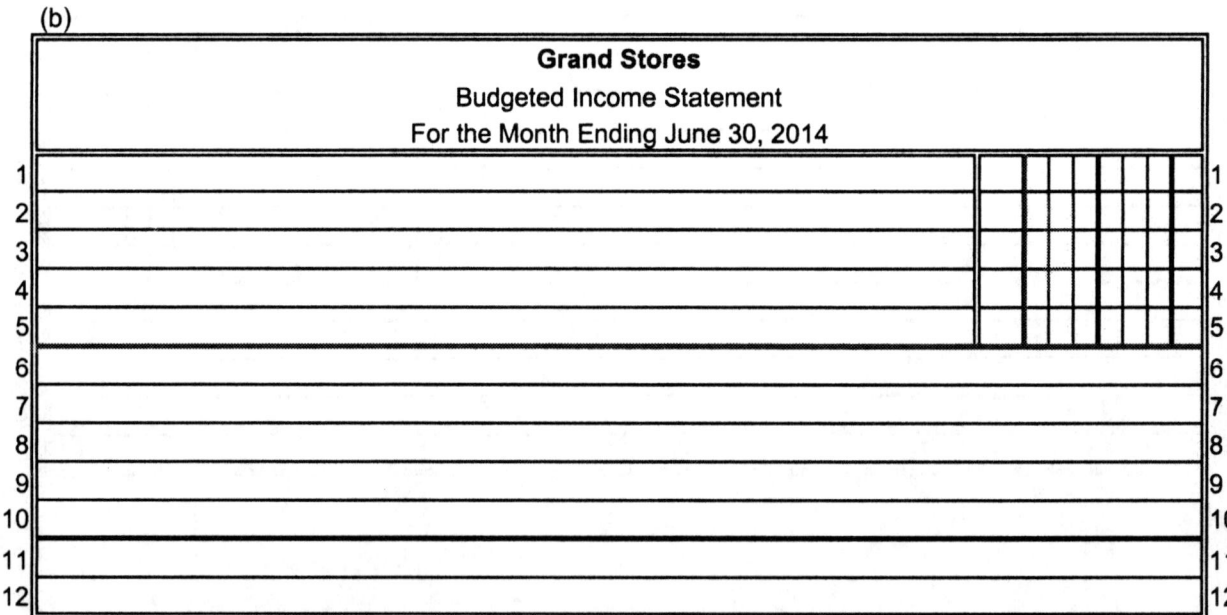

Grand Stores

Budgeted Income Statement

For the Month Ending June 30, 2014

Glendo Farm Supply Company Sales Budget For the Six Months Ending June 30, 2014	Quarter		Six Months
	1	2	
1			
2			
3			
4			

Glendo Farm Supply Company Production Budget For the Six Months Ending June 30, 2012	Quarter		Six Months
	1	2	
1			
2			
3			
4			
5			
6			

Glendo Farm Supply Company Direct Materials Budget-Gumm For the Six Months Ending June 30, 2014	Quarter		Six Months
	1	2	
1			
2			
3			
4			
5			
6			
7			
8			
9			
10			
11			
12			
13			
14			

Glendo Farm Supply Company
Direct Labor Budget
For the Six Months Ending June 30, 2014

	Quarter		Six Months
	1	2	
1			
2			
3			
4			
5			
6			
7			
8			
9			
10			

Glendo Farm Supply Company
Selling and Administrative Expense Budget
For the Six Months Ending June 30, 2014

	Quarter		Six Months
	1	2	
1			
2			
3			
4			
5			

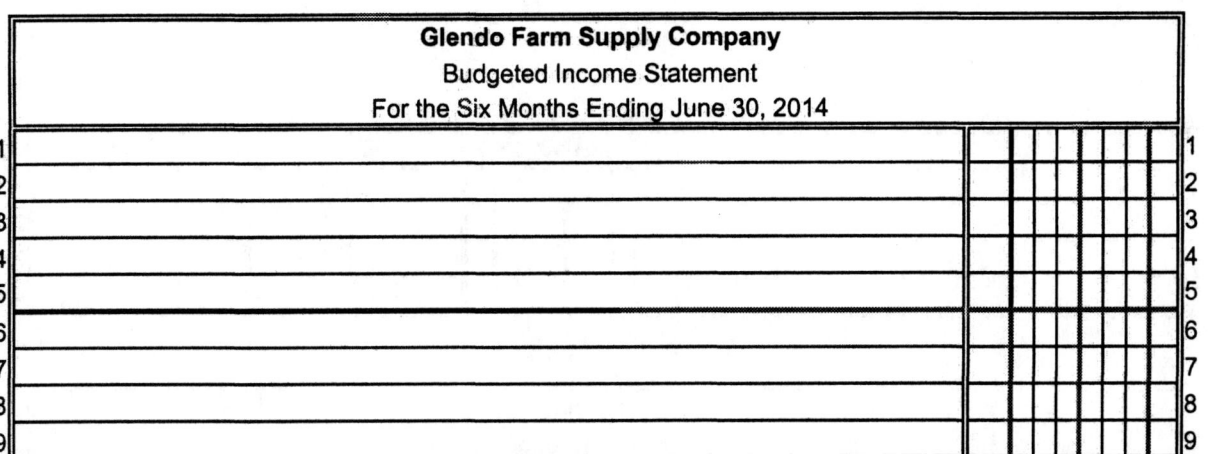

Glendo Farm Supply Company			
Budgeted Income Statement			
For the Six Months Ending June 30, 2014			

Glendo Farm Supply Company			
Schedule-Standard Cost Per Bag			
Cost Element	Quantity	Unit Cost	Total

(a)

		JB 50	JB 60	Total	
	Deleon Inc.				
	Sales Budget				
	For the Year Ending December 31, 2014				
1					1
2					2
3					3
4					4

(b)

		JB 50	JB 60	Total	
	Deleon Inc.				
	Production Budget				
	For the Year Ending December 31, 2014				
1					1
2					2
3					3
4					4
5					5
6					6
7					7

(c)

		JB 50	JB 60	Total	
	Deleon Inc.				
	Direct Materials Budget				
	For the Year Ending December 31, 2014				
1					1
2					2
3					3
4					4
5					5
6					6
7					7
8					8
9					9
10					10
11					11
12					12
13					13
14					14

(d)

	JB 50	JB 60	Total
Deleon Inc. Direct Labor Budget For the Year Ending December 31, 2014			
1			
2			
3			
4			
5			
6			
7			
8			
9			
10			

(e)

	JB 50	JB 60	Total
Deleon Inc. Budgeted Income Statement For the Year Ending December 31, 2014			
1			
2			
3			
4			
5			
6			
7			
8			
9			
10			
11			
12			
13			
14			
15			
16			
17			
18			
19			
20			

(a)

Marsh Industries Sales Budget For the Year Ending December 31, 2014		
	Plan A	Plan B
1			1
2			2
3			3

(b)

Marsh Industries Production Budget For the Year Ending December 31, 2014		
	Plan A	Plan B
1			1
2			2
3			3
4			4
5			5
6			6

(c) and (d)

	Plan A	Plan B
1 (c) Total variable costs			1
2			2
3 Total fixed costs			3
4			4
5 Total costs			5
6			6
7 Total units			7
8 Cost per unit			8
9			9
10			10
11 (d) Gross profit			11
12			12
13			13
14			14
15			15
16			16
17			17
18			18

(a)

	January	February	
1 (1) Expected collections from customers			1
2			2
3			3
4			4
5			5
6			6
7 (2) Expected payments for direct materials			7
8			8
9			9
10			10
11			11

(b)

Colter Company
Cash Budget
For the Two Months Ending February 29, 2014

	January	February	
1 Beginning cash balance	$ 6 0 0 0 0		1
2			2
3			3
4			4
5			5
6			6
7			7
8			8
9			9
10			10
11			11
12			12
13			13
14			14
15			15
16			16
17			17
18			18
19			19
20			20
21			21
22			22
23			23

(a)

Litwin Company - San Miguel Store
Merchandise Purchases Budget
For the Months of May and June, 2014

	May	June
1		
2		
3		
4		
5		
6		
7		
8		

(b)

Litwin Company - San Miguel Store
Budgeted Income Statement
For the Months of May and June, 2014

	May	June
1		
2		
3		
4		
5		
6		
7		
8		
9		
10		
11		
12		
13		
14		
15		
16		
17		
18		
19		
20		
21		
22		
23		
24		
25		

	Krause Industries																		
	Budgeted Income Statement																		
	For the Year Ending December 31, 2014																		
1																			1
2																			2
3																			3
4																			4
5																			5
6																			6
7																			7
8																			8
9																			9
10																			10
11																			11
12																			12
13																			13
14																			14
15																			15
16																			16
17																			17
18																			18
19																			19
20																			20
21																			21
22																			22
23																			23
24																			24
25																			25

Krause Industries							
Budgeted Balance Sheet							
December 31, 2014							
Assets							
Current assets							
Cash							
Accounts receivable							
Finished goods inventory							
Total current assets							
Property, plant, and equipment							
Equipment							
Less: Accumulated depreciation							
Total assets							
Liabilities and Stockholders' Equity							
Liabilities							
Notes payable							
Accounts payable							
Income taxes payable							
Total liabilities							
Stockholders' equity							
Common stock							
Retained earnings							
Total stockholders' equity							
Total liabilities and stockholders' equity							

Mercer Farm Supply Company
Sales Budget
For the Six Months Ending June 30, 2014

	Quarter		Six Months
	1	2	
1			
2			
3			
4			

Mercer Farm Supply Company
Production Budget
For the Six Months Ending June 30, 2014

	Quarter		Six Months
	1	2	
1			
2			
3			
4			
5			
6			

Mercer Farm Supply Company
Direct Materials Budget-Crup
For the Six Months Ending June 30, 2014

	Quarter		Six Months
	1	2	
1			
2			
3			
4			
5			
6			
7			
8			
9			
10			
11			
12			
13			
14			

Mercer Farm Supply Company			
Direct Labor Budget			
For the Six Months Ending June 30, 2014			
	Quarter		Six Months
	1	2	
1			
2			
3			
4			
5			
6			
7			
8			
9			
10			

Mercer Farm Supply Company			
Selling and Administrative Expense Budget			
For the Six Months Ending June 30, 2014			
	Quarter		Six Months
	1	2	
1			
2			
3			
4			
5			

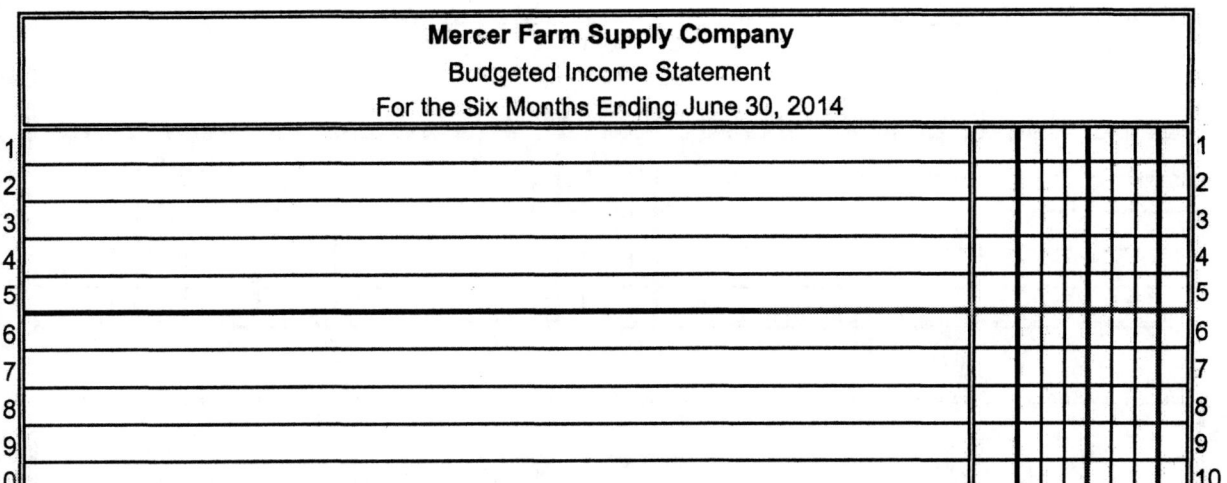

Mercer Farm Supply Company
Budgeted Income Statement
For the Six Months Ending June 30, 2014

		1
1		
2		
3		
4		
5		
6		
7		
8		
9		
10		

Mercer Farm Supply Company
Schedule-Standard Cost Per Bag

Cost Element	Quantity	Unit Cost	Total
1			
2			
3			
4			
5			
6			
7			
8			
9			
10			

(a)

	LN 35	LN 40	Total	
Urbina Inc.				
Sales Budget				
For the Year Ending December 31, 2014				
1				1
2				2
3				3
4				4

(b)

	LN 35	LN 40	Total	
Urbina Inc.				
Production Budget				
For the Year Ending December 31, 2014				
1				1
2				2
3				3
4				4
5				5
6				6
7				7

(c)

	LN 35	LN 40	Total	
Urbina Inc.				
Direct Materials Budget				
For the Year Ending December 31, 2014				
1				1
2				2
3				3
4				4
5				5
6				6
7				7
8				8
9				9
10				10
11				11
12				12
13				13
14				14

(d)

Urbina Inc. Direct Labor Budget For the Year Ending December 31, 2014	LN 35	LN 40	Total
1			
2			
3			
4			
5			
6			
7			
8			
9			
10			

(e)

Urbina Inc. Budgeted Income Statement For the Year Ending December 31, 2014	LN 35	LN 40	Total
1			
2			
3			
4			
5			
6			
7			
8			
9			
10			
11			
12			
13			
14			
15			
16			
17			
18			
19			
20			

(a)

Ogleby Industries
Sales Budget
For the Year Ending December 31, 2014

	Plan A	Plan B

(b)

Ogleby Industries
Production Budget
For the Year Ending December 31, 2014

	Plan A	Plan B

(c) and (d)

	Plan A	Plan B
(c) Total variable costs		
Total fixed costs		
Total costs		
Total units		
Cost per unit		
(d) Gross profit		

ame

ection

ate   Derby Company

(a)

	January	February	
1 (1) Expected collections from customers			1
2			2
3			3
4			4
5			5
6			6
7 (2) Expected payments for direct materials			7
8			8
9			9
10			10
11			11

(b)

Derby Company
Cash Budget
For the Two Months Ending February 29, 2014

	January	February	
1 Beginning cash balance	$ 5 0 0 0 0		1
2			2
3			3
4			4
5			5
6			6
7			7
8			8
9			9
10			10
11			11
12			12
13			13
14			14
15			15
16			16
17			17
18			18
19			19
20			20
21			21
22			22
23			23

(a)

Widner Company - Westwood Store Merchandise Purchases Budget For the Months of July and August, 2014	July	August
1			1
2			2
3			3
4			4
5			5
6			6
7			7
8			8

(b)

Widner Company - Westwood Store Budgeted Income Statement For the Months of July and August, 2014	July	August
1			1
2			2
3			3
4			4
5			5
6			6
7			7
8			8
9			9
10			10
11			11
12			12
13			13
14			14
15			15
16			16
17			17
18			18
19			19
20			20
21			21
22			22
23			23
24			24
25			25

Name

Section

Date

Current Designs
Production Budget
For the Year Ending December 31, 2013

	Quarter 1	Quarter 2	Quarter 3	Quarter 4	Total
1					
2					
3					
4					
5					
6					
7					

Name

Section

Date

Current Designs

Direct Materials Budget

For the Year Ending December 31, 2013

	Quarter 1	Quarter 2	Quarter 3	Quarter 4	Total
1					
2					
3					
4					
5					
6					
7					
8					
9					
10					
11					
12					
13					
14					
15					
16					
17					
18					
19					
20					
21					
22					

Name

Section

Date

Current Designs
Direct Labor Budget
For the Year Ending December 31, 2013

	Quarter 1	Quarter 2	Quarter 3	Quarter 4	Total
1					
2					
3					
4					
5					
6					
7					
8					
9					
10					
11					
12					
13					
14					
15					
16					
17					
18					
19					
20					
21					
22					

Name

Section

Date

Current Designs

Manufacturing Overhead Budget

For the Year Ending December 31, 2013

	Quarter 1	Quarter 2	Quarter 3	Quarter 4	Total	
						1
						2
						3
						4
						5
						6
						7
						8
						9
						10

Current Designs

Selling and Administrative Budget

For the Year Ending December 31, 2013

	Quarter 1	Quarter 2	Quarter 3	Quarter 4	Total	
						1
						2
						3
						4
						5
						6
						7

1					1
2					2
3					3
4					4
5					5
6					6
7					7
8					8
9					9
10					10
11					11
12					12
13					13
14					14
15					15
16					16
17					17
18					18
19					19
20					20
21					21
22					22
23					23
24					24
25					25
26					26
27					27
28					28
29					29
30					30
31					31
32					32
33					33
34					34
35					35
36					36
37					37
38					38
39					39
40					40

BE24-1

Maris Company

Sales Budget Report

For the Quarter Ended March 31, 2014

Product line	Budget	Actual	Difference
1			
2			
3			
4			

BE24-2

Maris Company

Sales Budget Report

For the Quarter Ended June 30, 2014

Product Line	Second Quarter			Year to Date		
	Budget	Actual	Difference	Budget	Actual	Difference
9						
10						
11						
12						
13						
14						

BE24-3 (a)

	Paige Company				
	Static Direct Labor Budget Report				
	For the Month Ended January 31, 2014				
1		Budget	Actual	Difference	1
2					2
3					3
4					4
5					5
6	(b)				6
7	Paige Company				7
8	Flexible Direct Labor Budget Report				8
9	For the Month Ended January 31, 2014				9
10		Budget	Actual	Difference	10
11					11
12					12
13					13
14					14
15					15
16					16
17					17
18					18
19					19
20					20
21					21

BE24-4

Gundy Company
Monthly Flexible Manufacturing Budget
For the Year 2014

Activity level			
Finished units	80000	100000	120000

BE24-5

Gundy Company
Manufacturing Budget Report
For the Month Ended March 31, 2014

	Budget	Actual	Difference	
			Favorable	F
Units produced	100000	100000	Unfavorable	U

BE24-6

Hannon Company
Assembly Department
Manufacturing Overhead Cost Responsibility Report
For the Month Ended April 30, 2014

Controllable Cost	Budget	Actual	Difference Favorable Unfavorable	F U

BE24-7

Elbert Company
Water Division
Responsibility Report
For the Year Ended December 31, 2014

	Budget	Actual	Difference Favorable Unfavorable	F U

BE24-8

Cobb Company - Plastics Division
Management Responsibility Report
For the Year Ended December 31, 2014

	Budget	Actual	Difference Favorable Unfavorable	F U

Units produced	Budget at 6,000 units	Actual 6,000 units	Difference Favorable (F) Unfavorable (U)	
1				1
2				2
3				3
4				4
5				5
6				6
7				7
8				8
9				9
10				10
11				11
12				12
13				13
14				14
15				15
16				16
17				17
18				18
19				19
20				20
21				21
22				22
23				23
24				24
25				25

Wellstone Division Responsibility Report For the Year Ended December 31, 2014				
	Budget	Actual	Difference Favorable (F) Unfavorable (U)	
1				1
2				2
3				3
4				4
5				5
6				6
7				7
8				8
9				9
10				10

1	(a) Return on investment for 2011:	1
2		2
3		3
4		4
5		5
6		6
7		7
8		8
9	(b) Expected return on investment for alternative 1:	9
10		10
11		11
12		12
13		13
14		14
15	Expected return on investment for alternative 2:	15
16		16
17		17
18		18
19		19
20		20
21		21
22		22
23		23
24		24
25		25
26		26
27		27
28		28
29		29
30		30
31		31
32		32
33		33
34		34
35		35

(a)

Crede Company
Selling Expense Report
For the Quarter Ended March 31

		By Month			Year to Date	
Month	Budget	Actual	Difference	Budget	Actual	Difference
January						
February						
March						

(b) and (c)

(b)

(c)

E24-3

Thome Company				
Monthly Flexible Manufacturing Overhead Budget				
For the Year 2014				
Activity level				
Direct labor hours	7000	8000	9000	10000

E24-4 (a)

		Actual	Difference	
	Budget at	Costs	Favorable (F)	
Direct labor hours (DLH)	9,000 DLH	9,000 DLH	Unfavorable (U)	

(b)

Thome Company				
Manufacturing Overhead Flexible Budget Report				
For the Month Ended July 31, 2014				
			Difference	
	Budget at	Actual Costs	Favorable (F)	
Direct labor hours (DLH)	8,500	8,500	Unfavorable (U)	

(c)

E24-5

	Dewitt Company Monthly Flexible Selling Expense Budget For the Year 2014				
1	Activity level					1
2	Sales	$ 170000	$ 180000	$ 190000	$ 200000	2
3						3
4						4
5						5
6						6
7						7
8						8
9						9
10						10
11						11
12						12
13						13
14						14
15						15

E24-6 (a)

	Dewitt Company Selling Expense Flexible Budget Report For the Month Ended March 31, 2014	Budget at $170,000	Actual Costs $170,000	Difference Favorable (F) Unfavorable (U)	
1					1
2					2
3	Sales				3
4					4
5					5
6					6
7					7
8					8
9					9
10					10
11					11
12					12
13					13
14					14
15					15
16					16
17					17
18					18
19					19
20					20

(b)

Dewitt Company Selling Expense Flexible Budget Report For the Month Ended March 31, 2014			
	Budget	Actual Costs	Difference Favorable F Unfavorable U
Sales	$ 180000	$ 180000	

(c)

(a)

	Kitchen Help Inc. Flexible Production Cost Budget			
Activity level:				
Production levels		90000	100000	110000

(b)

(a)

		Rensing Groomers		
		Flexible Budget		
Activity level:				
Direct labor hours	550	600	700	

(b)

(c)

(d)

(a)

Lowell Company Manufacturing Overhead Flexible Budget Report For the Quarter Ended March 31, 2014			Difference	
			Favorable F	
	Budget	Actual Costs	Unfavorable U	

(b)

Lowell Company Manufacturing Overhead Responsibility Report For the Quarter Ended March 31, 2014			Difference	
			Favorable F	
Controllable Costs	Budget	Actual Costs	Unfavorable U	

(a)

Soria Company - Clothing Department					
Selling Expense Flexible Budget Report					
For the Month Ended October 31, 2014					
		Budget	Actual Costs	Difference Favorable F Unfavorable U	
Sales in units		10000	10000		

(b)

(a)

Kirkland Plumbing Company
Home Plumbing Services Segment
Responsibility Report
For the Quarter Ended March 31, 2014

	Budget	Actual	Difference Favorable F Unfavorable U	
Service revenue	$ 25000	$ 26000	$	

(b)

(a)			
To Dallas Department Manager - Finishing			Month: July
Controllable Costs	Budget	Actual	Fav/Unfav

(b)			
To Assembly Plant Manager - Dallas			Month: July
Controllable Costs	Budget	Actual	Fav/Unfav

(c)			
To Vice President - Production			Month: July
Controllable Costs	Budget	Actual	Fav/Unfav

E24-14 (a)

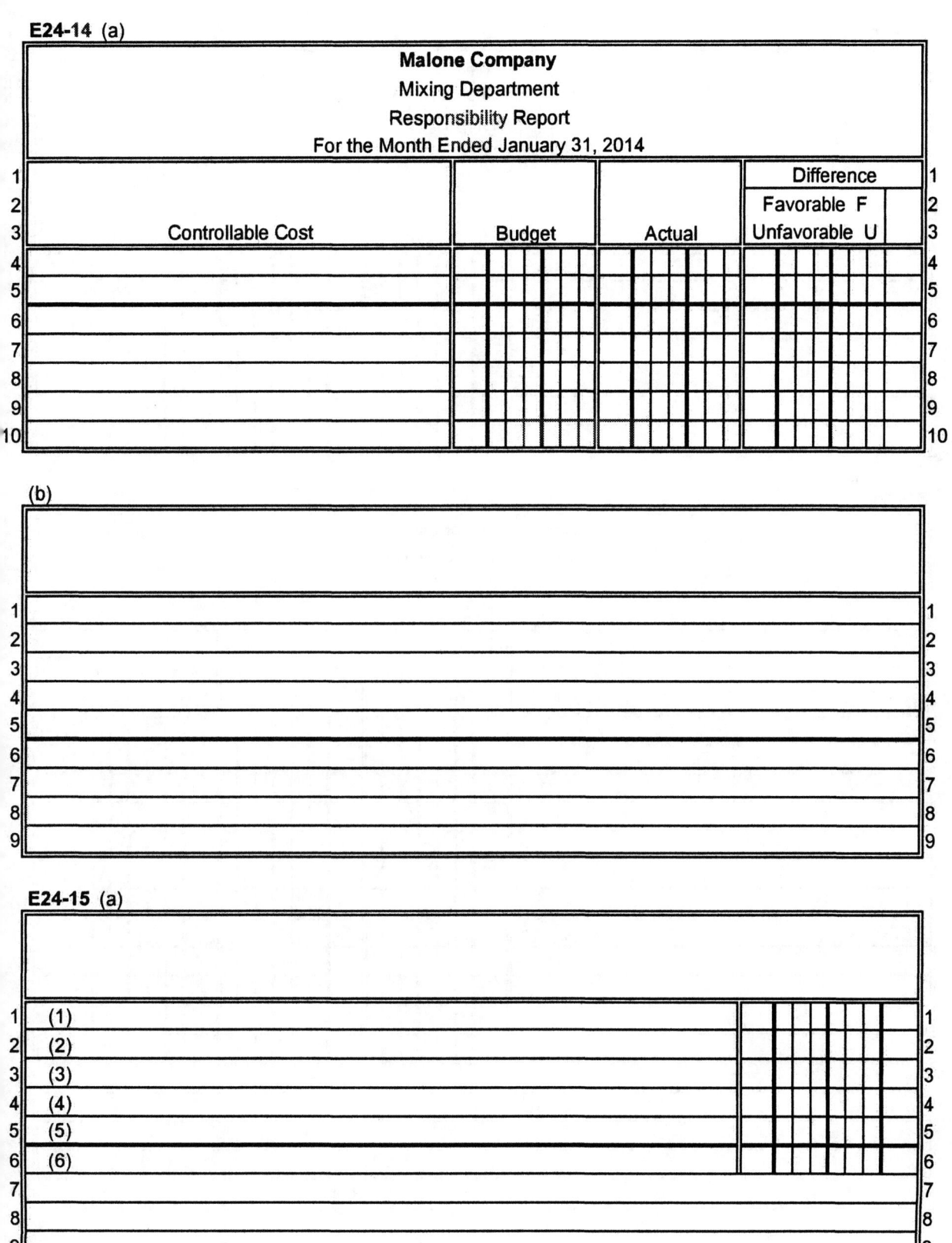

	Malone Company				
	Mixing Department				
	Responsibility Report				
	For the Month Ended January 31, 2014				
	Controllable Cost	Budget	Actual	Difference Favorable F Unfavorable U	
1					1
2					2
3					3
4					4
5					5
6					6
7					7
8					8
9					9
10					10

(b)

1		1
2		2
3		3
4		4
5		5
6		6
7		7
8		8
9		9

E24-15 (a)

1	(1)		1
2	(2)		2
3	(3)		3
4	(4)		4
5	(5)		5
6	(6)		6
7			7
8			8
9			9
10			10

E24-15 (b)

Deitz Inc. Women's Shoe Division Responsibility Report For the Month Ended June 30, 2014				
			Difference Favorable F Unfavorable U	
	Budget	Actual		

E24-16

Harrington Company Sports Equipment Division Responsibility Report 2014				
			Difference Favorable F Unfavorable U	
(a)	Budget	Actual		
(b)				

(a)

Dinkle and Frizell Dental Clinic Preventive Services Responsibility Report For the Month Ended May 31, 2014			
	Budget	Actual	Difference Favorable F Unfavorable U
Service revenue			

(b)

1	1
2	2
3	3
4	4
5	5
6	6
7	7
8	8
9	9
10	10
11	11
12	12
13	13
14	14
15	15
16	16
17	17
18	18
19	19
20	20
21	21
22	22
23	23
24	24
25	25
26	26
27	27
28	28
29	29
30	30
31	31
32	32
33	33
34	34
35	35
36	36
37	37
38	38
39	39

	Planes	Taxis	Limos	
1 Service revenue		$50 00 00		1
2 Variable costs	55 00 00 0		30 00 00	2
3 Contribution margin		25 00 00	48 00 00	3
4 Controllable fixed costs	15 00 00 0			4
5 Controllable margin		80 00 0	24 00 00	5
6 Average operating assets	25 00 00 00		15 00 00 0	6
7 Return on investment	13%	10%		7
8				8
9				9
10				10
11				11
12				12
13				13
14				14
15				15
16				16
17				17
18				18
19				19
20				20
21				21
22				22
23				23
24				24
25				25
26				26
27				27
28				28
29				29
30				30
31				31
32				32
33				33
34				34
35				35
36				36
37				37
38				38
39				39
40				40

1	1
2	2
3	3
4	4
5	5
6	6
7	7
8	8
9	9
10	10
11	11
12	12
13	13
14	14
15	15
16	16
17	17
18	18
19	19
20	20
21	21
22	22
23	23
24	24
25	25
26	26
27	27
28	28
29	29
30	30
31	31
32	32
33	33
34	34
35	35
36	36
37	37
38	38
39	39
40	40

	Lager	Lite Larger	
1 Contribution margin	$500000	$300000	1
2 Controllable margin	200000		2
3 Average operating assets		1200000	3
4 Minimum rate of return		13%	4
5 Return on investment	20%		5
6 Residual income	$100000	$204000	6
7			7
8			8
9			9
10			10
11			11
12			12
13			13
14			14
15			15
16			16
17			17
18			18
19			19
20			20
21			21
22			22
23			23
24			24
25			25
26			26
27			27
28			28
29			29
30			30
31			31
32			32
33			33
34			34
35			35
36			36
37			37
38			38
39			39
40			40

(a)

Cook Company Packaging Department Monthly Manufacturing Overhead Flexible Budget For the Year 2014				
Activity level Direct labor hours	27000	30000	33000	36000
1				
2				
3				
4				
5				
6				
7				
8				
9				
10				
11				
12				
13				
14				
15				
16				
17				
18				

(b)

Cook Company Packaging Department Manufacturing Overhead Flexible Budget Report For the Month Ended October 31, 2014				
			Difference	
	Budget at	Actual Costs	Favorable F	
Direct labor hours (DLH)	27,000 DLH	27,000 DLH	Unfavorable U	
1				
2				
3				
4				
5				
6				
7				
8				
9				
10				
11				
12				
13				
14				
15				
16				
17				

(c)

1	
2	
3	
4	
5	

(a)

Zelmer Company Monthly Manufacturing Overhead Flexible Budget Ironing Department For the Year 2014				
Activity level Direct labor hours	35,000	40,000	45,000	50,000
1				
2				
3				
4				
5				
6				
7				
8				
9				
10				
11				
12				
13				
14				

(b)

Zelmer Company Ironing Department Manufacturing Overhead Flexible Budget Report For the Month Ended June 30, 2014			Difference	
Direct labor hours (DLH)	Budget at 42,000 DLH	Actual Costs 42,000 DLH	Favorable F Unfavorable U	
1				
2				
3				
4				
5				
6				
7				
8				
9				
10				
11				
12				
13				
14				

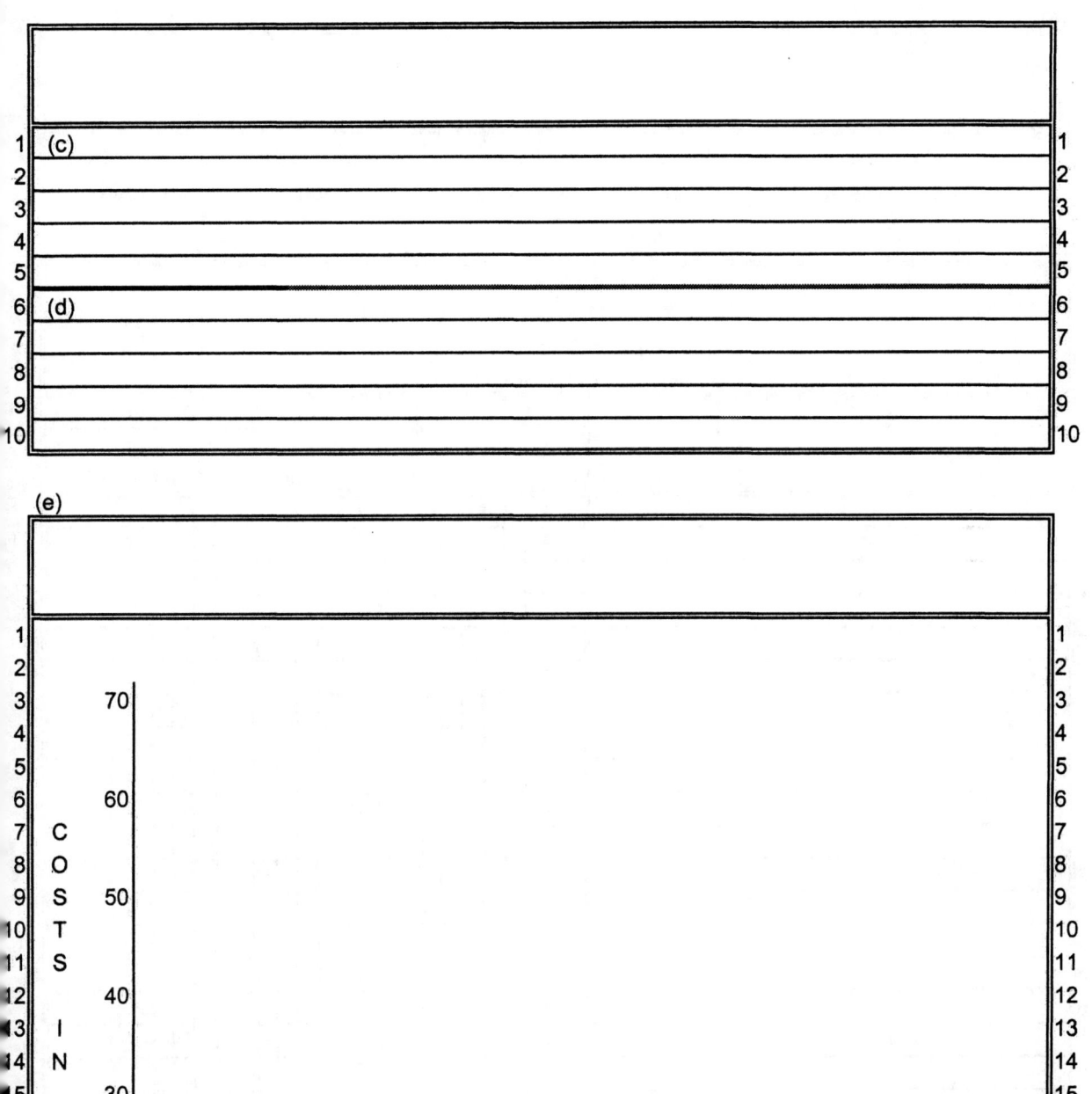

(c)

1

2

3

4

5

(d)

6

7

8

9

10

(e)

(a)

1	1
2	2

(b)

Hill Company
Assembling Department
Flexible Budget Report
For the Month Ended August 31, 2014

Units	Budget at ___ Units	Actual Costs ___ Units	Difference Favorable F Unfavorable U	
1				1
2				2
3				3
4				4
5				5
6				6
7				7
8				8
9				9
10				10
11				11
12				12
13				13
14				14
15				15
16				16
17				17
18				18
19				19
20				20
21				21
22				22
23				23
24				24
25				25
26				26
27				27
28				28
29				29

(c)

Hill Company
Assembling Department
Flexible Budget Report
For the Month Ended September 30, 2014

Units	Budget at 64,000 Units	Actual Costs 64,000 Units	Difference Favorable F Unfavorable U	

(a)

Clarke Inc. Patio Furniture Division Responsibility Report For the Year Ended December 31, 2014				
	Budget	Actual	Difference Favorable F Unfavorable U	
1				1
2				2
3				3
4				4
5				5
6				6
7				7
8				8
9				9
10				10
11				11
12				12
13				13
14				14
15				15

(b)

1	1
2	2
3	3
4	4
5	5
6	6
7	7
8	8
9	9
10	10
11	11

(c)

12	12
13	13
14	14
15	15
16	16
17	17

(a)

Suppan Company Home Division Responsibility Report (in thousands of dollars) For the Year Ended December 31, 2014				
	Budget	Actual	Difference Favorable F Unfavorable U	
1				1
2				2
3				3
4				4
5				5
6				6
7				7
8				8
9				9
10				10
11				11
12				12
13				13
14				14
15				15

(b)

1	1
2	2
3	3
4	4
5	5
6	6
7	7
8	8
9	9
10	10
11	11
12	12
13	13
14	14
15	15
16	16

(c)

(a)

To Cutting Department Manager - Seattle Division			Month: January
Controllable Costs	Budget	Actual	Fav/Unfav
1			
2			
3			
4			
5			
6			
7			
8			
9			

To Division Production Manager - Seattle			Month: January
Controllable Costs	Budget	Actual	Fav/Unfav
1			
2			
3			
4			
5			
6			
7			
8			
9			
10			

To Vice - President - Production			Month: January
Controllable Costs	Budget	Actual	Fav/Unfav
1			
2			
3			
4			
5			
6			
7			
8			
9			
10			

(a) (Continued)   No. 4

To President						Month: January
Controllable Costs		Budget		Actual		Fav/Unfav

(Ruled worksheet rows 1–10, blank)

(b)

1.

(Ruled worksheet rows 1–5, blank)

2.

(Ruled worksheet rows 6–10, blank)

3.

(Ruled worksheet rows 11–20, blank)

(a)

Speier Company Assembly Department Flexible Monthly Manufacturing Overhead Budget For the Year 2014				
Activity level Direct labor hours	18,000	20,000	22,000	24,000
1				
2				
3				
4				
5				
6				
7				
8				
9				
10				
11				
12				
13				
14				
15				
16				
17				
18				

(b)

Speier Company Assembly Department Manufacturing Overhead Budget Report (Flexible) For the Month Ended January 31, 2014				
Direct labor hours (DLH)	Budget at 20,000 DLH	Actual Costs 20,000 DLH	Difference Favorable F Unfavorable U	
1				1
2				2
3				3
4				4
5				5
6				6
7				7
8				8
9				9
10				10
11				11
12				12
13				13
14				14
15				15
16				16
17				17

(c)

1	1
2	2
3	3
4	4
5	5

(a)

Gonzalez Company				
Flexible Monthly Manufacturing Overhead Budget				
Assembly Department				
For the Year 2014				
Activity level Direct labor hours	22,500	25,000	27,500	30,000
1				
2				
3				
4				
5				
6				
7				
8				
9				
10				
11				
12				
13				
14				

(b)

Gonzalez Company			
Assembly Department			
Manufacturing Overhead Budget Report (Flexible)			
For the Month Ended July 31, 2014			
Direct labor hours (DLH)	Budget at 27,500 DLH	Actual Costs 27,500 DLH	Difference Favorable F Unfavorable U
1			
2			
3			
4			
5			
6			
7			
8			
9			
10			
11			
12			
13			
14			

1	(c)	1
2		2
3		3
4		4
5		5
6	(d)	6
7		7
8		8
9		9
10		10

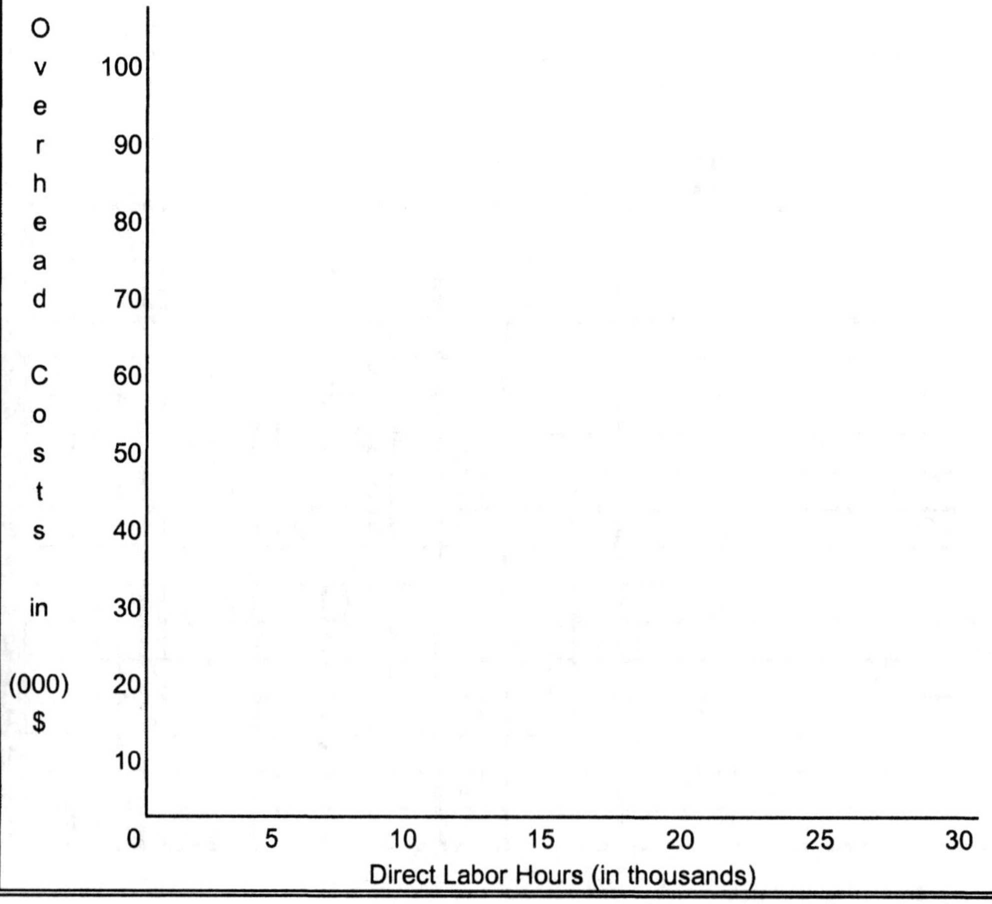

(e)

Name

Section

Date

(a)

(b)

Hardesty Company Packaging Department Budget Report (Flexible) For the Month Ended May 31, 2014			
	Budget at ____ Units	Actual Costs ____ Units	Difference Favorable F Unfavorable U
1			
2			
3			
4			
5			
6			
7			
8			
9			
10			
11			
12			
13			
14			
15			
16			
17			
18			
19			
20			
21			
22			
23			
24			
25			
26			
27			
28			

(c)

	Hardesty Company
	Packaging Department
	Budget Report (Flexible)
	For the Month Ended June 30, 2014

Units	Budget at 40,000 Units	Actual Costs 40,000 Units	Difference Favorable F Unfavorable U	
1				1
2				2
3				3
4				4
5				5
6				6
7				7
8				8
9				9
10				10
11				11
12				12
13				13
14				14
15				15
16				16
17				17
18				18
19				19
20				20
21				21
22				22
23				23
24				24
25				25
26				26
27				27
28				28
29				29
30				30
31				31
32				32
33				33
34				34
35				35
36				36

ame

ection

ate

Guzman Inc.

(a)

Guzman Inc. Home Appliance Division Responsibility Report For the Year Ended December 31, 2014			Difference Favorable F Unfavorable U	
	Budget	Actual		
1				
2				
3				
4				
5				
6				
7				
8				
9				
10				
11				
12				
13				
14				

(b)

(c)

(a)

Strauss Company Lawnmower Division Responsibility Performance Report (in thousands of dollars) For the Year Ended December 31, 2014			
	Budget	Actual	Difference Favorable F Unfavorable U
1			
2			
3			
4			
5			
6			
7			
8			
9			
10			
11			
12			
13			

(b)

1	
2	
3	
4	
5	
6	
7	
8	
9	
10	

(c)

(1)

(2)

(3)

(a)

To Cutting Department Manager - Phoenix Division	Budget	Actual	Fav/Unfav	Month: January
Controllable Costs	Budget	Actual	Fav/Unfav	
1				1
2				2
3				3
4				4
5				5
6				6
7				7
8				8
9				9

To Division Production Manager - Phoenix	Budget	Actual	Fav/Unfav	Month: January
Controllable Costs	Budget	Actual	Fav/Unfav	
1				1
2				2
3				3
4				4
5				5
6				6
7				7
8				8
9				9
10				10

To Vice - President - Production	Budget	Actual	Fav/Unfav	Month: January
Controllable Costs	Budget	Actual	Fav/Unfav	
1				1
2				2
3				3
4				4
5				5
6				6
7				7
8				8
9				9
10				10

(a) (Continued)   No. 4

To President			Month: January			
Controllable Costs	Budget	Actual	Fav/Unfav
1				1
2				2
3				3
4				4
5				5
6				6
7				7
8				8
9				9
10				10

(b)

1.	
1	1
2	2
3	3
4	4
5	5
6 2.	6
7	7
8	8
9	9
10	10
11 3.	11
12	12
13	13
14	14
15	15
16	16
17	17
18	18
19	19
20	20

(a)

Current Designs Rotomolded Line Manufacturing Budget For the Year Ended December 31, 2013	
Units to be produced	4,000 Kayaks
	Amount
Costs:	Budgeted

(b)

Current Designs Rotomolded Line Manufacturing Flexible Budget For the Quarter Ended March 31, 2013			
Units to be produced	900 Kayaks	1,000 Kayaks	1,050 Kayaks
Costs:			

(c)

	Current Designs Rotomolded Line Maufacturing Flexible Budget Report For the Quarter Ended March 31, 2013			
			Difference	
	Budget for 1,050 Kayaks	Actual Costs 1,050 Kayaks	Favorable Unfavorable	F U
Units to be produced				
Costs:				

(a)

1	(1)	1
2		2
3		3
4		4
5		5
6		6
7		7
8		8
9		9
10		10
11	(2)	11
12		12
13		13
14		14
15		15
16		16
17		17
18		18
19		19
20		20
21		21
22		22
23		23
24		24
25		25
26	(3)	26
27		27
28		28
29		29
30		30
31		31
32		32
33		33
34		34
35		35
36		36
37		37
38		38
39		39
40		40

(b)

Green Pastures Income Statement Flexible Budget Report For the Year Ended December 31, 2014			
Boarding days (BD)	Budget at 19,000 BD	Actual Costs at 19,000 BD	Difference Favorable F Unfavorable U
1			
2			
3			
4			
5			
6			
7			
8			
9			
10			
11			
12			
13			
14			
15			
16			
17			
18			
19			
20			
21			
22			
23			
24			
25			

(c)

1	(1)
2	
3	
4	
5	
6	
7	
8	
9	
10	(2)
11	
12	
13	
14	
15	
16	(3)
17	
18	
19	
20	
21	(d)
22	
23	
24	
25	
26	
27	
28	
29	
30	
31	
32	
33	
34	
35	
36	
37	
38	
39	
40	

	1
(a)	1
	2
	3
	4
	5
(b)	6
	7
	8
	9
	10
	11

(c)

Fleming Company
Production Department
Manufacturing Overhead Flexible Budget Report
For the Month Ended _____

	Budget at 1,500 Units	Actual at 1,500 Units	Difference Favorable F Unfavorable U	
1				
2				
3				
4				
5				
6				
7				
8				
9				
10				
11				
12				
13				
14				
15				
16				
17				
18				
19				
20				

(d)

1					1
2					2
3					3
4					4
5					5
6					6

Fleming Company
Production Department
Manufacturing Overhead Responsibility Report
For The Month Ended _____

Controllable Cost	Budget	Actual	Difference Favorable F Unfavorable U

*BE25-8

	Account Titles	Debit	Credit	
1	(a)			1
2				2
3				3
4				4
5				5
6	(b)			6
7				7
8				8
9				9
10				10
11				11
12				12

*BE25-9

	Account Titles	Debit	Credit	
14				14
15				15
16				16
17	(a)			17
18				18
19				19
20				20
21				21
22	(b)			22
23				23
24				24
25				25
26				26
27				27
28				28
29				29
30				30
31				31
32				32
33				33
34				34
35				35
36				36
37				37
38				38
39				39
40				40

Manufacturing Cost Element	Standard Quantity x	Standard Price =	Standard Cost
1			
2			
3			
4			
5			
6			
7			
8			
9			
10			
11			
12			
13			
14			
15			
16			
17			
18			
19			
20			
21			
22			
23			
24			
25			
26			
27			
28			
29			
30			
31			
32			
33			
34			
35			
36			
37			
38			
39			
40			

1	(a)								1
2									2
3									3
4									4
5									5
6									6
7	(b)								7
8									8
9									9
10									10
11									11
12									12
13	(c)								13
14									14
15									15
16									16
17									17
18									18
19									19
20									20
21									21
22									22
23									23
24									24
25									25
26									26
27									27
28									28
29									29
30									30
31									31
32									32
33									33
34									34
35									35
36									36
37									37
38									38
39									39
40									40

E25-2

Ingredient	Amount Per Gallon	Standard Waste	Standard Usage	Standard Price	Standard Cost Per Gallon
1 Grape concentrate						1
2 Sugar						2
3 Lemons						3
4 Yeast						4
5 Nutrient						5
6 Water						6
7						7
8						8
9						9
10						10

E25-3

1 Direct materials:			1
2			2
3			3
4			4
5			5
6 Direct labor:			6
7			7
8			8
9			9
10 Manufacturing overhead:			10
11			11
12			12
13			13
14			14
15			15
16			16
17			17
18			18
19			19
20			20
21			21
22			22
23			23
24			24
25			25

(a)								
(b)								
(c)	Standard direct labor cost							
	per oil change =							
(d)	Direct labor quantity variance =							

You will find this working paper at the end of this booklet.

(a)

Picard Landscaping
Variance Report - Purchasing Department
For the Current Month

Project	Actual Pounds Purchased	(1) Actual Price	(2) Standard Price	Price Variance	Explanation	
Remington						4
Chang						5
Wyco						6
						7
						8
						9
						10

(b)

Picard Landscaping
Variance Report - Production Department
For the Current Month

Project	Actual Pounds	Standard Pounds	Standard Price	Quantity Variance	Explanation	
Remington						3
Chang						4
Wyco						5
						6
						7
						8

Burte Corporation

Variance Report - Purchasing Department

For the Week Ended January 9, 2012

	Type of Materials	Quantity Purchased	Actual Price	Standard Price	Price Variance		Explanation
1							
2							
3	Rogue 11		$ 5 20	$ 5 00	$ 5 2 0 0		Price increase
4	Storm 17			3 30	1 0 5 0	U	Rush order
5	Beast 29		0 40		4 4 0	F	Bought larger quantity
6							
7							
8							
9							
10							
11							
12							
13							
14							
15							

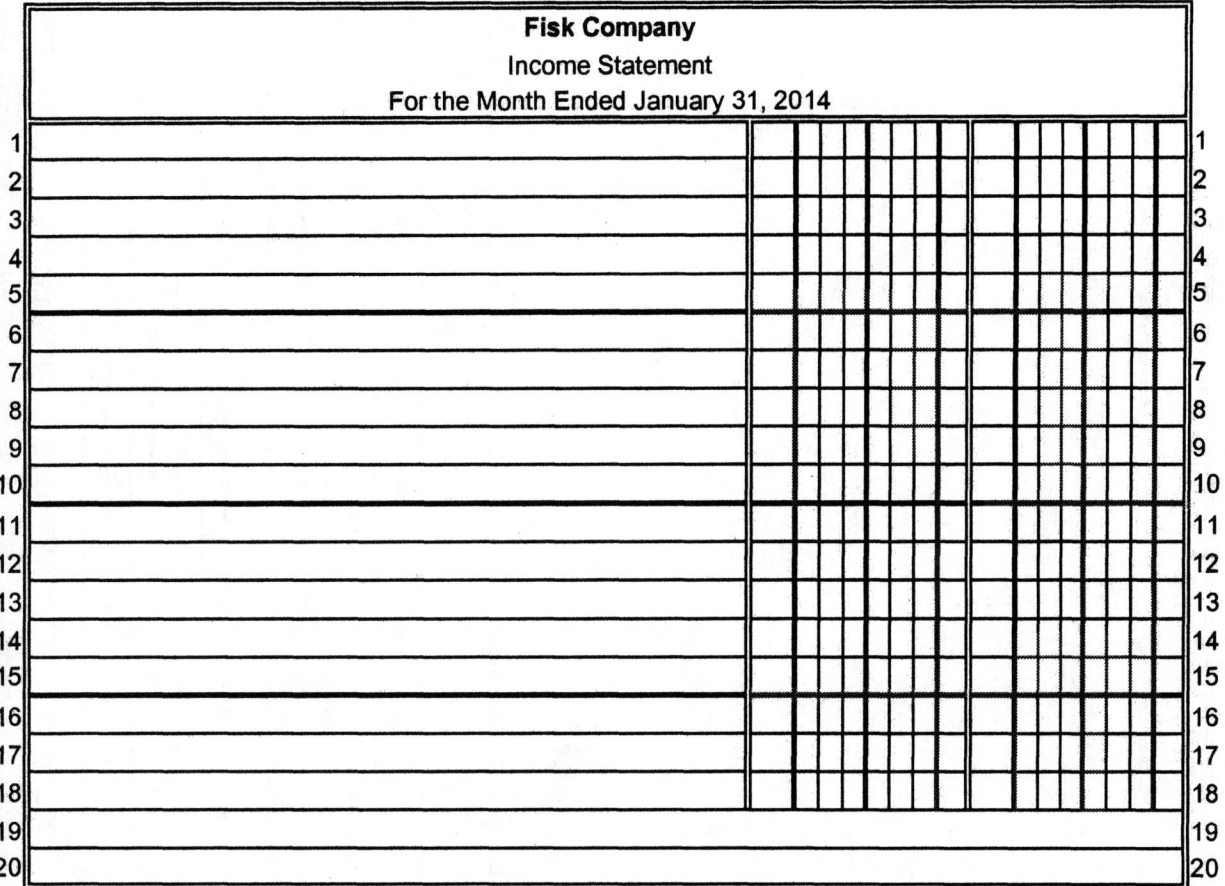

Fisk Company
Income Statement
For the Month Ended January 31, 2014

		Account Titles	Debit	Credit	
1	1.				1
2					2
3					3
4					4
5	2.				5
6					6
7					7
8					8
9	3.				9
10					10
11					11
12					12
13	4.				13
14					14
15					15
16					16
17	5.				17
18					18
19					19
20					20
21					21
22					22
23					23
24					24
25					25
26					26
27					27
28					28
29					29
30					30
31					31
32					32
33					33
34					34
35					35
36					36
37					37
38					38
39					39
40					40

ame

ection

ate

Nona Inc.

		Account Titles	Debit	Credit	
1					1
2					2
3					3
4					4
5					5
6					6
7					7
8					8
9					9
10					10
11					11
12					12
13					13
14					14
15					15
16					16
17					17
18					18
19					19
20					20
21					21
22					22
23					23
24					24
25					25

(a) Item	Amount	Hours	Rate	
1				1
2				2
3				3
4 (b)				4
5			F	5
6 Total overhead variance:			U	6
7				7
8				8
9				9
10				10
11 Overhead controllable variance:				11
12				12
13				13
14				14
15				15
16 Overhead volume variance:				16
17				17
18				18
19				19
20				20
21				21
22				22
23				23
24				24
25 (c)				25
26				26
27				27
28				28
29				29
30				30
31				31
32				32
33				33
34				34
35				35

(a)

	F U
(1) Total materials variance:	
Materials price variance:	
Materials quantity variance:	
(2) Total labor variance:	
Labor price variance:	
Labor quantity variance:	
(b)	
Total overhead variance:	

(c)

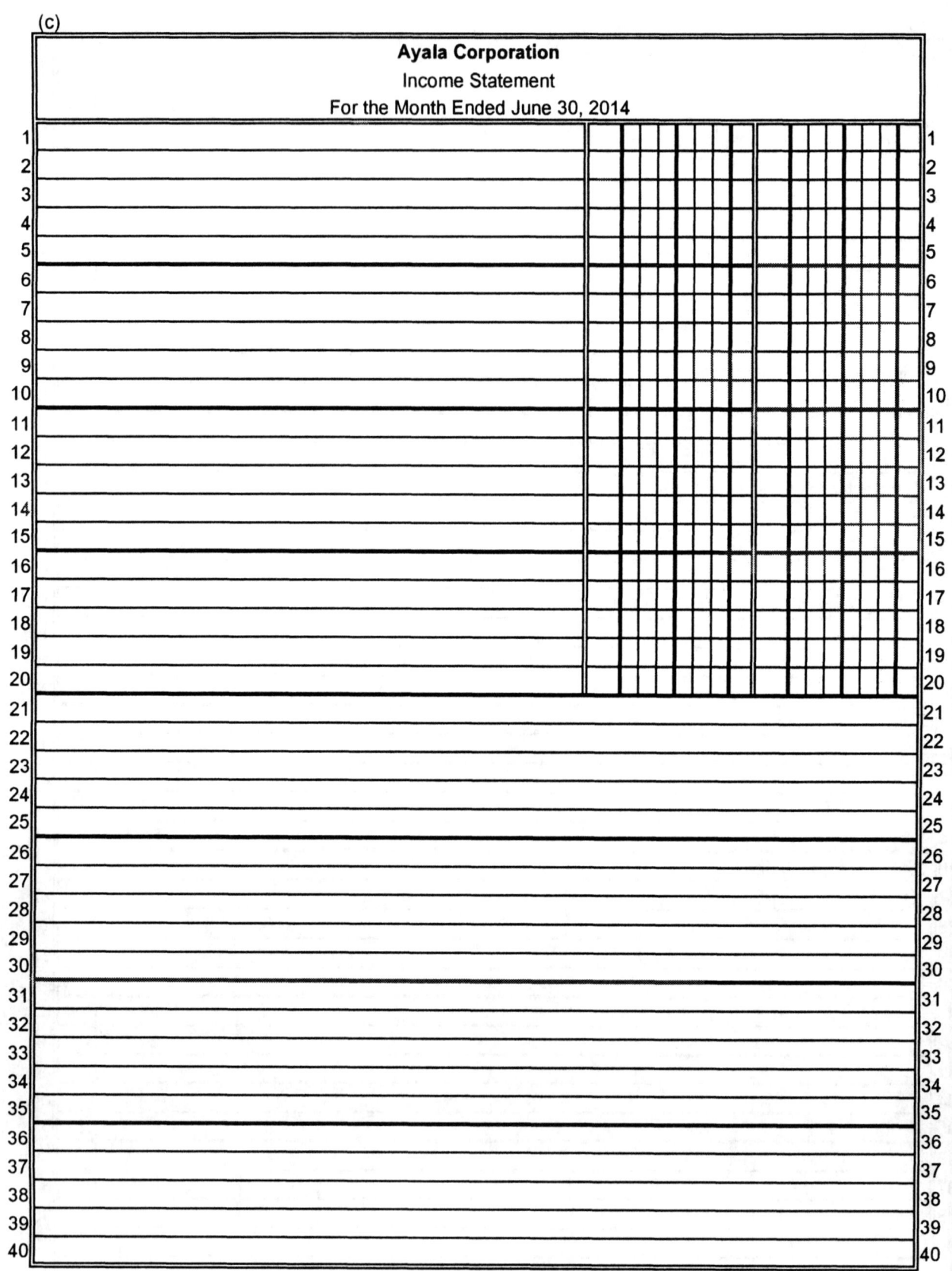

Ayala Corporation
Income Statement
For the Month Ended June 30, 2014

(a)

	F U
1 Materials price variance:	1
2	2
3	3
4	4
5 Materials quantity variance:	5
6	6
7	7
8	8
9 Labor price variance:	9
10	10
11	11
12	12
13 Labor quantity variance:	13
14	14
15	15
16	16
17 (b)	17
18 Total overhead variance:	18
19	19
20	20
21	21
22	22
23	23
24	24
25	25
26	26
27	27
28	28
29	29
30	30
31	31
32	32
33	33
34	34
35	35
36	36
37	37
38	38
39	39
40	40

(c)

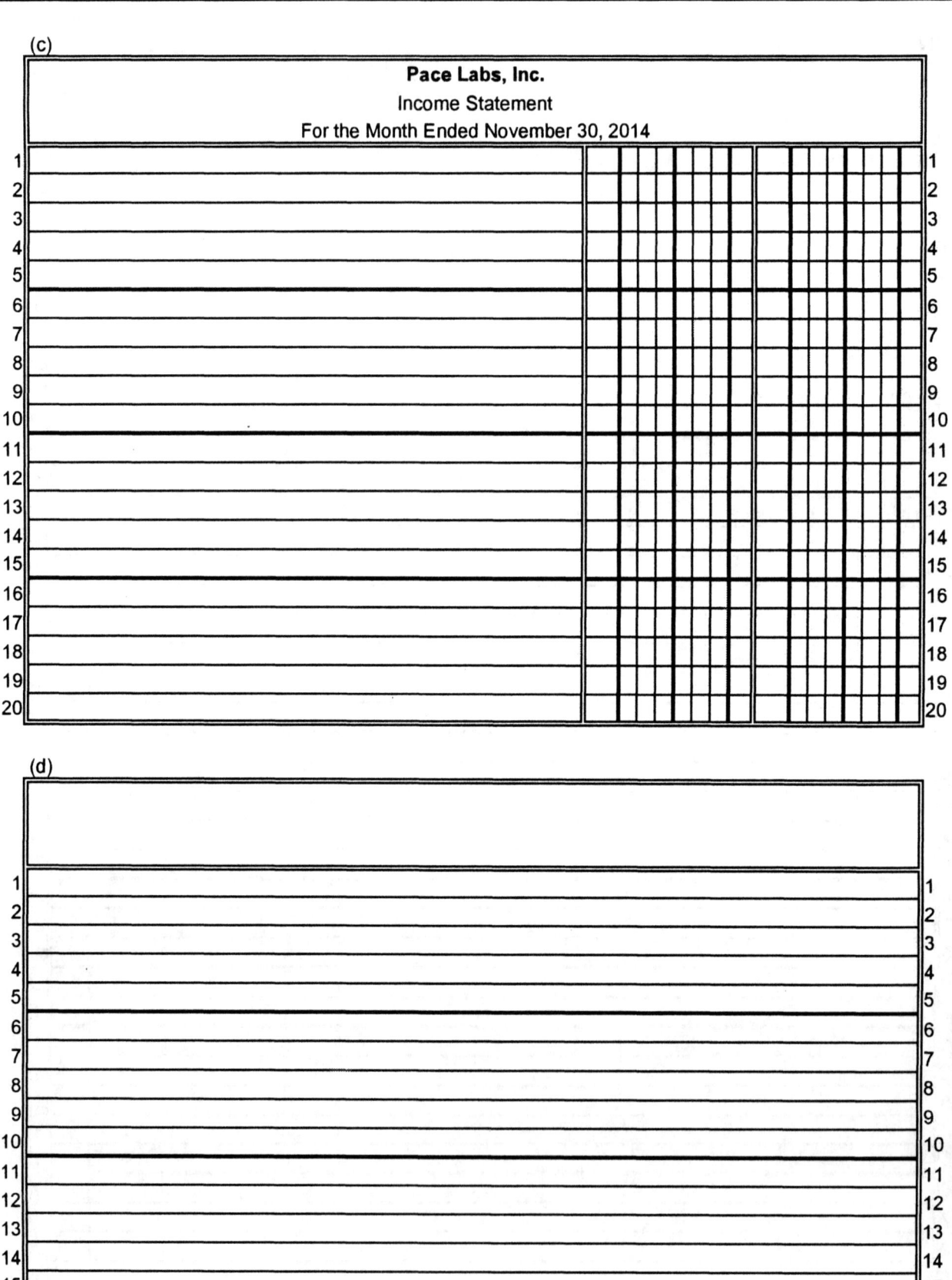

Pace Labs, Inc.

Income Statement

For the Month Ended November 30, 2014

(d)

(a)

		Account Titles	Debit	Credit	
1	1.				1
2					2
3					3
4					4
5	2.				5
6					6
7					7
8					8
9	3.				9
10					10
11					11
12					12
13	4.				13
14					14
15					15
16					16
17	5.				17
18					18
19					19
20	6.				20
21					21
22					22
23	7.				23
24					24
25					25
26	8.				26
27					27
28					28
29					29
30					30
31					31
32					32
33					33
34	9.				34
35					35
36					36
37					37
38					38
39					39
40					40

(b)

Raw Materials Inventory	Work in Process Inventory
Materials Price Variance	Materials Quantity Variance
Factory Labor	Manufacturing Overhead
Labor Price Variance	Labor Quantity Variance
Finished Goods Inventory	Cost of Goods Sold

(c)

	Account Titles	Debit	Credit	
1				1
2				2
3				3
4				4
5				5
6				6
7				7
8				8
9				9
10				10
11				11
12				12
13				13
14				14
15				15

(d)

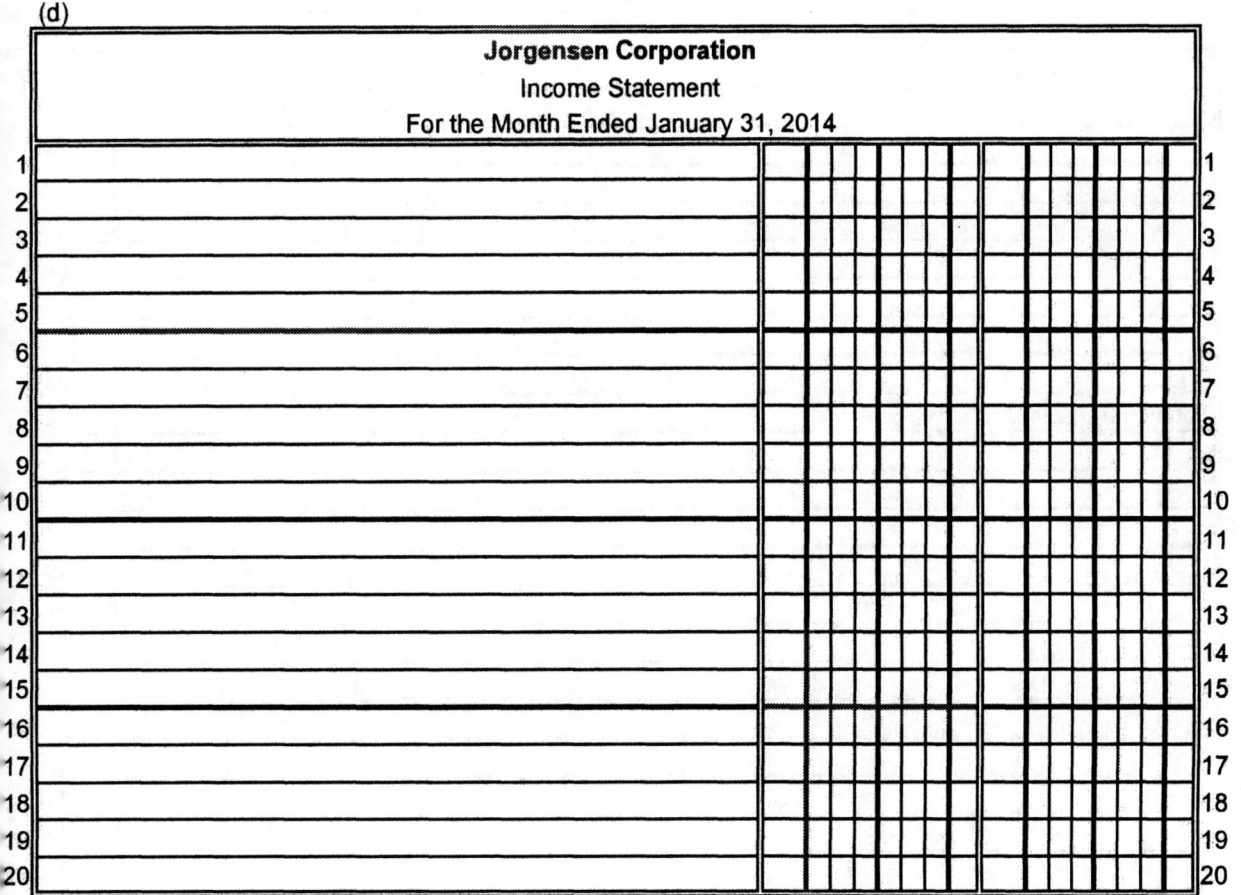

Jorgensen Corporation
Income Statement
For the Month Ended January 31, 2014

1			1
2			2
3			3
4			4
5			5
6			6
7			7
8			8
9			9
10			10
11			11
12			12
13			13
14			14
15			15
16			16
17			17
18			18
19			19
20			20

(a)

	F U
1 (1) Total materials variance:	1
2	2
3	3
4	4
5 Materials price variance:	5
6	6
7	7
8	8
9 Materials quantity variance:	9
10	10
11	11
12	12
13 (2) Total labor variance:	13
14	14
15	15
16	16
17 Labor price variance:	17
18	18
19	19
20	20
21 Labor quantity variance:	21
22	22
23	23
24	24
25	25
26 (b)	26
27 Total overhead variance:	27
28	28
29	29
30	30
31	31
32	32
33	33
34	34
35	35
36	36
37	37
38	38
39	39
40	40

(c)

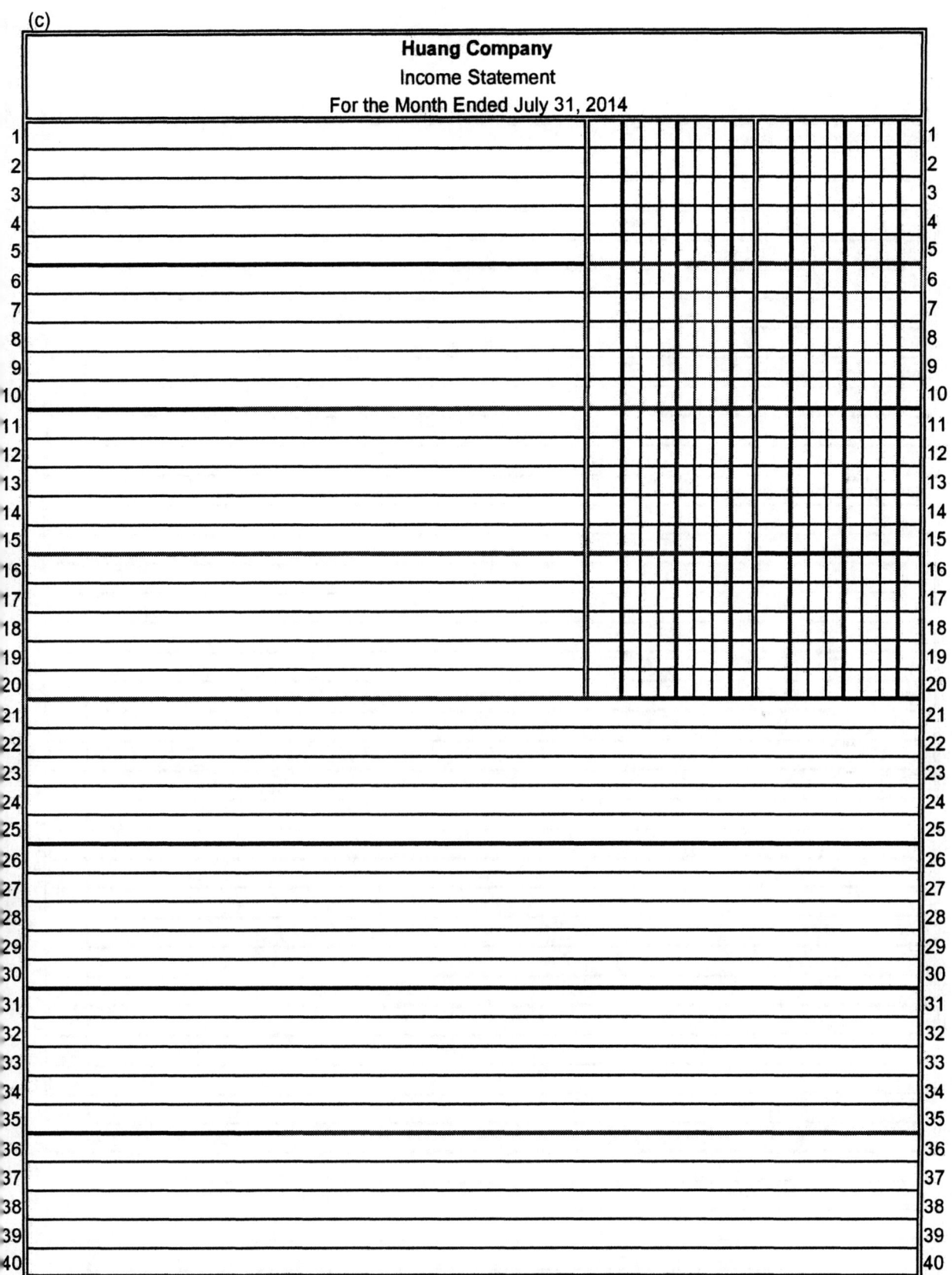

Huang Company

Income Statement

For the Month Ended July 31, 2014

(a)

	F U
1 Materials price variance:	1
2	2
3	3
4	4
5 Materials quantity variance:	5
6	6
7	7
8	8
9 Labor price variance:	9
10	10
11	11
12	12
13 Labor quantity variance:	13
14	14
15	15
16	16
17	17
18	18
19 (b)	19
20 Total overhead variance:	20
21	21
22	22
23	23
24	24
25	25
26	26
27	27
28	28
29	29
30	30
31	31
32	32
33	33
34	34
35	35
36	36
37	37
38	38
39	39
40	40

(c)

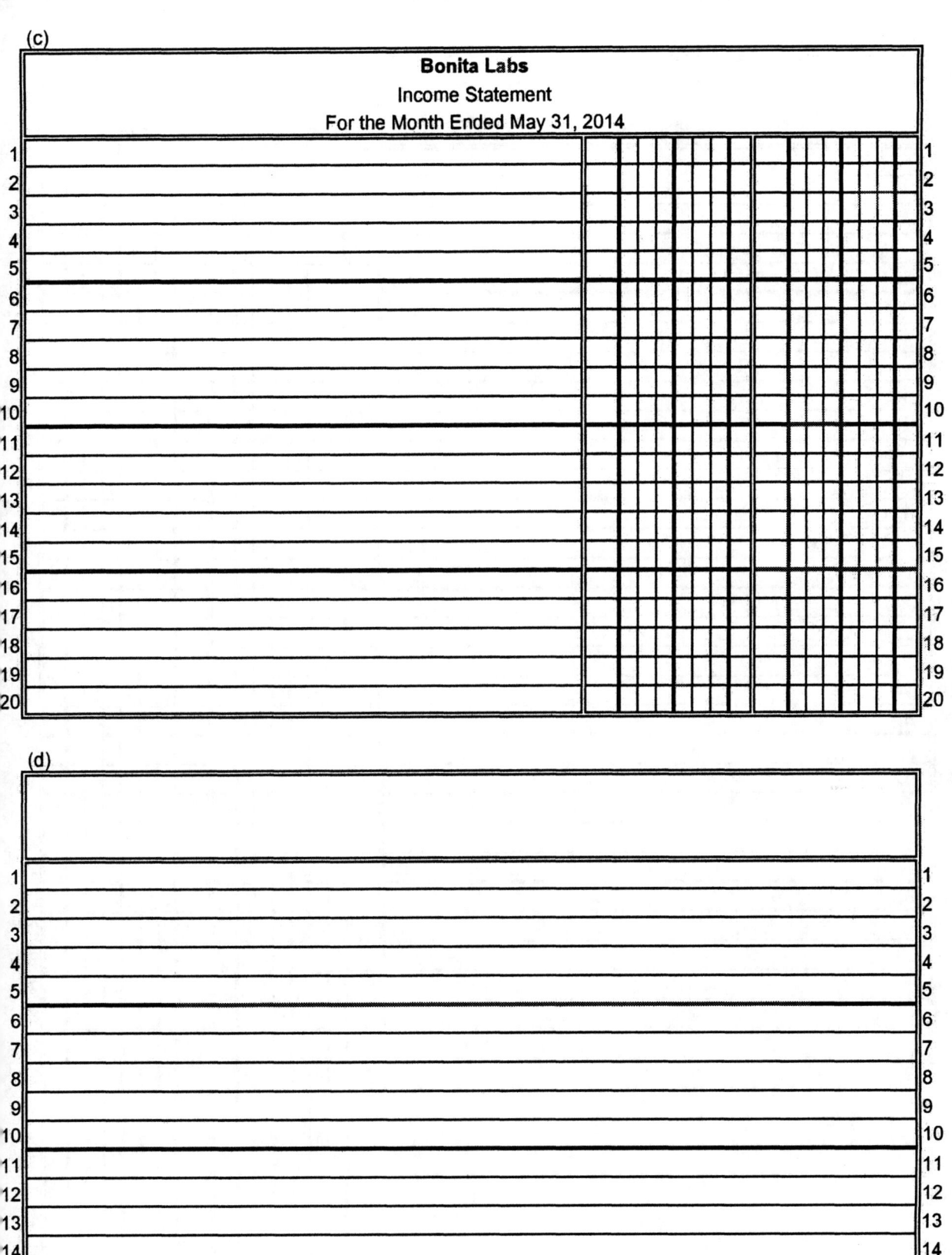

Bonita Labs
Income Statement
For the Month Ended May 31, 2014

(d)

(a)

Account Titles	Debit	Credit
1.		
2.		
3.		
4.		
5.		
6.		
7.		
8.		
9.		

(b)

Raw Materials Inventory	Work in Process Inventory

Materials Price Variance	Materials Quantity Variance

Factory Labor	Manufacturing Overhead

Labor Price Variance	Labor Quantity Variance

Finished Goods Inventory	Cost of Goods Sold

(c)

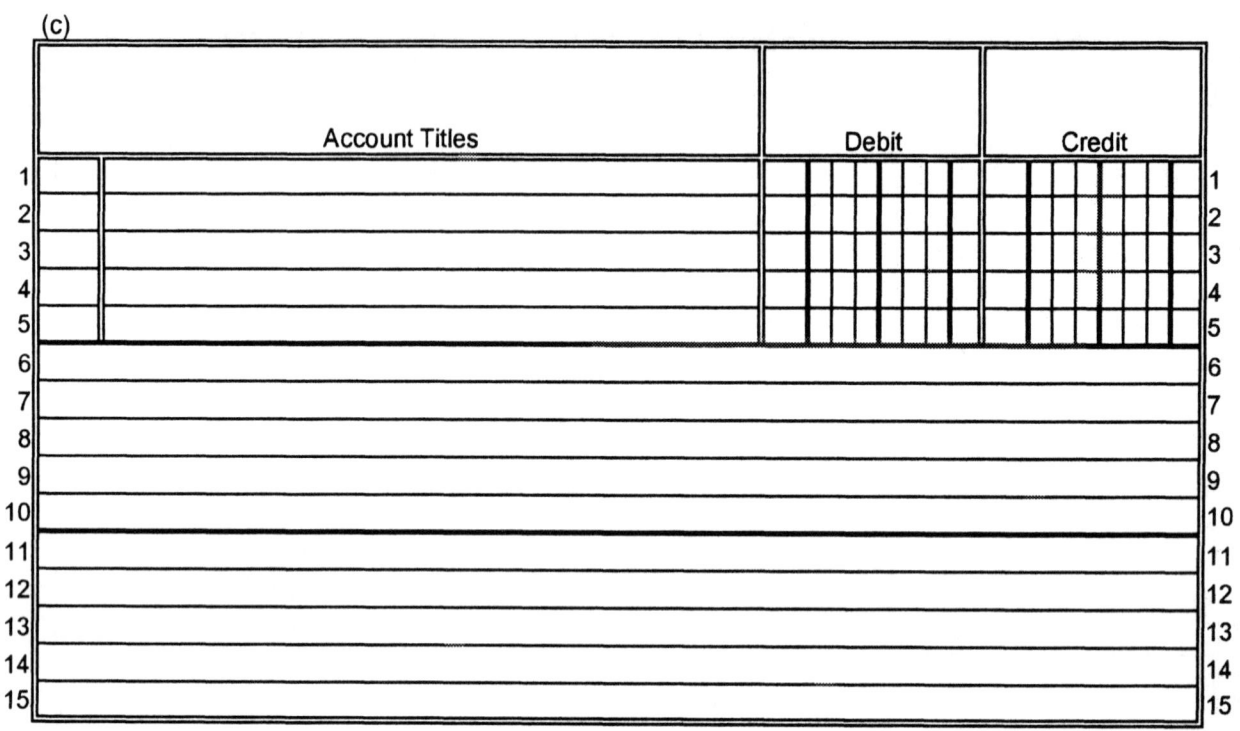

	Account Titles	Debit	Credit	
1				1
2				2
3				3
4				4
5				5
6				6
7				7
8				8
9				9
10				10
11				11
12				12
13				13
14				14
15				15

(d)

Frio Company
Income Statement
For the Month Ended January 31, 2014

1				1
2				2
3				3
4				4
5				5
6				6
7				7
8				8
9				9
10				10
11				11
12				12
13				13
14				14
15				15
16				16
17				17
18				18
19				19
20				20

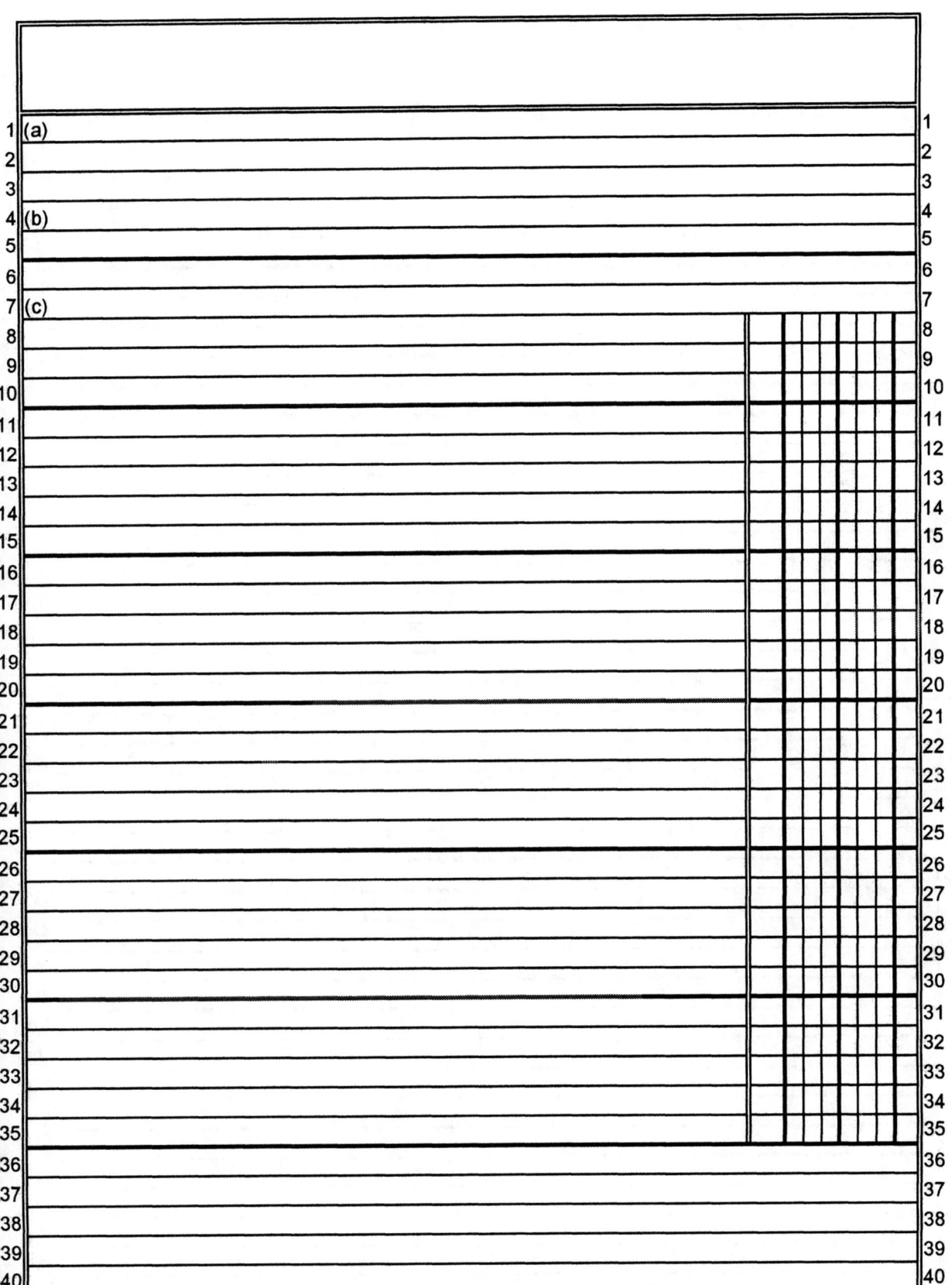

1	(d)	1
2		2
3		3
4		4
5		5
6		6
7	(e)	7
8		8
9		9
10		10
11		11
12		12
13		13
14		14
15		15
16		16
17		17
18		18
19		19
20		20
21		21
22		22
23		23
24		24
25		25
26		26
27		27
28		28
29		29
30		30
31		31
32		32
33		33
34		34
35		35
36		36
37		37
38		38
39		39
40		40

BE26-2

	Cash Flows	Discount Factor	Present Value	
1				1
2				2
3				3
4				4
5				5
6				6

BE26-3

	Cash Flows	10% Discount Factor	Present Value	
7				7
8				8
9				9
10				10
11				11
12				12
13				13
14				14
15				15

BE26-4

	Cash Flows	9% Discount Factor	Present Value	
16				16
17				17
18				18
19				19
20				20
21				21
22				22
23				23
24				24

BE26-5 Project A

	Cash Flows	9% Discount Factor	Present Value	
25				25
26				26
27				27
28				28
29				29
30				30
31				31
32				32
33	Profitability index =			33
34				34
35				35
36				36
37				37
38				38
39				39
40				40

BE26-5 (Continued)

Project B	Cash Flows	9% Discount Factor	Present Value	
1				1
2				2
3				3
4				4
5				5
6				6
7 Profitability index =				7
8				8
9				9
10				10
11				11
12				12
13				13
14				14

BE26-6 (Original estimate)	Cash Flows	10% Discount Factor	Present Value	
15				15
16				16
17				17
18				18
19				19
20				20
21				21
22				22

Revised estimate	Cash Flows	10% Discount Factor	Present Value	
23				23
24				24
25				25
26				26
27				27
28				28
29				29
30				30
31				31
32				32
33				33
34				34
35				35
36				36
37				37
38				38
39				39
40				40

BE26-8

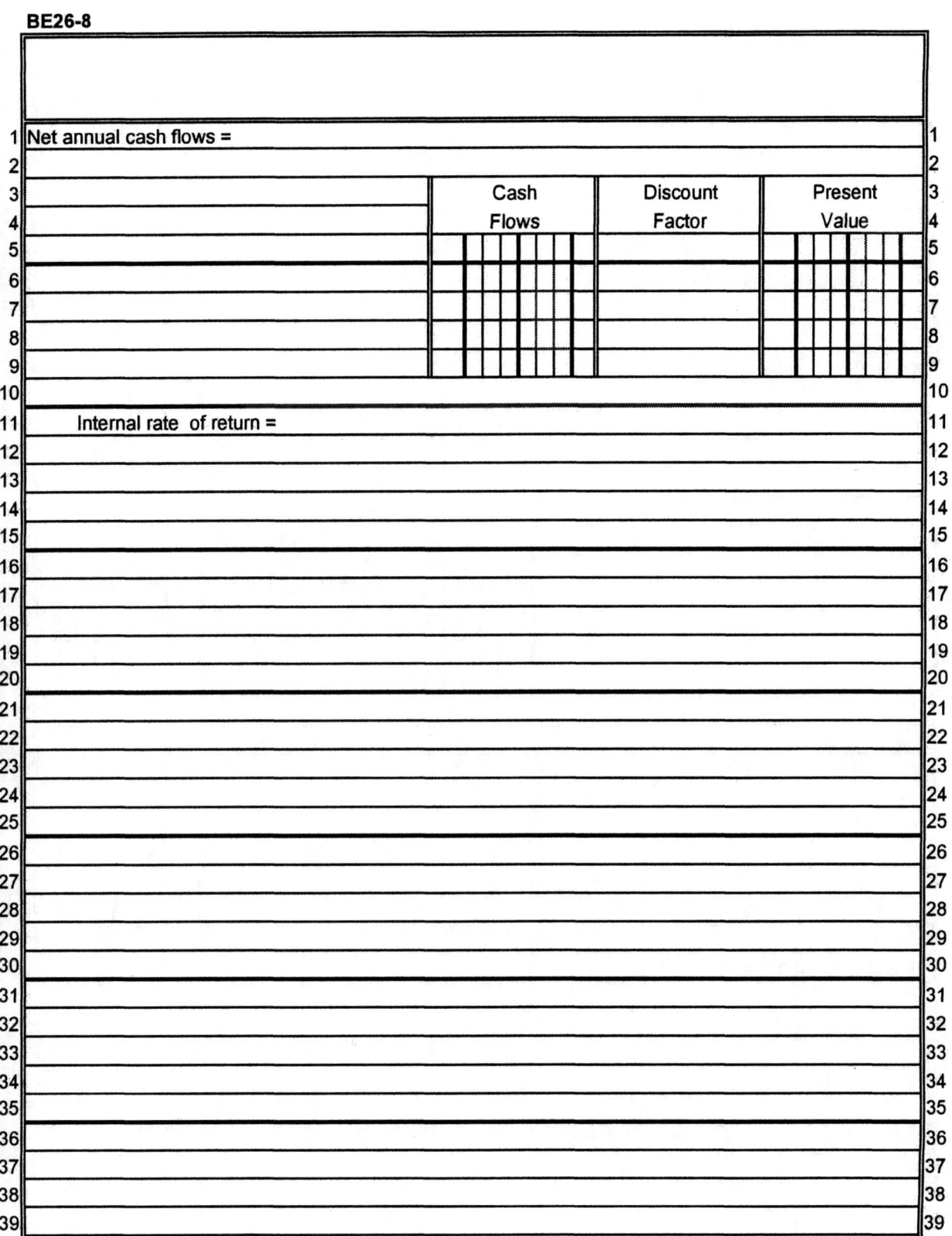

			Cash Flows	Discount Factor	Present Value	
1	Net annual cash flows =					1
2						2
3						3
4						4
5						5
6						6
7						7
8						8
9						9
10						10
11	Internal rate of return =					11

DO IT! 26-1

1	
2	
3	
4	
5	
6	Cash payback period =
7	
8	

DO IT! 26-2

	Cash Flow	12% Discount Factor	Present Value

DO IT! 26-3

Internal rate of return =

1	
2	
3	
4	
5	
6	
7	
8	Average investment =
9	
10	Annual rate of return =
11	
12	
13	
14	
15	
16	
17	
18	
19	
20	
21	
22	
23	
24	
25	
26	
27	
28	
29	
30	
31	
32	
33	
34	
35	
36	
37	
38	
39	
40	

			Cash Flows	8% Discount Factor	Present Value	
1	(a)	Cash payback period =				1
2						2
3						3
4		Net present value is:				4
5						5
6						6
7						7
8						8
9						9
10						10
11						11
12						12
13	(b)					13
14						14
15						15
16						16
17						17
18						18
19						19
20						20
21						21
22						22
23						23
24						24
25						25
26						26
27						27
28						28
29						29
30						30
31						31
32						32
33						33
34						34
35						35
36						36
37						37
38						38
39						39
40						40

Exercise 202

Doug's Custom Manufacturing Company

(a) Computation of each project's payback period:

	AA		BB		CC	
Year	Net Annual Cash Inflow	Cumulative Cash Flow			Net Annual Cash Inflow	Cumulative Cash Flow
1						
2						
3						
4						
5	Payback		Payback		Payback	
6	Period =		Period =		Period =	
7						
8	Most desirable project is:				Least desirable project is:	

(b) Computation of each project's net present value:

	AA			BB		CC	
Year	Discount Factor	Cash Inflow	Present Value	Cash Inflow	Present Value	Cash Inflow	Present Value
1							
2							
3							
4	Total present value						
5	Investment						
6	Net present value						
7							
8							
9	Most desirable product is:				Least desirable project is:		
10							
11							

	Cash Flows	Year	9% Discount Factor	Amount	Present Value	
1						1
2						2
3						3
4						4
5						5
6						6
7						7
8						8
9						9
10						10
11						11
12						12
13						13
14						14
15						15
16						16
17						17
18						18
19						19
20						20
21						21
22						22
23						23
24						24
25						25
26						26
27						27
28						28
29						29
30						30
31						31
32						32
33						33
34						34
35						35
36						36
37						37
38						38
39						39
40						40

Machine A	Cash Flows	9% Discount Factor	Present Value	
1				1
2				2
3				3
4				4
5				5
6				6
7				7
8 Profitability index =				8
9				9
10				10
11				11

Machine B	Cash Flows	9% Discount Factor	Present Value	
12				12
13				13
14				14
15				15
16				16
17				17
18				18
19				19
20				20
21 Profitability index =				21
22				22
23				23
24				24
25				25
26				26
27				27
28				28
29				29
30				30
31				31
32				32
33				33
34				34
35				35
36				36
37				37
38				38
39				39
40				40

(a)		
1	Total net investment =	
2		
3	Annual net cash flow =	
4		
5	Payback period =	
6		
7		

(b)	Item	Amount	Years	PV Factor	Present Value
8					
9					
10					
11					
12					
13					
14					

(c)		
15		
16		
17		
18		
19		
20		

(a)

		Net Annual Cash Inflows		Internal Rate of Return Factor	Closest Discount Factor	Internal Rate of Return
Project	Capital Investment	Annual Income +	Depreciation Expense			
22A							1
23A							2
24A							3
							4
							5
							6
							7
							8
							9
							10

(b)

					11
					12
					13
					14
					15

E26-9

	(a)		
1	Cost of hoist:		1
2	Net cash flows:		2
3			3
4			4
5			5
6			6
7			7
8	Cash payback period =		8
9			9
10			10
11	(b)		11
12	Average investment =		12
13			13
14	Annual depreciation =		14
15			15
16	Annual net income =		16
17			17
18	Annual rate of return =		18
19			19
20			20

E26-10

	(a)					
1	(1) Cash payback period =					1
2						2
3						3
4	(2) Annual rate of return =					4
5						5
6						6
7	(b)					7
8				12% Discount	Present	8
9	Item	Amount	Years	Factor	Value	9
10						10
11						11
12						12
13						13
14						14
15						15

(a)

Cash Flows		Year	Net Annual Cash Flow	Cumulative Cash Flow
1				
2				
3				
4				
5				
6	Payback period =			
7				
8				
9	(b) Average annual net income =			
10				
11				
12	Average investment =			
13				
14				
15	Annual rate of return =			
16				
17				
18				
19				

(c)

Net Cash Flows	Year	12% Discount Factor	Amount	Present Value

(a)

	Project Kilo						
Payback period =							

Project Lima

	Year		Cash Flow		Cumulative Cash Flow		
	1						
	2						
	3						
	4						
	5						

Payback period =

Project Oscar

	Year		Cash Flow		Cumulative Cash Flow		
	1						
	2						
	3						
	4						
	5						

Payback period =

Problem 26-1A Continued

Henkel Company

(b)

Project Kilo

Item	Amount	Years	PV Factor	Present Value
				1
1				2
2				3
3				4
4				

Osc.

Project Lima | | | | | | | | Project | | Osc.

Year	Discount Factor	Cash Inflow	PV	Cash Inflow	PV	
1						1
2						2
3						3
4						4
5						5
6 Totals						6
7 Capital investment						7
8 Positive (negative) net present value						8
9						9
10						10
11						11
12						12
13						13
14						14

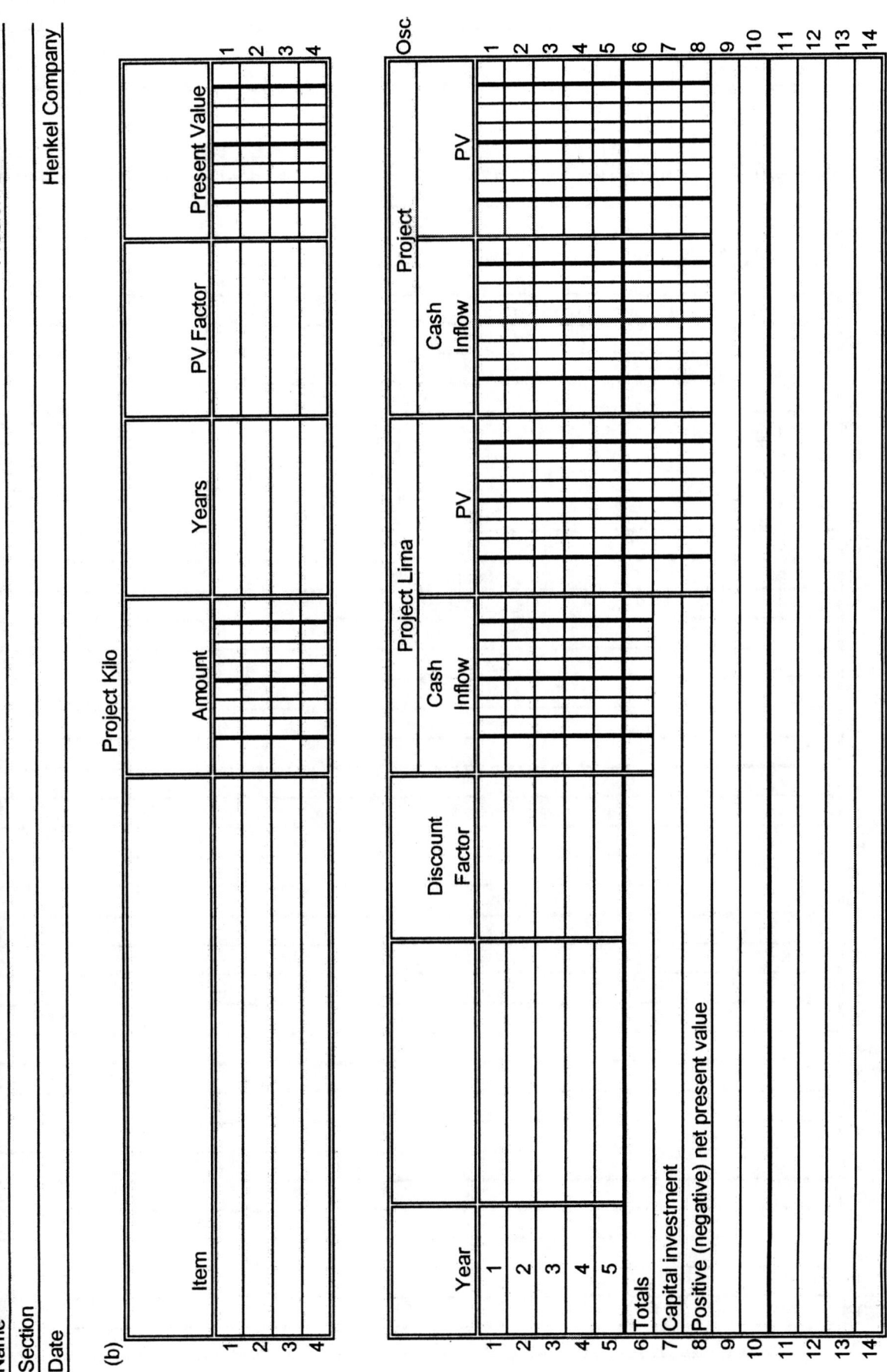

(c) and (d)

(c) Annual Rate of Return

Project Kilo =

Project Lima =

Project Oscar =

(d)

Project	Cash Payback	Net Present Value	Annual Rate of Return
Kilo			
Lima			
Oscar			

(a)

	(1) Annual Net Income	(2) Annual Cash Inflow
1		
2		
3		
4		
5		
6		
7		
8		
9		
10		
11		
12		

(b), (c), and (d)

1	(b) (1) Cash payback period =			
2				
3				
4				
5	(2) Annual rate of return =			
6				
7				
8				

	(c)	Cash Flow	15% Discount Factor	Present Value
9				
10				
11				
12				
13				
14				
15				
16	(d)			
17				
18				
19				
20				
21				
22				
23				

(a)

(1) Option A	Cash Flows	8% Discount Factor	Present Value
1			
2			
3			
4			
5			
6			
7			
8			
9 (2) Profitability index =			
10			

(3)	Cash Flows	Discount Factor	Present Value
12			
13			
14			
15			
16			
17			
18			
19			
20 Internal rate of return =			
21			
22			

(1) Option B	Cash Flows	8% Discount Factor	Present Value
25			
26			
27			
28			
29			
30			
31			
32			
33 (2) Profitability index =			
34			
35			
36			
37			
38			
39			
40			

(a)   (Continued)

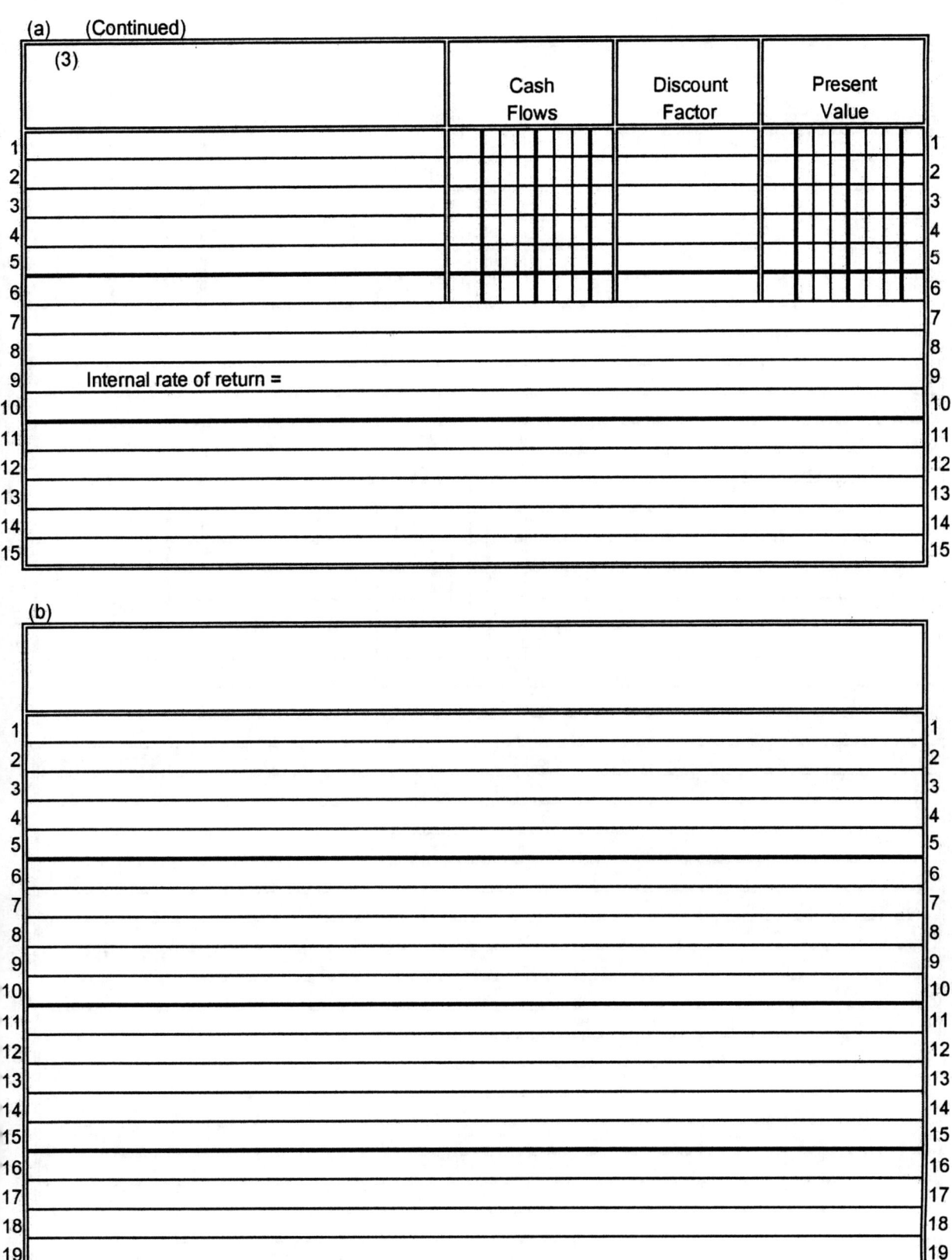

(3)

	Cash Flows	Discount Factor	Present Value	
1				1
2				2
3				3
4				4
5				5
6				6
7				7
8				8
9	Internal rate of return =			9
10				10
11				11
12				12
13				13
14				14
15				15

(b)

1		1
2		2
3		3
4		4
5		5
6		6
7		7
8		8
9		9
10		10
11		11
12		12
13		13
14		14
15		15
16		16
17		17
18		18
19		19
20		20

(a)

Original estimates	Cash Flows	9% Discount Factor	Present Value	
1				1
2				2
3				3
4				4
5				5
6				6
7				7
8				8
9				9
10				10

(b)

Revised estimates	Cash Flows	9% Discount Factor	Present Value	
13				13
14				14
15				15
16				16
17				17
18				18
19				19
20				20
21				21
22				22
23				23
24				24
25				25

(c)

(a)

Original estimates	Cash Flows	8% Discount Factor	Present Value
1			
2			
3			
4			
5			
6			
7			
8			
9			
10			

(b)

Revised estimates	Cash Flows	8% Discount Factor	Present Value
13			
14			
15			
16			
17			
18			
19			
20			
21			
22			
23			
24			

(c)

Original estimates at 11%	Cash Flows	11% Discount Factor	Present Value
27			
28			
29			
30			
31			
32			
33			
34			
35			
36			
37			
38			
39			
40			

(d)

	Cash Flows	Discount Factor	Present Value
1			
2			
3			
4			
5			
6			
7			
8			
9			
10	Internal rate of return =		
11			
12			
13			
14			
15			
16			
17			
18			
19			
20			
21			
22			
23			
24			
25			
26			
27			
28			
29			
30			
31			
32			
33			
34			
35			
36			
37			
38			
39			
40			

(a)

	Project Mary

1	
2	Payback period =
3	
4	

5	Project Winnie

				Cash		Cumulative Cash	
	Year			Flow		Flow	
	1						
	2						
	3						
	4						
	5						

15	Payback period =

20	Project Sarah

				Cash		Cumulative Cash	
	Year			Flow		Flow	
	1						
	2						
	3						
	4						
	5						

31	Payback period =

Problem 26-1B Continued

Borders and Noble

(b)

Project Mary

Item	Amount	Years	PV Factor	Present Value

Project Winnie

Year	Discount Factor	Cash Inflow	PV
1			
2			
3			
4			
5			
Totals			

Project Sarah

	Cash Inflow	PV

Capital investment

Positive (negative) net present value

(c) and (d)

(c)	Annual Rate of Return			
Project Mary =				
Project Winnie =				
Project Sarah =				

(d)		Project	Cash Payback	Net Present Value	Annual Rate of Return
		Mary			
		Winnie			
		Sarah			

(a)

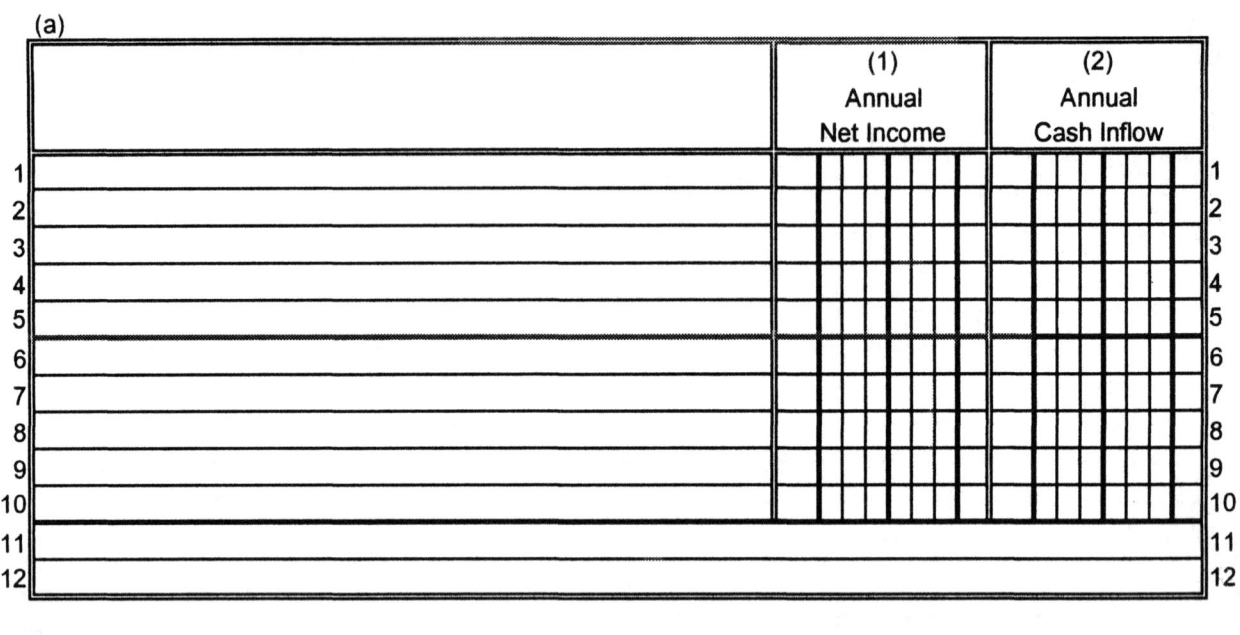

	(1) Annual Net Income	(2) Annual Cash Inflow
1		
2		
3		
4		
5		
6		
7		
8		
9		
10		
11		
12		

(b), (c), and (d)

		Cash Flow	15% Discount Factor	Present Value	
1	(b) (1) Cash payback period =				1
2					2
3					3
4					4
5	(2) Annual rate of return =				5
6					6
7					7
8					8
9	(c)				9
10					10
11					11
12					12
13					13
14					14
15					15
16	(d)				16
17					17
18					18
19					19
20					20
21					21
22					22
23					23

(a)

(1) Option A	Cash Flows	11% Discount Factor	Present Value
1			
2			
3			
4			
5			
6			
7			
8			
(2) Profitability index =			

(3)	Cash Flows	Discount Factor	Present Value
Internal rate of return =			

(1) Option B	Cash Flows	11% Discount Factor	Present Value
(2) Profitability index =			

(a)   (Continued)

(3)

	Cash Flows	Discount Factor	Present Value	
1				1
2				2
3				3
4				4
5				5
6				6
7				7
8				8
9	Internal rate of return =			9
10				10
11				11
12				12
13				13
14				14
15				15

(b)

1		1
2		2
3		3
4		4
5		5
6		6
7		7
8		8
9		9
10		10
11		11
12		12
13		13
14		14
15		15
16		16
17		17
18		18
19		19
20		20

(a)

Original estimates	Cash Flows	10% Discount Factor	Present Value	
1				1
2				2
3				3
4				4
5				5
6				6
7				7
8				8
9				9
10				10

(b)

Revised estimates	Cash Flows	10% Discount Factor	Present Value	
11				11
12				12
13				13
14				14
15				15
16				16
17				17
18				18
19				19
20				20
21				21
22				22
23				23
24				24
25				25

(c)

26	26
27	27
28	28
29	29
30	30
31	31
32	32
33	33
34	34
35	35
36	36
37	37
38	38
39	39
40	40

(a)

Original estimates	Cash Flows	12% Discount Factor	Present Value
1			
2			
3			
4			
5			
6			
7			
8			
9			
10			

(b)

Revised estimates	Cash Flows	12% Discount Factor	Present Value
13			
14			
15			
16			
17			
18			
19			
20			
21			
22			
23			
24			

(c)

Original estimates at 15%	Cash Flows	15% Discount Factor	Present Value
27			
28			
29			
30			
31			
32			
33			
34			
35			
36			
37			
38			
39			
40			

(d)

	Cash Flows	Discount Factor	Present Value	
1				1
2				2
3				3
4				4
5				5
6				6
7				7
8				8
9				9
10	Internal rate of return =			10
11				11
12				12
13				13
14				14
15				15
16				16
17				17
18				18
19				19
20				20
21				21
22				22
23				23
24				24
25				25
26				26
27				27
28				28
29				29
30				30
31				31
32				32
33				33
34				34
35				35
36				36
37				37
38				38
39				39
40				40

1	(a)	Average investment =				
2						
3		Annual rate of return =				
4						
5						
6	(b)	Net annual cash flow =				
7						
8		Payback period =				
9						
10						

	(c) Event	Time Period	Cash Flows	9% Discount Factor	Present Value	
11						
12						
13						
14						
15						
16						
17						
18						
19						

	(d) Event	Time Period	Cash Flows	15% Discount Factor	Present Value	
20						
21						
22						
23						
24						
25						
26						
27						
28						
29						
30						
31						
32						
33						
34						
35						
36						
37						
38						
39						
40						

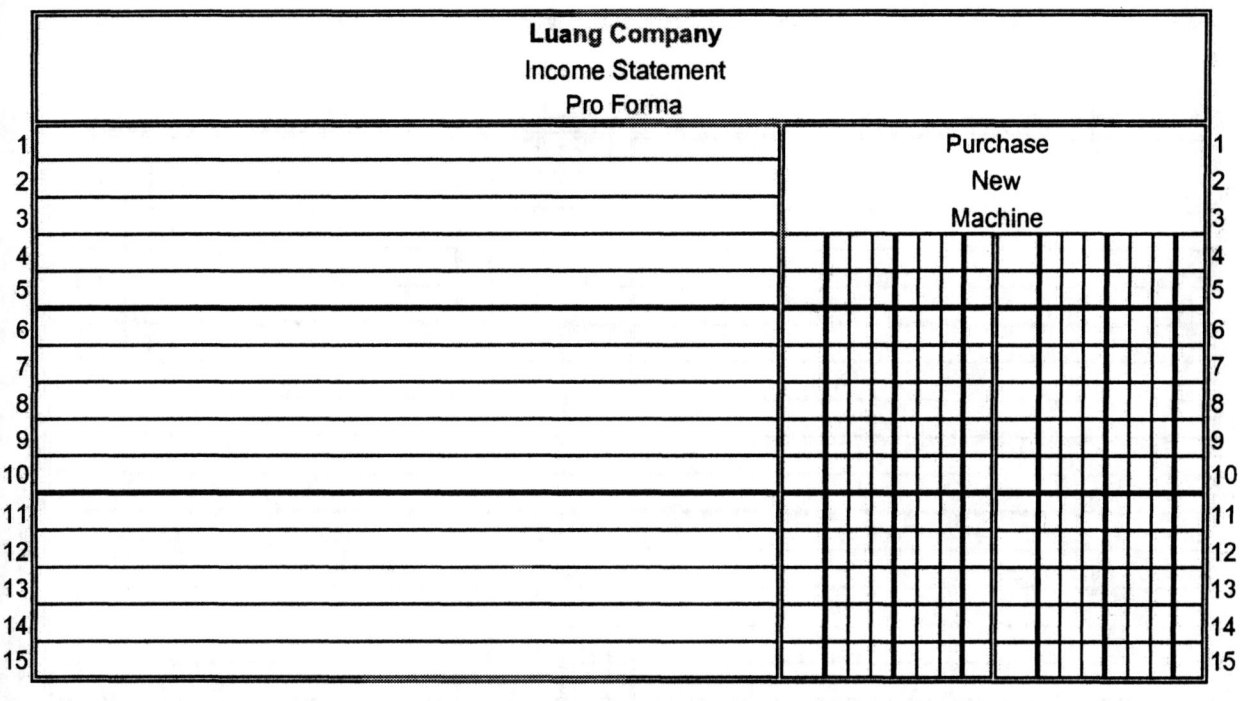

	Luang Company Income Statement Pro Forma		Purchase New Machine
1			
2			
3			
4			
5			
6			
7			
8			
9			
10			
11			
12			
13			
14			
15			

			Cash Flows	15% Discount Factor	Present Value
1	(a)	Annual rate of return =			
2					
3					
4					
5	(b)	Cash payback period =			
6					
7					
8					
9	(c)		Cash Flows	15% Discount Factor	Present Value
10					
11					
12					
13					
14					
15	(d)				
16					
17					
18					
19					
20					

(a)

Original estimates	Cash Flows	11% Discount Factor	Present Value
1			
2			
3			
4			
5			
6			
7			
8			
9			
10			

(b)

Revised estimates	Cash Flows	11% Discount Factor	Present Value
13			
14			
15			
16			
17			
18			
19			
20			
21			
22			
23			
24			

(c)

Original estimates at 9%	Cash Flows	9% Discount Factor	Present Value
27			
28			
29			
30			
31			
32			
33			
34			
35			
36			
37			
38			
39			
40			

(d)

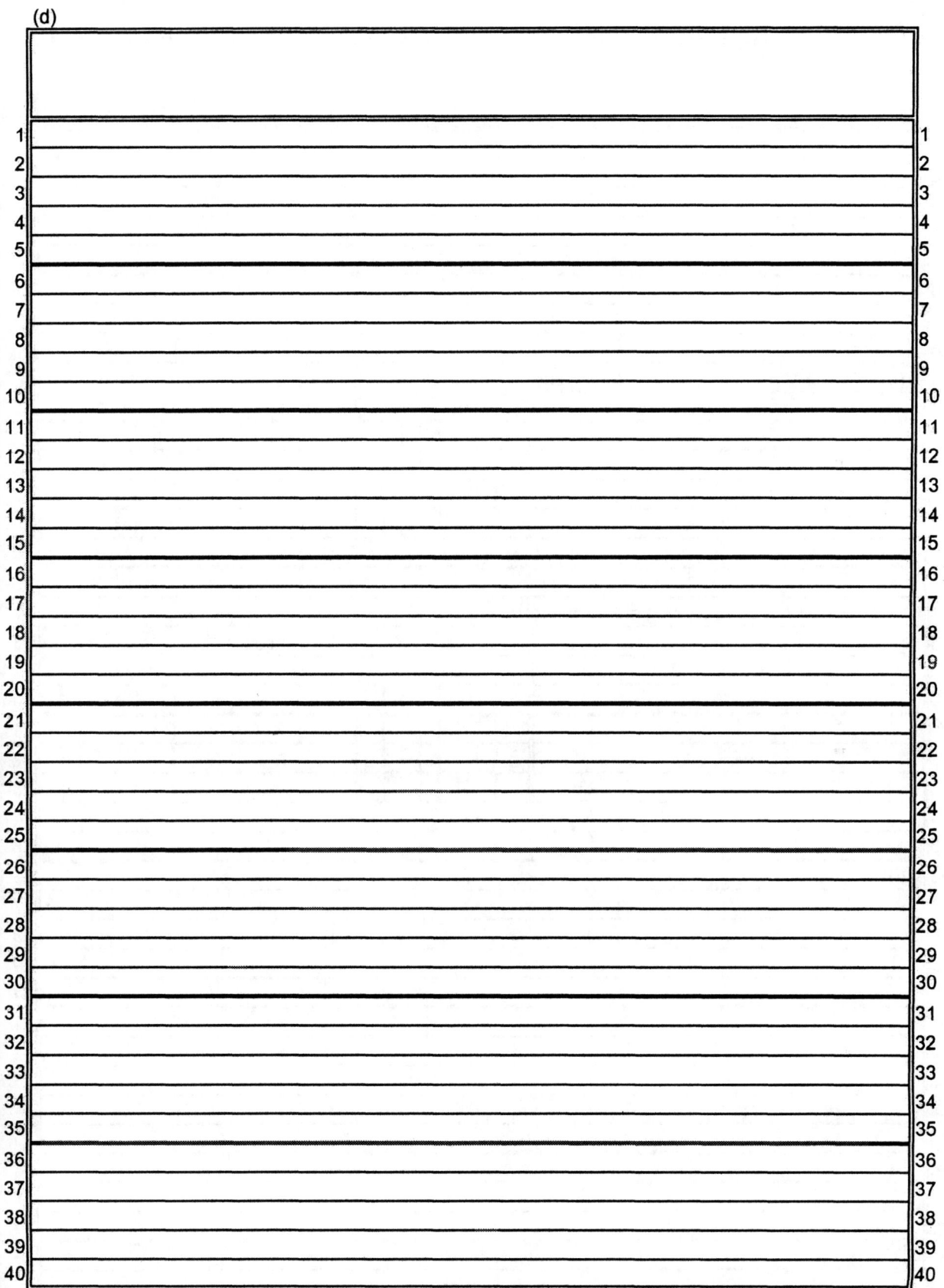

	(a)			
1				
2				
3				
4	(b)			
5				
6				
7				
8				

	(c) The NPV of project using the total cost	Cash Flows	6% Discount Factor	Present Value
9				
10				
11				
12				
13				
14				
15				

	The NPV of project using out-of-pocket cost:	Cash Flows	6% Discount Factor	Present Value
16				
17				
18				
19				
20				
21				
22				
23				
24				
25				

(d)

		Edington Electronics Inc.									
		Sales Budget									
		For the Six Months Ending June 30, 2014									
Product	Quarter 1			Quarter 2			Six Months		
	Units	Selling Price	Total Sales	Units	Selling Price	Total Sales	Units	Selling Price	Total Sales
1									
2									
3									
4									
5									
6									
7									
8									
9									
10									
11									
12									
13									
14									
15									

Garza and Neely, CPAs
Sales Revenue Budget
For the Year Ending December 31, 2014

Dept.	Quarter 1			Quarter 2			Quarter 3		
	Billable Hours	Billable Rate	Total Revenue	Billable Hours	Billable Rate	Total Revenue	Billable Hours	Billable Rate	Total Revenue
1 Auditing									
2 Tax									
3 Consulting									
4 Totals									
5									

Dept.	Quarter 4			Year		
	Billable Hours	Billable Rate	Total Revenue	Billable Hours	Billable Rate	Total Revenue
1 Auditing						
2 Tax						
3 Consulting						
4 Totals						
5						

				Toby Tool & Die Company							
				Direct Labor Variance Report							
				For the Month Ended March 31, 2014							
Job No.	Actual Hours	Standard Hours	Quantity Variance		Actual Rate	Standard Rate	Price Variance		Explanation	
A257	2 2 1	2 2 5								
A258	4 5 0	4 3 0								
A259	3 0 0	3 0 0								
A260	1 1 6	1 1 0								